W9-CXN-572

The author in Central Park in New York City, complete with fishing rod and reel. (*Edward Pierat, Christian Science Monitor*)

THE COMPLETE BOOK
OF KITES AND KITE FLYING
by WILL YOLEN

A Fireside Book
Published by Simon and Schuster

Copyright © 1976 by Will Yolen
All rights reserved
including the right of reproduction
in whole or in part in any form

Published by SIMON and SCHUSTER
A Division of Gulf & Western Corporation
Simon & Schuster Building
Rockefeller Center
1230 Avenue of the Americas
New York, New York 10020

Manufactured in the United States of America

1 2 3 4 5 6 7 8 9 10

Library of Congress Cataloging in Publication Data

Yolen, Will H   1908-
    The complete book of kites and kite flying.

    (A Fireside book)
    Bibliography: p.
    Includes index.
    1. Kites.   I. Title.
TL759.Y58   1979   629.133′32   78-27295
ISBN 0-671-22191-4
ISBN 0-671-24852-9 Pbk.

ACKNOWLEDGMENTS

Special thanks to Caleb Crowell, friend and technical adviser, whose expertise and invaluable contributions to kite construction and other technical aspects of kite flying are limitless; Kenneth Anderson for research; Robert Scott, who gave gracious help in outlining the book; Robert Ingraham, inspired kite flier and leader of the American Kitefliers Association, whose special material was invaluable; my loving daughter, Jane Yolen Stemple; my son, Steven, Fairchild Publications Bureau chief in Brazil, who helped so ably with South American kite lore; and Julie Houston, assisted by Roselyne Gregor, who edited this book to success.

Here are some other wonderful kite people who helped with advice, anecdotes and design ideas: Paul Garber, curator emeritus of the Smithsonian flight section; Francis Rogallo, who gave aeronautic advice; Domina Jalbert, the Boca Raton parachute maker and inventor of many ingenious kites; Benn Blinn, Ed Grauel and Al Hartig, whose unstinted contributions are in this book; Harry Sauls and Max Coombs of Florida, who opened my eyes to the possibilities of kite riding; Ed Hanrahan as well as the Jimmy Swartzes of Baltimore. In New York, former Mayor John Lindsay and Katie and Dallas Coke encouraged us, and ran the police lines with me to establish kite flying as a legal sport in New York City. Much appreciation goes to Red Smith, Harry Galloway, director of the Sheraton-Sandcastle in Sarasota, Florida, and Stephen Brener, who have acted as sponsors of annual kite flights. Thanks also to Walter Hickel, former Secretary of the Interior, who helped remove legislation against kite flying in Washington, D.C.; Wyatt Brummitt, whose technical advice is always valuable, as is the research of Clive Hart, as well as his friendship, and Bob Gonter, whose data processing material was so helpful; and some of the commercial kite people such as Harvey Sellers of Hi-Fliers, Les Phillips of Gayla Kites in Houston, Texas, Ray Holland of Airplane Kite Company in Roswell, New Mexico, and Hal Levine of Alan-Whitney Company. Thanks to William Morris, president of the Dutch Treat Club, who let me address this sophisticated and prestigious literary group on the subject of kites, and to members of the Explorers and Adventurers Clubs who have taken my efforts seriously, as have the Overseas Press Club, The Players and the Ischoda Yacht Club of Norwalk, Connecticut.

Finally, thanks to Benjamin Franklin, patron saint of kite fliers.

WILL HYATT YOLEN

Kite flying is exhilarating for all ages.

To all kite
fliers whose soaring ideals
are part of their everyday life.

The fun of kite flying can be shared. This family sends a huge bird version of the French military kite aloft from the top of East Rock in New Haven, Connecticut. (*Alan Whitney Kite Company*)

CONTENTS

The end of a summer's day. (*Tom Lesley*)

Even birds do it. . . . A bird kite soaring alongside a sea gull at Compo Beach, Connecticut.
(*Tom Lesley*)

INTRODUCTION

Will Yolen is the John Peter Zenger of kite fliers. In 1966, about 230 years after Zenger came out of solitary confinement to score the first major victory for freedom of the press in the American colonies, Yolen strode into Criminal Court in New York and struck a telling blow for self-expression in the skies. During the mayoralty campaign a few months earlier, he had got himself arrested in Central Park for flying a kite with a banner reading: "Vote for John Lindsay."

In a landmark decision Judge James L. Watson upheld the right of freeborn Americans to state their convictions in this fashion, even if it caused passersby to stare and tap their brows significantly.

Modest to a fault, Yolen seldom refers to himself as a crusader. He prefers the simple designation that appears in the 1972–73 edition of *Who's Who in America*— "kite-flying champion of the world."

He has held this title since 1959 after a thrilling victory over the Maharajah of Bharatpur in a five-hour duel on the lawn of the maharajah's hunting palace in India. (Employing a maneuver he had perfected against Pablo Diablo, a wickedly ingenious kite-fighter in Central Park who had the edges of his kites studded with razor blades to sever an adversary's string, Yolen tricked the maharajah into diving his kite into a rain forest.)

It was shortly after this coup that I became acquainted with the Master. At lunch in the Overseas Press Club, of which he is a past president, he leaned back, closed his eyes, and recounted such a tale of tiger hunting, kite flying and derring-do that I, who had hoped to get one sports column for the New York *Herald Tribune* out of the meeting, had to write it as a serial that filled the column for four or five days hand running. This may help explain what eventually happened to the *Herald Tribune*.

It might be mentioned that in 1959 the Chicago White Sox were champions of the American League, Ingemar Johansson was heavyweight champion of the world, Billy Casper won the United States Open golf championship and Neale Fraser of Australia took the United States singles championship in tennis. Out of this redoubtable company, only Will Yolen retains his title today.

Not that Will has rested on his laurels, or on anything else. Even as champion, he

11

has striven unceasingly to improve. In 1962 he flew 30 kites on a single string over the rooftops of Adamant, Vermont, and coolly proclaimed this a world record. In 1971 he headed a team that kept a kite aloft for 37 hours, 17 minutes, which the same unimpeachable authority certifies as a world record. And finally he achieved Nirvana by putting an exaltation of 50 kites in the sky.

It should not be assumed that all of Yolen's activities have been extraterrestrial. He has been an author, playwright, radio executive, journalist, press agent and editor, but it is as a kite flier that he has gained immortality, the most celebrated kite flier since Benjamin Franklin.

That is a comparison the Master would not applaud. He respects Franklin as a libertarian and admires him as a libertine, but blames him for luring countless God-fearing kite fliers to death by electrocution. Will says that when anybody tries that funny business with lightning as Franklin described it, it is even money that a thunderbolt will flatten him permanently. Furthermore, although Will gives Franklin full credit as inventor of bifocals and daylight saving time, he hints darkly that when Ben flew a kite in a thunderstorm he had already read an account of this experiment by a French scientist.

This is Will's third and most comprehensive book on kites. It includes descriptions of his favorite kites and instructions for making them, yet when he was asked whether he constructed his own, his lip curled. "Did Babe Ruth make his own bats?" he demanded. "Does Heifetz build violins?"

This is a man with his world on a string. You might think that here, if anywhere, is the man who has everything, but in truth Will Yolen aches with unfulfilled longing. At boxing matches in Madison Square Garden he has watched handlers doctoring their fighters between rounds and has yearned to possess that healing skill.

Nothing in the world could make him so happy as to walk down Broadway and hear somebody say, "There goes the best cut man in New York."

RED SMITH
Sports columnist, *The New York Times*

FOREWORD

Since the renaissance of the art of building and flying kites, which occurred in the early 1960s after six decades of seeming lack of interest on the part of adults, several books on kites and kite flying have been written.

Although most of such publications have been excellent and welcomed by today's kite-flying fraternity, virtually all have covered only that period of kite history that began at an undetermined time in antiquity and barely extended into the beginning of the twentieth century.

The kite renaissance is more or less a phenomenon. While kites were the first true heavier-than-air man-made flying objects and the direct forerunner of the airplane, they were all but abandoned after the first powered flight by the Wright brothers. For more than sixty years after the event at Kill Devil, only children flew kites and only in the windy days of spring. For some reason, without foundation or logic, it was believed throughout these six decades that adults who flew kites other than in the company of children were short of masculinity or ill of some psychotic disease. There are few sillier inhibitions than that. But now it is all over.

It may have been the space program that inspired men to fly kites once more. No one really knows. But in every normal being there is a love for flight that has frustrated mankind since the beginning of time and the first bird escaped from the quickly thrust hand. In flying a kite there is an expression of that love for flying in the most personal way possible other than piloting an airplane, soaring plane or balloon.

Will Yolen has written a book that credits those good men and women who "pioneered" kiting throughout the past sixty or more years and continued pursuit of the sport even though furtively. No one knows more about the struggle with self-consciousness that caused the kite flier to remain hidden from view at the end of the line below a dancing kite than this apostle of all tethered aircraft.

Kite flying is a way that those with artistic souls can temporarily decorate the sky, leaving it unmarred at nightfall, containing no debris to impede the passage of the night winds. Kite flying is a means to tame the power of the wind and convert it to a force that lofts artistic handmade creations toward the clouds. Kite flying is a key to greater and badly needed human sociability without sinister or commercial goal. It is unpolitical, nonsectarian and a means of the soul's better expressions.

In the kite are man's finest desires.

BOB INGRAHAM
Executive Director
American Kitefliers Association

Auxiliary kites (right) were needed to lift the massive kite into the airstream. This innovation in kite flying was used by NASA to launch the first space vehicles, something the Russians never thought of when they first raised their Sputniks. (*George Cardozo*)

It took 12 men to launch this military kite, which measured 144 square feet. Lofted on March 8, 1959, it was the largest ever flown in Connecticut and brought a crowd of more than 5,000 people to witness its flight—more than would come to witness the launching of the first 747. (*George Cardozo*)

This amazing picture of me seemingly flying through the skies via balloon kite illustrated my story on early kite flying for **Life** magazine. Actually, I descended into a mound of hay, after jumping from a cherry picker fifteen times before the photographer got the picture he wanted. (*Yale Joel*)

1 MEMOIRS OF A KITE-FLYING GENTLEMAN

In "The Kite" Somerset Maugham tells the story of a man who was so inflamed with passion for kite flying he rotted in prison rather than pay alimony to his wife who had broken his favorite prize-winning kite.

My passions don't run so high—my late wife never flew with me, or against me, for that matter—but I do have moments of ecstasy which make me realize that Maugham's kite flier was correct in his behavior. Other kite fliers I have talked to all over the world agree with this point of view—although most of them wouldn't go so far as to divorce their wives. Most kite fliers aren't violent men, which is one of the reasons that the sport attracts them. It is a contemplative sport rather than a violent one and there is little body contact.

It was Francis Rogallo who introduced me to kite flying. One fine autumn day Rogallo appeared in my apartment across the street from Central Park in New York City in the company of my brother-in-law Edward Garrick, chief physicist of NACA, which later became NASA, in the Langley Field installation, where Rogallo was chief of one of the giant wind tunnels.

The two scientists were in New York to read papers before a distinguished group of fellow aerospace scientists. Rogallo's paper had to do with his work in wind tunnels and his experiments with the nonrigid kite.

"Let me show you how this works," exclaimed the scientist. We went into the park across the street and Rogallo opened the kite and handed it to me.

"It doesn't even look like a kite" I said as the three square feet of plastic was handed to me. "Where are the sticks?" I asked.

"No sticks," Rogallo answered. "I got tired of placing rigid kites into the wind tunnels to test the turbulence. The kites would smash against the side of the wind tunnels. Now when the kite hits the side of the tunnel it just reshapes itself. There's nothing in these kites that can break."

I put the kite into an eight-knot breeze and the kite whooshed into the air. I had flown my first nonrigid kite with the inventor himself as my observer. It was a feeling of elation as though I had stepped ashore in America with Christopher Columbus.

I was hooked.

When I first started flying kites, I was very self-conscious. I always thought it was a sport or game for kids. I had never seen a grown man flying a kite. I couldn't get my son, Steve, age five at the time, or my nine-year-old daughter, Jane, to go flying with me. I tried to bribe some of the kids in the park to fly with me. They thought I was some kind of a park nut, and they stayed away from me on instructions from their mothers.

My shyness about flying kites on my own was having a deleterious effect on my new found hobby. I tried flying early in the morning, at sunrise, when there were few people around in the park; but at that hour it attracted the attention of the cops. They viewed me with great suspicion. Furthermore, there was a law against kite flying, a law that I destroyed years later. It was meant to prevent kite flying in the 1880s and early 1900s when kites frightened horses.

I finally solved this problem by making a cutout figure of a small boy out of papier-mâché. At the foot of this papier-mâché figure I inserted a spike, which I then planted in the ground. This figure had his arm extended as though he were holding a kite string. From the walks and paths in the park this cutout figure looked like a small boy flying a kite while I, the fond father, instructed him.

Kite fliers all wear caps. It tends to make them look boyish, they hope.

Soon after I began flying kites seriously, I discovered that running and reeling were taking much of the fun out of my kite flying. Furthermore, on a good wind, the kite's upward progress was impeded with the slow hand-over-hand reels then in use. I thought I had discovered something new in the way of reels when I attached the line to an empty Schaefer beer can. The line slid off the shiny surface of the can very rapidly, and when I brought it in I could gain about eight inches of line every time I made a full turn of the can. But even this method was awkward, for as I became more skillful I wanted to do more than just fly kites; I wanted to do some target kiting. That is, I wanted to be able to hit a target three or four hundred feet away on the ground or in a treetop. Maneuverability of the line was what I needed.

The answer to this, of course was a conventional fishing rod and reel. I immediately took possession of the family rod and reel, attached three thousand feet of thin, but strong, nylon sewing thread (No. 10) and began a new career of kite flying.

Many times in Central Park, with the kite extended the full three thousand feet, it was out of sight and there I was standing in the middle of the meadow with a fishing rod and reel looking to all the world as though I were a fisherman who had lost his way. Interested spectators would taunt me with "What fish did you catch today?" I would reply snappily, "Flying fish!"

The rod-and-reel technique eliminated all running in order to get the kite into the wind. Instead I would whirl the kite overhead letting out a little bit of line and thus cast it into the wind and catch a happy thermal or upward draft.

After a couple of years of flying in Central Park I became a well-known sportsman in that area. All the little kids, except my own, helped me fly kites from time to time. The cops stopped chasing me. In the spring the baseball players tolerated me and no longer did outfielders blame my kite for their losing a line drive. In the fall I danced around the football players. They tolerated me, and once in a while a passer would throw the ball at a low-flying kite to show off his skill. They never hit it. Everybody liked me.

Everybody but Pablo Diablo. Pablo Diablo, Paul the devil, flew kites from the rooftops above 110th Street. He used glass-encrusted line on a heavy-frame rigid kite. The frame was studded with razor blades. He was the scourge of the rooftops. Nobody could withstand an assault from his razor-studded kite with the glass-encrusted line. He was a killer.

After months of viewing my kite aloft, he descended from the rooftops and approached me. The little kids cried, *"Mire, mire!* Pablo Diablo, Pablo Diablo!" and scattered as they screamed, clutching their kites.

Without a word he shot his five-foot, diamond-shaped kite into the air on a fifteen-mile southwest breeze. I sent my nonrigid kite up rapidly another one thousand feet to get out of his way as fast as possible, but maintaining a belly in the string so that he could not run a tight line against mine and cut me. I went up to four thousand feet. He continued to try to lean on my string, but he couldn't take hold. My kite just drifted away, carrying my line out of the grasp of his. Nor could he reach mine with his razor-studded kite. We fought each other for five hours.

The sun was beginning to fade and the wind was coming out of the northwest. Pretty soon, I knew, there would be a sudden drop of wind and then there would be a stillness in the air.

I began to reel in my kite one thousand feet, then two thousand feet. Pablo Diablo reeled his in from one thousand feet to eight hundred feet and then six hundred feet, waiting to meet me when I came down within his fighting range. As the wind shifted, our kites began to fly over a copse of trees in the southeast area of the park. I brought my kite down another five hundred feet. Pablo brought his to two hundred feet. I knew that the wind was soon to die down entirely. All of a sudden the wind stopped dead. Pablo Diablo, who had no experience in the park, flying above treetops, looked shocked as the wind stopped dead. His kite fell into the trees, and was disintegrated by the branches. I spun out my kite on my fast reel in a victory flourish, and the kids cheered and cheered. I was champion of New York.

Pablo slunk out of the park carrying a bunch of junk, which was once a kite, under his arm. He was never seen in the park again.

Following my victory over Senõr Diablo, I found myself the hero of the kite fliers of the park. I should have left well enough alone, but on the momentum of this crushing defeat of the Attila of kite flying, I overreached myself and began to experiment with huge target kites designed by Paul Garber, at that time curator of the Smithsonian Institution's flight section.

This type of kite, a rigid, heavier-than-air flying vehicle, was almost the size of a Piper Cub airplane. It had a rudder, and its direction could be changed by pulley lines attached to the lead line and to both wings. On it was painted a Nazi warplane. These kites were being sold in all the army and navy surplus stores and were a drug on the market because neither the army nor the navy was practicing shooting or identifying Nazi planes anymore. Furthermore, one of the reasons why none of them were sold to the conventional kite flier was that it took a ground crew to assemble one of them.

I finally managed to put one together on a fine spring day and sailed it aloft in the baseball field above 96th Street in Central Park. The West Side Rats, a pickup baseball team of neighborhood sports, were in the field for their early spring training. A crowd of onlookers watched the team, scouting them for bets they would make later in the season when the semipro hardball league opened.

Another shot that appeared in **Life**, imitating the famous photograph of Alexander Graham Bell leading a group of his young friends in raising a huge multicellular kite. The kite in this picture is a big French military vehicle, like those used in the Franco-Prussian War to signal troop movements. The French lost that war and the current wisdom of that time was that the French should have been fighting instead of kiting. (*Yale Joel*)

All of a sudden my mammoth kite, with Nazi markings on its underbelly, roared across the park out of control, dragging me in its wake on a thirty-mile wind of tornado size. The startled ballplayers and spectators began to scream as the kite yawed and slipped toward the ground from a height of 350 feet. "Pearl Harbor!" screamed one of them as he dived to the ground. "Hit the ditches!" cried the captain of the baseball team as he led his men in a tumbling roll into a nearby gully. The spectators scrambled as, with a terrific roar, the kite swooped to home plate on the diamond and crashed. The lead line and I were still in the outfield.

The shaken players and spectators returned to view the wreckage and looked for bullet holes. It wasn't until I reeled myself in on the lead line that they realized that it was nothing but a kite.

I never flew a Garber kite again.

Years later I met an air force man, who had introduced the Garber kite into the army's target and identification program. He said, "If we could have put engines into these kites we would have won the war a year earlier."

At about this time of my kite-flying career, I was not working. I had decided that I had enough money to live a gracious life with my wife and two children in a nine-room, three-bathroom apartment on Central Park West. I was determined to maintain the pose of a man of leisure, a club man whose main preoccupation was to get through the day.

But there was nothing to do all day but fly kites. I flew kites in the morning, in the afternoon and even in the evenings. Kite flying is a lonely profession, and my

One of the huge Bell tetrahedrals that set the stage for the flying machine is shown here being lofted by the inventor, children and friends. This is the picture that Yale Joel simulated for **Life** magazine.
(*National Geographic Society*)

kids were at school during the day. Therefore, I embarked on a program of recruiting other kite fliers.

The greatest pool of nonworking talent was centered at Toots Shor's Restaurant at that time at 51 West 51st Street. After my morning flights I drifted down to Toots' in the traditional manner of all the club members. I sat at the bar, discussed contemporary problems with the bartender and other club men.

I'd usually come up with at least two or three recruits. Instead of going to the ball game that afternoon, they went with me to the kite-flying field of Central Park. In this way I built a coterie of kite fliers, which included theater people (Fredric March, Nanette Fabray, and Errol Flynn when he was in New York); writers, who were dying for an excuse not to write, such as MacKinlay Kantor, Peter Maas, Cornelius Ryan, as well as half the staff of the late *Collier's* and *Woman's Home Companion*, whose offices were nearby; and some professional men, doctors and lawyers, who joined us at twilight, just after office hours.

Among this clutch of kite fliers was one eager beaver, a curiosity-seeking, mixed-up kid who wanted to mingle with the kite-flying greats, a natural athlete of the muscle-beach type. He turned out to be totally unfit for classic kite flying, but he was so eager for the company that formed around the flying activities of this group that he suffered all types of humiliation in order to go out with us on our daily rounds. The youngster of the crowd, he acted as the "tree boy," which meant that in case a kite was entangled in the trees, it was his duty to climb and retrieve the kite.

The author perfects a unique style of kite casting in Central Park. (*Barrett Gallagher*)

In fact he was the only one with the muscle power to climb the tree. He is known today as Vince Edwards, star of many TV shows.

I flew kites in the park along the Hudson River and in the various country meadows for many years, but it was not until 1958 that I went outside the United States.

The occasion was a casual trip to Nassau in the Bahamas. I took a kite along, for I had heard through the kite-flying grapevine that some of the greatest fliers of our time were to be there.

I stopped at the British Colonial Hotel and found that the other kite fliers had made it their headquarters also. This greatest congregation of kite fliers amounted to exactly six: a gentleman from Nationalist China, a man from the Barbados Islands, a Texas lawyer, a representative from South Africa and one from England. This world kite tourney lasted three days. We flew against each other in the morning and in the afternoon. We drank in the evening.

At the end of three days of competition, which I must admit was of a languorous type, I was declared Western Hemisphere Champion. The rest of the world was divided among the other contestants.

Otherwise the town of Nassau failed to recognize the event as a landmark of any kind. The director of public relations of the island replied as follows when later queried about the significance of the world kite tournament:

"Regarding the kite-flying championship tests in Nassau last year, please note that as far as Nassau is concerned they were hardly that. The kite-flying contest as such was less than a world-shaking event.

"In fact, there is so little interest in this event that no records are kept on it, nor is a man assigned to it, except for a curious photographer named Roland Rose, who insisted that he might be able to make some interesting pictures in case he ever decided to write a book on 'The Dullest Sports I Ever Covered.'"

Following my triumph at Nassau, I was invited to participate in the dedication ceremonies of the swank Boca Raton Club polo field in Florida.

One of the prize kites I carried with me to this high society nonsense was a Papagaio, recently sent to me from Brazil by Inez Robb, a newspaper columnist and a kite buff herself. The Papagaio, called a Falcon in the United States, has a wing-spread of six feet and is shaped like a bird.

With a loud blast of a horn and a roll of drums, the ceremonies were started and the beautiful, sleek ponies were trotted out past the reviewing stand. At the same time, the field marshal signaled me to send up a few kites. I sent up a leash of small kites which hung listlessly in the air, and then I whipped the Papagaio into the air by swirling it over head on my rod and reel. I kept letting out line and soon the Papagaio bit into a thermal which zoomed it into the air and across the field toward the ponies.

The ponies began to rear and jump as this tremendous bird swept among them. They tore loose from the grooms and stampeded across the field. It looked like a film of a wild west stampede, run in reverse. The more I tried to bring the kite down, the more violently it yawed and sideslipped.

The field was in panic. The polo players were frantically signaling the grooms to do something about the ponies. The grooms spotted me at the other end of the field with the kite and chased after me. As they got closer I panicked also, and without waiting for the speechmaking or the rest of the ceremonies, I cut my kite string and leaped over a fence and disappeared.

I have not been invited to another polo field dedication.

I carry kites in the back of my car. Fishermen carry their equipment wherever they go, but can fish only if they find a good pond or stream. I can fly kites on a good breeze in any meadow or any clear area one hundred feet square.

One day I visited the Avco plant in Stratford, Connecticut on a public relations survey tour. I was met by scientists who were working on some of the most esoteric problems in space travel, Avco being one of the leading manufacturers of air space hardware.

I had to be checked in with clearance passes and a report from NASA, which controls some phases of the Avco operation. Before we checked in at the office, I opened the luggage compartment of the car and the scientists' eyes bugged out. The back of the car was full of kites—kites like they had never seen before.

Fortunately it was near lunchtime, and we repaired to the huge parking lot across the street from the research labs. For the next hour, these scientists, who in their workday dealt with the most sophisticated and recondite space vehicles, gamboled about the parking lot, flying the classic kid's kites.

Refreshed from their adventures in lower space with kites, these scientists went back to their drawing boards, according to some of their non-kiting colleagues at Avco, to invent the famous Avco nose cone, which carrys the most sensitive instruments in our space exploration vehicles.

Kite contests are not well organized, either in America or in India, where I went in 1959 to participate in a tiger hunt which ended in a kite tourney because our tiger got away.

The maharajah of Bharatpur, with whom I hunted, was accepted in India as the world's kite-flying champion. In all other countries where kite flying has developed into a sport, it is generally thought of as a fun-loving, amiable, peaceful endeavor. Not so in India. Though they profess love and peaceful aims in every other aspect of their lives, Indian kite fliers are savages.

There is only one kind of kite in India, a fighting kite. Paper thin and with a round cross spar, the kite ascends rapidly in an eccentric jerky manner. The lead string is glazed and impregnated with abrasives. This type cannot be bought in any Western country. It's as lethal as a switchblade knife in the hands of a hopped-up killer.

I used a conventional number-ten nylon string and flew a three-foot nonrigid kite on a fishing rod and reel.

Flying against a maharajah is an awe-inspiring proposition. In the first place the prince has a kite bearer—a huge Indian, white-turbaned, wearing a blue uniform of the royal house, but barefooted. The kite bearer gets the kite into the air, then hands it to the maharajah. His excellency insists on all the honors due his noble birth; therefore his kite must go up first and be positioned before his opponent of lesser rank may launch a kite.

His kite bearer took the kite to 200 feet and handed it to his highness. I had to get my own kite up in a hurry to 300 feet to stay away from his cutting line.

I went three hours against the Prince of Hunting and Kite Flying, using my rod-and-reel technique against his glazed string. We felt each other out and I avoided Bharatpur's wide sweeps. I stayed steadily anchored in the sky.

The kite bearer had now become the martini bearer, and was plying me with same. The prince, very Westernized, though religious—he was head of a sect known as the Jhats, one of my partners pointed out—was not averse to having a martini also because, as he explained it, he had gone to school in Cambridge.

With a rush and swoop after the martinis had taken hold, I found my kite embracing the prince's. He brought it out of danger but I followed him at great speed because of my rod-and-reel technique. He outmaneuvered me, came out from under me and flew clear and began to pursue me. He was beginning to get his glazed string across me in the classic T formation of naval warfare when I tore from under him and brought myself over a copse of trees, where he followed.

That was his big mistake. I kept my kite dancing over the trees about 70 feet high, and he began to maneuver his kite and line into a cutting position—again in an effort to cross my line in a T.

My experience with Pablo Diablo stood me well. I tantalized the prince to play after me above the trees; then when I felt the wind falling off, I began to reel in. He followed me down, but couldn't sustain his kite in the thin air without more room in which to maneuver. Down he crashed into the treetops. I ducked my kite away from his and yelled my triumph, as his kite was now a piece of broken spars and crumpled paper.

I was the world's champion.

We did exchange kites even though the prince was not entitled to mine, the

For the world's championship. The Maharajah of Bharatpur on the lawn of his hunting palace in Central India (Uttar Pradesh Province) is attended by his martini and kite bearer. The Western champ is at his right feeding a line to him. Nevertheless, when the chips were down, friendship and a five-day tiger hunt didn't count. Yolen beat the prince and captured the world title for the United States. (*Baldev of India*)

custom being that the winner is presented with the loser's kite. Thus, he was the first to fly the Rogallo flexible kite after me in the entire Far East.

Reports from his home say that when the sun is setting in the sky and the soft breezes are playing about the minarets of his hunting palace, the prince is out there flying his Western-type modern kite. There is a look of wonderment on his face, says one observer, as though he is still puzzling over the fact that a piece of flexible plastic, with no sticks in it, brought down his traditional, nonpareil, fearsomely unbeatable kite even though it was carrying a deadly cutting string.

Crazy American kite fliers!

2 THE ROMANCE OF KITES

The true origin of the kite is as lost in antiquity as the discovery of acupuncture or alcohol, the invention of the arrowhead or the fishhook, or the reason for man's fear of snakes and lightning bolts. It is easier to document the development of agriculture and man's control of fire than to trace the genealogy of the kite. The oldest legends of the earliest cultures are sprinkled with references that suggest the use of kites.

The story of the flight of Icarus in Greek mythology, for example, has been interpreted by some scholars as a description of an effort to fly a man-lifting kite. According to the legend, the heat of the sun melted the wax used by Icarus in constructing the bird-like wings of his airfoil and he fell into the Aegean Sea and drowned. The best available evidence, however, indicates that kites evolved somewhere in the southwest Pacific, around the Malay Peninsula, thousands of years ago. And it is most likely that the kite originally had a function in primitive religious ceremonies.

The people of primitive cultures have always been absorbed in the mysteries of nature. The sun, the moon and the stars represented forces beyond comprehension. The early dwellers of this planet were fascinated if not frightened by storms, earthquakes, volcanoes and floods. When the sun declined in the northern latitudes at the onset of winter, religious ceremonies were staged to coax the sun high in the sky again; circles of evergreen boughs were set afire and the burnt boughs and ashes were swept upward as an offering to the sun god. Springtime was the reward.

In ancient Europe, other gods were conceived to explain lightning, thunder and other natural phenomena. And in the tropical ocean regions, where weather extremes were comparatively rare, the constantly unseen and unexplainable force of Nature was the wind that swept along the beaches and whipped through the treetops. This was the work of the wind god, and the natives of the region, like their distant cousins far to the north, used the foliage at hand to send up in the air as offerings to their god. Reports of the early explorers of the Malaysian area tell of the sight of green kites fluttering above the island shores as they sailed toward the land. But when the sailors made landfall, the kites had disappeared and the only evidence

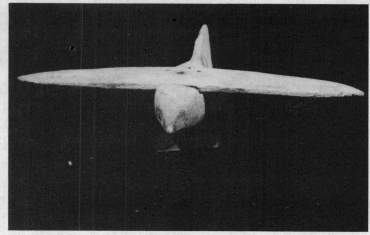

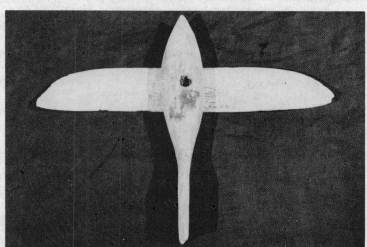

The oldest manmade flying vehicle—a kite—is shown in model form in the Cairo museum. It is 2,200 years old and made of clay. This original was actually flown, according to aviation editor Kamal Naguib, of **Al Ahram**, who delivered the picture to me by special messenger when I was in Egypt in May of 1974. When I visited the museum in person, I was not allowed to see it—or it couldn't be found. It was only through the special intervention of Naguib that I was able to obtain these pictures.

of the display they had viewed from a distance was an occasional bamboo kite frame floating along an inlet.

Some years later, after traders and explorers had established rapport with the natives, it was learned that the kites—made of palm fronds fastened to light bamboo frames—were used in secret ceremonies honoring the wind god, who, when angered, could lash the seas and land with destructive typhoon power. To conceal the ritual from foreign eyes, the palm leaf kites were reeled in on their lines, made of twisted vines, and hidden. Only when a piece of vine broke and a kite fell into the sea did outsiders get a glimpse of the ceremonial device.

Elsewhere in the Pacific, the Polynesians used kites in similar religious ceremonies for at least hundreds of years before European explorers reached their shores. The Polynesians, however, made no effort to conceal their kite ceremonies. In fact, when new materials such as cloth became available, they were adapted to use in kite building. Some of the Polynesian kites were as tall as a man and had long tails ornamented with colorful feathers, flowers, or other materials.

It should be noted that the Malaysian kites ordinarily required no tails because they were designed with a bowed, or curved, rather than a flat surface. The curvature gave the Malaysian kites greater stability against wind fluctuations. The modern bowed kites still use that basic ancient design and sometimes are sold under the name of Malay kites.

The Polynesians had two wind gods, brothers named Tane and Rongo. One of

The Maori were serious early fliers, according to Polynesian lore and history. Their kite flying was part of their religion until the missionaries discovered them. Special songs were sung during kite-flyng sessions. Only the right hand was used for holding the kite, the left hand being considered unclean, as in many Arab countries. Women were not allowed to fly kites.

The Maori kite-flyer's kite was considered part of his soul and his fate. "The flying kite foretells a man's luck" is an old New Zealand Maori apothegm. "If it swoops, it is bad luck, if it is steady, then truly the sun shines."

Kites were also involved with magic. It was believed that a trailing kite line could destroy a man's enemies by just touching them.

Herewith a Maori kite from the Bay of Plenty. These kites were made of a vine called raupo. The male bird figure is used in religious ceremonies, especially in fertility rites.

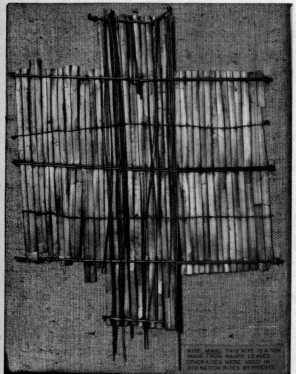

Kite, **Manu.** This kite is a toy made from raupo leaves. Other kites were used in divination rites by priests. (*Dominion Museum, New Zealand*)

the ceremonies depicted a contest in which Tane challenged his older brother to a kite-flying contest. Because Rongo had a longer line and Tane's kite tail became entangled in a tree, Rongo won the match. As the Polynesians played out this religious drama with their own kites, the first one to reach a certain height was designated Rongo.

Some experts contend that China was the birthplace of kites, offering as evidence certain Chinese writings dating back to the pre-Christian era. But there are equally ancient Egyptian references to kites, recorded in hieroglyphics carved in stone as well as on papyrus. One of the earliest Chinese descriptions tells of a battle that occurred around 200 B.C. when General Han Hsin flew what apparently was a man-lifting kite over the walls of a besieged castle. A forerunner of the observation kites used by European armies some 2,000 years later, General Han's kite maneuver provided enough information about the deployment of forces within the castle walls to enable the general to tunnel into the fortress and capture it. This may have been a popular ploy of Chinese military leaders in those days because other old Chinese manuscripts tell of similar flights of manned kites over enemy forces during various sieges of 2,000 or more years ago.

Kite flying was recognized as an art form in China as early as the twelfth century when the contemporary artist Su Han-Ch'en painted this scroll. The kite at the top is still used today in China as well as in other parts of the Far East. It is believed that the kite in China began as a standard or flag or banner flown by nobles two or three thousand years ago. (*Division of Photography Field Museum of Natural History*)

The Elephantine papyrus, dated about 500 B.C., contains a story about a pharaoh who plotted against one of his court officials by ordering him to build a stone palace midway between heaven and earth. The story relates that the court executive accepted the challenge and trained two eagles, tethered by lines attached to their legs, to fly to a height of about 100 feet. On the back of each of the eagles was a boy. From the altitude that had been judged as midway between heaven and earth, the boys called down to the pharaoh that they were ready to build the palace and they needed only stone and mortar. Then they invited the pharaoh to fly up to the building site with the materials so he could lay the cornerstone; if the pharaoh was truly a god, as he claimed, he certainly could fly.

The pharaoh, who had planned to execute his court official on the pretense that he had failed to obey an order to build the palace in the sky, was faced with a dilemma. If he did not fly up to the building site, the people would know he was not a god. The pharaoh resolved the problem by calling off the project and announcing that he had merely been testing the loyalty of his vizier. Since archeologists believe the papyrus version followed a similar Egyptian story found carved in stone, the incident upon which the tale was based may quite easily have been much older than 2,500 years.

What is fascinating here is that although the story tells of boys being carried into the sky on tethered eagles, some scholars have pointed out that the boys actually could have been raised into the sky on kites. In many languages, the words for kite and bird are either the same or quite similar. And the story may have described an early use of man-lifting kites in that part of the world. In any case, the stone carving

Miniature paintings of this type began to appear in technical publications as far back as 1405. This is a dragon balloon created by Konrad Kyeser Von Eichstat. The rider holds it on a string. The head is made of parchment, the body of linen and the tail of silk. Very ingenious: a small oil lamp in the mouth warms the air inside the body and lifts the dragon into the air as a hot-air balloon.

clearly shows men on the ground with what appear to be kite lines extending upward from their raised arms.

Since it would be unlikely that kites were invented independently in several scattered parts of the earth more than 2,000 years ago, we must assume that there was some commerce among the early peoples leading to a diffusion of kite knowledge from a single point of origin, and at a time much more ancient than would be indicated by early written descriptions of rather sophisticated man-lifting kites in China and Egypt. Because of the nearly constant onshore and offshore winds of tropical islands and the concern of primitive peoples for the godlike influences of natural forces, the Malayan Peninsula would have been a logical site for the earliest interest in kites. From that point of origin, the art of kite flying could have spread northward to the Chinese mainland and directly or indirectly to such distant places as Egypt and the Pacific Islands to the east.

There are a number of fanciful stories relating to the origin of kites in the literature of the Chinese. One story tells of a Chinese farmer, Meng Chia, who was attending a picnic when his hat was blown from his head and carried aloft. Because a string was tied to the hat, it sailed about like a kite, according to one rendering of the tale. Another story based on the aerodynamics of Chinese coolie straw hats tells of a young man who became the intended murder victim of relatives, who locked him in a granary and set the grain afire. The quick-thinking Oriental saved himself by leaping from the top of the building and gliding safely to the ground by holding his coolie hat like a parachute.

Separating fact from fiction about early Chinese kites is difficult. One document describes a craftsman in the time of Confucius, about 500 B.C., who devoted three years to the construction of a kite made of wood. Unfortunately, the kite crashed to the ground and was destroyed after the first day of flight. Other stories suggest that paper kites were flown before the invention of paper.

Nevertheless, the Chinese probably could lay undisputed claim to the discovery of kites for amusement. Their history is filled with tales of kite festivals and kite games; they even used kites for telling fortunes: the higher one's kite rose in the sky, the higher that individual would rise in wealth and fame. And at one point in Chinese history, kite flying had become so popular that such festivals were banned by the emperor because they threatened the nation's food production. Instead of planting and cultivating crops, everybody was involved in flying kites and trampling the young stalks of vegetables and grain with the destructive fury of a horde of locusts.

One traditional Chinese kite festival was called the "Festival of Ascending on High," and commemorates the legend of a farmer who was spared his own life and the lives of his wife and children because of their love of kite flying. According to the story, the farmer dreamed that a terrible disaster would befall his home on the ninth day of the ninth month. The farmer was so disturbed that he took his family on a picnic in the hills on that particular day. During the afternoon, they sailed a kite high into the sky and were so intrigued by the kite's performance that they lost track of time until darkness had enveloped the countryside.

When the farmer and his family returned home, they found that their house had collapsed, destroying all their possessions. Each year after that the farmer and his family flew kites on the ninth day of the ninth month. And as word spread of the good fortune of the kite-flying event, other Chinese began flying kites on that date. Even-

Kite flying at Hae-kwan on the ninth day of the ninth moon, similar to Boys' Day on May 5 in Japan. The drawing by T. Allom shows Chinese peasants flying bird and dragon kites. In the early days of kite flying in China—as in Japan—the sport was banned because kite flying addicts ran across newly planted grain fields and destroyed them in their flying enthusiasm. The penalty was death—but it was also death by starvation for the peasant whose field was destroyed.

tually, the custom was observed by hundreds of thousands of Chinese whose kites literally flooded the skies each year on the ninth day of the ninth month.

There also is the story of an Emperor Huan Theng of the Han Dynasty whose palace was surrounded by enemy soldiers. The emperor ordered everybody to build kites—specially designed kites carrying bamboo instruments that would produce moans and wails when the wind blew through them. The kites were sent up over the enemy troops that night, which was dark and moonless, and by the following morning all of the enemy soldiers had fled in terror.

One well-known author, Clive Hart, has suggested still another possible beginning for modern kites. In various writings, including a paper in the British *Aeronautical Journal* (December, 1969), Hart has noted the similarities between kites and windsock pennants carried by military units in battle or to identify traveling dignitaries. He also has pointed out that, particularly in medieval documents, there seemed to be some confusion by writers and illustrators as to whether they were describing military banners or pennants attached to the end of a pole or perhaps kites attached to lines extending from the hands of soldiers. In certain situations, it is conceivable that such banners may have been reinforced with frameworks of sticks of bamboo or other materials to keep them unfurled in the absence of a stiff breeze. That idea was employed as recently as the 1970s by astronauts on the moon who carried the United States flag, which was displayed in that windless atmosphere in an unfurled manner, with the aid of wires. A banner displayed in that position within a framework of stiff materials on earth could become "flyable" in a breeze.

The Roman legions are known to have carried standards, some of which are believed to have been hollow windsocks, as early as the first century A.D. Because they frequently were designed and painted to resemble dragons or serpents, they were called *draci*, plural of the Latin word *draco*, for dragon. But there is scattered evidence that the Romans got the idea from armies they encountered in the Middle East, who may have borrowed the concept in turn from soldiers from the Orient. There also is an account of Romans acquiring kite standards, as they are sometimes described, as war booty during battles with the Dacians who inhabited the Danube region nearly 2,000 years ago.

Although the draco standards may have originally been truly hollow windsocks that would billow out with the wind, the windsocks portrayed in manuscripts of the ninth to fifteenth centuries appear to have undergone a transition to become flat or plane-surfaced. And they are controlled by lines that loop around reels in the hands of soldiers, rather than being attached to stiff poles. And while early draco standards may have been used to identify military units or to frighten a naive enemy with their dragonlike appearance, the later, kitelike dragon standards probably were used for signaling and to help archers estimate wind direction and speed. Because of the loss of certain manuscripts during the years that World War II raged in Europe, the complete details of the story of the draco windsock standards may never be assembled. But Hart believes, on the basis of available evidence, that the standards represent a type of kite introduced in Europe from the Middle East before A.D. 1000.

Historians have noted that the earliest record of kite flying in the Western world dates to the year 400 B.C. when a kite was raised over the Greek city of Tarentum by an individual named Archytas. However, some investigators contend the object described was not a kite at all but a wooden dove; the confusion may be due to the inability of ancient observers to comprehend the principles of kite flying. Kites made with wooden materials have been used throughout history, and as noted elsewhere, the names of birds have frequently been used to describe kites. If the dove of Archytas was indeed a kite, perhaps imported to Greece from Egypt or the Orient, there is no further mention of kites in that region for more than a thousand years.

Kites of Chinese origin made an appearance in Arabian countries in the ninth century. Although identified as "flags," construction details in the literature of Islam definitely describe the devices as paper kites with tails.

One of the enigmas of kite history is that Marco Polo spent many years in China, where kites apparently were flown by tens of thousands of citizens during the festivals, but he brought back to Europe no important knowledge of the flat-surfaced kites used in the Orient. Only one brief reference to the kite is found in one of Polo's manuscripts, which describes a type of "hurdle" on a long rope which rose in the wind and was used to predict whether a ship would have a quick and prosperous voyage.

Even after the death of Marco Polo, European kites were of the windsock type with wings attached for improved lift in the wind. One such kite is seen in the Milemete manuscript of 1326–27, which shows a fourteenth-century air raid on a European city. The illustration reveals a fire bomb being dropped from a winged airsock flying above the city. The fire bomb was suspended and controlled by a chain hanging from beneath a large draco-type windsock which appears to be tethered by a rope held by three knights with the help of a winch.

Ironically, when flat kites finally came into popular use in Europe, around the

This is war! As early as 1326 a war kite was sketched by Walter de Milemete in his **Treaties de Nobilitatibus Sapientis et Prudentiis Regum**. The drawing shows a besieged town with a kite above it. A fireball hangs below the kite and a trio of knights are flying the kite into position to make a direct hit. Little do they suspect that the beleaguered villagers are flying a fire bomb from a window and it's right over their heads. Fortunately, this is an unfinished sketch and neither fireball has been dropped.

sixteenth century, their purpose frequently was associated with displays of gunpowder—one of the Chinese inventions that Marco Polo did bring back from the Orient. In fact, from around the middle of the sixteenth century until the mid-seventeenth century, most of the published articles about flat kites were discussions about the use of kites in nocturnal displays of fireworks. An English-language book by John Bates, in 1634, for example, provides detailed instructions for making a firedrake, as such kites were called. The covering was made of linen cloth coated with linseed oil and varnish, the tail of a string of firecrackers separated by knots of paper shavings. As the kite went up, the end of the tail was ignited and the firecrackers exploded one after another until the burning gunpowder and paper finally reached the body of the kite which burst into flames.

In some communities, the firedrakes of the seventeenth century were used by Christian religious leaders to simulate celestial apparitions such as illuminated dragons or "comets" accompanied by the sounds of musical devices attached to the kites. Such a phenomenon was almost guaranteed to put the "fear of God" into backsliding parishioners of that era. An account of Athanasius Kircher in the 1640s tells of the use of an illuminated kite to release Christian missionaries held captive by natives of an Indian village. A warning of the wrath of God was painted on the sides of a dragon kite with a mixture of sulfur, pitch and wax. The kite, with the mixture ignited, was launched in the darkness and the natives were terror-stricken by the appearance of the message that blazed from the heavens. They quickly opened the prison and allowed the captives to go free.

Shortly after publication of Bates' instructions for building a firedrake, the term *kite* began to appear in the English language, although no source has been found for the change in the name of the device. Since the days of the Romans, until about 1635, it had been called *draco*, flying dragon, or a variation of that terminology in most European languages. The word *kite* had been used to describe birds, particularly hawks, and was derived from Old English. But kite, originally spelled with a capital K, quickly gained preference, and the reference to kites as dragons quickly disappeared from the English language.

The introduction of terminology to suggest an identity with a graceful bird rather than the earlier association with a fiery dragon seemed to coincide with the use of kites in Europe for recreation. The public obsession for competitive kite flying grew to such intensity in some parts of Europe that political leaders, in the fashion of the ancient Chinese emperor who was concerned about crop damage, tried to ban the use of kites. Because of riots spawned by competition in French cities, kite fliers of that country were required by a 1736 law to hold their tournaments in rural areas.

Sailors returning to England, Holland and other seafaring nations of Europe brought home the flat or bowed kites that were used in festivals and ceremonies of the Orient, the Malay-Java region and Polynesia. From the middle of the seventeenth century, the literature began to show kites as children's toys rather than as military weapons or as a tool for religious sky writing. And men of the Western world echoed the mystical message of the Orient: "The sensation of flying a kite is that of having the wind in your hands."

"They shall have music wherever they fly . . ." The Chinese are credited with the invention of the musical kite. Specifically, Li Heh, a musician and kite flier, combined both his talents by attaching a bamboo flute to the head of a paper kite. As the kite flew upward, the wind struck the flute holes and the result was the sound of a heavenly harp. Li Heh was the Emperor's kite maker in the tenth century.

3 THE KITE GROWS UP

For years, since it departed from legend and lore, the kite has been thought of as a trivial toy, a plaything of gypsy wayfarers, for jongleurs and idlers. But history tells us that the kite is much more than a toy. In fact, the kite has been found useful in so many ways that it deserves a chapter of its own in almost any book of industry, war and peace.

The separate efforts begun by Benjamin Franklin and the Scottish team of Thomas Melville and Alexander Wilson to study the atmosphere with kites led to extensive meteorological work that continued for more than 150 years, until the airplane had been developed as a suitable vehicle for making weather observations. Man had always yearned for knowledge about the skies, filled with clouds and winds and other phenomena beyond his grasp. Sir Henry Cavendish would not discover the lighter-than-air properties of hydrogen until 1766, and Joseph Montgolfier would not invent the hot air balloon until 1782. But in 1749, the Scotsman Dr. Alexander Wilson conceived the notion that a train of kites could be used to measure the temperature of the air "in the higher regions of the atmosphere."

From the perspective of the late twentieth century, the idea of using kites to obtain weather data seems as obvious as the invention of the wheel or the discovery that water will douse a wood fire. But when Wilson and Thomas Melville met to discuss possible methods of measuring the temperature of the air at cloud level in 1748, the concept was as novel as the Dick Tracy and Diet Smith comic-strip journeys via gravity waves.

Evangelista Torricelli had only a century before invented a means of measuring atmospheric pressure with a mercury-filled glass tube. And Torricelli in turn was a pupil of Galileo, who had invented the thermometer. For the previous 2,000 years, the Western world's knowledge of meteorology had been based on the fanciful theories of the Greek philosopher Aristotle. John Dalton, whose research into atmospheric pressure, heating and cooling of air, wind, and rain led to modern concepts of weather, hadn't yet been born. Such was the relative ignorance of weather conditions when Wilson and Melville decided to "explore the temperature of the atmosphere in the higher regions" by attaching thermometers to kites. Since the feat had never

The innovative philosopher Benjamin Franklin is shown here with his son as they begin experimenting with the translation of lightning into electricity.

been attempted, the young researchers were "somewhat uncertain how far the thing might succeed," according to a document of the event published some years later. In fact, they worked from the spring of 1749 until the middle of July on the design of the experiment and construction of a half-dozen paper kites.

The kites, made of the strongest yet lightest materials available, ranged from four to seven feet in height and were to be raised as a train of kites. The order of launching began with the smallest kite. When it reached the limit of its line, the next kite was attached and carried into the sky, and so on until "the uppermost one ascended to an amazing height, disappearing at times among the white summer clouds."

When the complete train of kites finally was airborne, the uppermost of the half-dozen disappeared into the clouds and the lifting surfaces of the combined set of kites was so great that help was required from the small army of observers in maintaining control of the line.

Thermometers were attached to the highest kites and released at different altitudes by pullcords controlled from the ground. Each thermometer had a "bushy tassel of paper" tied to it; the tassel apparently served a double purpose of slowing the descent of the thermometer and allowing Wilson and Melville to keep an eye on the location of the instrument both in the air and after it reached the ground.

This first use of kites for weather observations was a great success and the meteorological kite experiments continued well into the following year.

Wilson and Melville might have been the first kite fliers of record to lure lightning down a kite line except for their safe and sane policy of conducting experiments only when the sky was free of storm clouds. When Melville finally learned of Benjamin Franklin's great performance in bringing atmospheric electricity down a kite line, about a year after the actual event, he tried to induce Wilson to join in experiments that might prove even more spectacular. After all, he suggested, the train of six

The scientific part of Ben Franklin's experiments was pretty shaky. Scientists still cannot understand why Ben and his son, shown here with him, weren't killed. They are standing outside the shed, instead of in it; there is no evidence of the wire being grounded—so it is astonishing that they survived. In any case, Franklin's experiments did demonstrate that lightning was in fact electricity.

kites could reach areas of the sky untouched by Franklin's tiny silk handkerchief kite. However, Wilson died in December, 1753, and the world's first weather kite team act came to an end.

Franklin's experiment was conducted in June, 1752, and was begun in some secrecy because, as Franklin later confided to his friend Joseph Priestley, the noted English scientist who discovered oxygen, he dreaded the "ridicule which too commonly attends unsuccessful attempts in science." It is not known if Franklin was aware of the atmospheric experiments by Wilson and Melville. But Priestley noted that Franklin did not know at the time of his famous lightning experiment that French researchers already had completed similar work that verified Franklin's theory.

Even today there are probably few people who realize that Franklin was trying to determine whether the earth and the sky functioned like the conducting layers of a Leyden jar in the presence of an electric charge. Franklin did not discover lightning; it had always been around. And he was not the first man to entice a lightning bolt from the sky; that had been done already by Buffon, Dalibard and De Lor.

According to some historians, the kite was a sort of spur-of-the-moment device used by Franklin to determine for himself the static electric nature of lightning. If he had lived in mountainous country, he could have stuck an iron rod into a peak to attract lightning. But Philadelphia is about as flat and as close to sea level as it is possible to get in North America, so he decided to launch a kite with a "very sharp pointed wire, rising a foot or more above the wood." The Leyden jar, developed at the University of Leyden in 1745, had been brought to America as an instrument to detect and demonstrate static electricity. And Franklin had obtained a Leyden jar which produced an electric spark and a crackling noise when touched by a metal object after being electrically charged. It was Franklin's intention to learn whether the electricity in lightning could be used to trigger the spark in the Leyden jar and if perhaps the electrical activity in the jar was in effect a tiny scale model of a lightning bolt.

In his autobiography, Franklin reported that he had been able to charge the Leyden jar with electricity carried by a silk thread from the kite as easily as if the electricity had been produced by a manmade friction machine—the usual way of putting an electric charge into the jar. He noted that "thereby the Sameness of the Electric Matter with that of Lightning [is] compleatly demonstrated."

One of the greatest authorities on Franklin's kite-flying experiments is Eugene Seder, who wrote the following in a recent issue of *Kite Tales*, the magazine of the American Kitefliers Association: "Over the last few months I have sought what information I could on the most famous of kite flights . . . in Philadelphia in 1752 in which he demonstrated memorably and forever that lightning is electricity. My research carried me to the Franklin Institute in Philadelphia and then back to New Haven where I found the most and really only fruitful source at Yale University where a special endowed department is devoted to Franklin's papers."

Mr. Seder claims that the kite-flying episode was ill recorded by Franklin himself, usually prolific with his pen. Franklin said almost nothing about this experiment to anyone. His son, then twenty-one, witnessed it on that blustery June day, but Franklin told none of the scientific journals. It is believed he wanted it as a scoop for his own *Poor Richard's Almanack*. However, he did tell his patron in England, Peter Collison, before sketchily reporting it in his own periodical.

Mr. Seder found that the first full description of what actually took place had to wait another fifteen years until Priestley himself set down an account of the famed flight in an article which biographers assume Franklin read before it was published.

According to Seder, Priestley wrote:

. . . as every circumstance relating to so capital a discovery (the greatest perhaps since the time of Sir Isaac Newton) can not but give pleasure to my readers.

The doctor, having published his method and verifying his hypothesis concerning the sameness of electricity with the matter of lightning, was waiting for the erection of a spire (on Christ Church) in Philadelphia to carry his views into execution; not imagining that a pointed rod of moderate length could answer that purpose when it occurred to him that by means of a common kite he could have better access to the regions of thunder than any spire whatsoever. Preparing therefore a large handkerchief and two cross sticks of a proper length on which to extend it, he took the opportunity of the first approaching thunderstorm to take a walk in the fields in which there was a shed convenient for his purpose. But dreading the ridicule which too commonly attends unsuccessful attempts in science, he communicated his intended experiment to no one but his son, then 21 years old [and not a child as in the paintings depicting the scene], who assisted him in the raising of the kite.

The kite being raised, a considerable time elapsed before there was any appearance of it being electrified. One very promising cloud had passed over it without any effect;

when at length, just as he was beginning to despair of his contrivance, he observed some loose threads of hempen strings to stand erect and to avoid one another, just as though they had been suspended on a common conductor. Struck with the promising appearance, he immediately presented his knuckle to the key (let the reader judge of the exquisite pleasure he must have felt at the moment) and the discovery was complete. He perceived a very evident electrical spark. Others succeeded [in perceiving the spark] even before the string was wet, so as to put the matter beyond all dispute, and when the rain had wet the string, he collected electrical fire very copiously. This happened in June of 1752, months after the electricians in France had verified the same theory but before he had heard of anything they had done.

It must be pointed out that Franklin's experiment with kites was questioned by many scientists. There was one theory that Franklin had witnessed the experiments earlier in France and had simulated them in America without remembering all the details. In his *Almanack* he did not describe it in scientific detail but rather popularized it.

Many people trying the experiment according to Franklin's instructions were knocked on their duffs. Even Franklin admits that he had killed many a turkey in his trials and had himself been knocked unconscious by a charge from one of his Leyden jars. After a while he learned to ground his wires.

Thanks are due to Mr. Seder for setting some of these records straight.

One Frenchman named De Romas published a book in an effort to prove that he

Still another rendering of Benjamin Franklin drawing electricity from the sky (c. 1805). Painting by Benjamin West. (*A.J. Wyatt, staff photographer Philadelphia Museum of Art*)

was the rightful discoverer of the electrical effects of lightning bolts, but records show that his first success at attracting electricity from lightning, using a kite, did not occur until June, 1753, a full year after Franklin's demonstration that electricity could be lured down a kite line.

Later Franklin, willing to share his scientific knowledge, published his instructions for others who might want to repeat his experiment. (See "The Handkerchief Kite," Chapter 6.)

The practical application of the kite experiment was the invention of the lightning rod, which offered, like the kite-borne "very sharp pointed wire," a pathway for the flow of static electricity from the thunderclouds above to the earth below. Within a few years after the Franklin kite experiment, hundreds of lightning rods appeared on buildings throughout Philadelphia.

Aside from the scientific benefits of Franklin's work, it triggered a fad of "electric kite" demonstrations on both sides of the Atlantic. Whereas the Leyden jar had frequently been used to give an electric shock to an unwitting spectator, the electric kite (with copper or brass wires wrapped around the kite line) became the source of jolting shocks offered by practical jokers. De Romas, among others, became obsessed with efforts to produce larger and larger sparks from lightning sources and, on one occasion, claimed to have lured enough lightning from the skies to make a spark eighteen feet in length. The so-called electric kites also were used in sadistic demonstrations to kill or violently shock birds, dogs, cows and other animals with giant sparks. In some instances, the experimenters themselves became victims of the electricity running earthward from a kite; the Russian researcher Georg Richmann was killed by lightning in 1753 as he tried to repeat the Ben Franklin feat while holding a metal rod. His assistant, who was standing nearby, was injured by the unexpected electric bolt traveling at the speed of light from the kite. Other fatalities from kite experiments in thunderstorms probably have been foiled by the simple fact that intense heat from a lightning strike vaporized the kite line before the electricity could reach the person holding the line.

In controlled tests with recording instruments attached, scientists have determined that a kite line can pick up as much as 50,000 volts of electricity during a thunderstorm. One recent Weather Bureau report stated that a bolt traveled down the kite line with a noise like a cannon report, and "the vaporized wire left a rocketlike trail of yellowish-brown smoke which remained visible for fifteen minutes throughout the entire length of the line." Highest voltage potentials apparently are associated with the higher kite altitudes, which may coincide with the general trend of thunderstorms to pack more violence when the storm clouds are higher in the sky.

Franklin's work was commemorated in 1835 by the organization of a Franklin Kite Club which met once a week at the Philadelphia City Hospital grounds to experiment with kites. Weather was an item of prime interest, and because there were no official forecasts available, everybody was his own weatherman. Even people like George Washington and Thomas Jefferson kept weather diaries; records of important meetings like the gathering of the Founding Fathers to sign the Declaration of Independence are punctuated by weather data. Kites became a common device for obtaining information about winds and rains. It has even been reported that small animals were sent up in baskets attached to kite lines, but the results of these early experiments are unrecorded. The members of the Franklin Kite Club devised glass insulators to protect themselves from shock when reeling kite lines out in stormy weather.

The public, however, misunderstood the principle of the electric kites, and many believed that the kite itself was the source of the electric charge. On one occasion, in 1759, a kite flier had left his kite in a café in the Bordeaux area of France. The patrons feared the kite would precipitate lightning bolts, and when by sheer coincidence lightning did strike the café during a storm, a near-riot ensued. To appease the patrons, the café proprietor had the kite ripped to shreds, thus ending the danger of further lightning bolts in the minds of the customers.

One of the members of the Franklin Kite Club, James P. Espy, used kites to study the properties of clouds and discovered the relation between convection currents of rising warm air and the condensation of water vapor in the atmosphere. He later wrote a treatise, *The Philosophy of Storms,* and initiated the preparation of weather maps for tracking storm systems across the nation.

In his book on storms, Espy wrote of a kite that "was sent up into the base of a cloud and its height ascertained by sextant and compared with the height calculated from the dew point, allowing 100 yards for every degree by which the dew point was below the temperature of the air, and the agreement of the two methods was within the limits of the errors of observation. In this case the base of the cloud was over 1,200 yards high. Moreover, the motions of the kite whenever a forming cloud came nearly over it proved that there was an upmoving column of air under it."

Some of Espy's ideas for weather control, based on his kite studies, were a bit irrational. For example, he was so enthusiastic about the relationship between upward-moving air columns and precipitation that he once proposed setting huge wood fires on the then western edge of the United States. He reasoned that heat from the fires, built along a north-south line, would produce convection currents resulting in rain clouds which would move in a generally eastward direction to provide moisture for farmers along the Atlantic Coast.

However, Espy did make a number of significant contributions to weather science through the use of kites and was, in fact, the first professional meteorologist to use kites in his work. His studies of vertical air currents and the role of cloud formations in storms and his use of weather maps were great innovative contributions to weather science in an era when forecasting was so rudimentary that hurricanes and typhoons were regarded as a succession of storms rather than one great cyclonic movement of stormy weather. As one observer noted, Espy was so far ahead of his time it was difficult to apply his meteorological discoveries; from his kite studies he learned how to predict storm paths but there was no telegraphy or radio communication at that time to warn people in the path of the storms.

Except for an effort to repeat the Wilson and Melville experiments of checking high-altitude temperatures with kites, much of the meteorological kite work in the first decades of the nineteenth century involved the continued interest in luring the electrical potential of lightning bolts from the skies. The major exception of note was the work of the Reverend George Fisher and Sir William Parry, the British explorer of the Arctic. The men had stopped at Igloolik in 1822 during the second attempt to find a "Northwest Passage" around North America and decided to use a kite to measure the temperature of the air several hundred feet above the ground.

They attached a U-shaped maximum-minimum thermometer to a kite which they raised to an altitude of about 400 feet and stood patiently in minus 24-degree cold waiting for the instrument to adjust to the temperature at kite height. When the thermometer finally was brought back to ground level, it was found that the reading was exactly the same—24 degrees below zero.

The balloon, introduced by the Montgolfiers in 1783 and first used for collecting weather data in 1785, continued its important meteorological work well into the 1970s; before the use of weather satellites, the U.S. Weather Bureau alone launched as many as two thousand balloons a day over various parts of the world. But the balloon had several shortcomings, the most common of which was that a free balloon might be carried by high altitude winds to a useless demise in an ocean or on an inaccessible mountain peak where the load of expensive instruments could not be recovered. If a balloon was, on the other hand, tethered like a kite it could not be controlled adequately; lateral winds would whip it about in a large arc or bring it down when it was supposed to be up.

On August 14, 1897, Sir Francis Reynolds and W. R. Birt of the Kew Gardens Observatory in England developed a six-sided meteorological kite that enabled meteorologists to raise and lower weather instruments along the kite lines through a system of pulleys.

In 1887, another British meteorologist, E. D. Archibald, had introduced the use of high-tensile piano-wire lines which had twice the strength but one-fourth the weight of fabric kite strings used earlier. Archibald also developed a diamond-shaped bamboo and silk weather kite with a tail. These kites were flown in trains with self-recording anemometers attached at various points to measure wind velocities at altitudes of up to 1,500 feet.

Unfortunately, the kites developed by the British meteorologists, as well as a variation of the hexagonal kite developed in 1892 by the American Alexander McAdie, were not practical for the increasing needs of weather forecasting. The McAdie kite, for example, proved to be unstable and difficult to control; and its most important function seemed to be that of continuing the study of static electricity, as it was flown with a surface covering of tinfoil to build up electric charges and an electrometer was attached to measure the electricity. However, Franklin had demonstrated that kites could attract electricity from storm clouds 140 years earlier and the scientific weather observers found themselves simply repeating the experiment with bigger and better kites.

The major breakthrough in meteorological kites came about in 1894 when William Eddy introduced the tailless bowed kite that was later named for him. Eddy had experimented with trains of tailed hexagonal kites but found them difficult to control, so he tried building a bowed kite of the sort used for hundreds of years by natives of the South Pacific. He had at that point never seen a Javanese-type bowed kite, but he had heard of them and tried to work out details using information obtained from the stories he had heard. His big break, or breaks, came in 1893 when he saw a native Javanese kite at the World's Fair in Chicago and at about the same time received a letter from a man in South Africa who described his experiences in flying bowed kites that had been brought to that region by a merchant returning from Indonesia. With the fresh inputs of data, Eddy set about redesigning his bowed kite and a year later introduced the Eddy kite to meteorologists at the U.S. Weather Bureau's Blue Hill Observatory near Boston.

For several years, the Weather Bureau used Eddy kites in trains to lift rather heavy instruments to altitudes of 1,000 to 1,500 feet. A train of five Eddy kites, each with a lifting surface of about two square yards, made it possible for weather observers to achieve a stable platform for recording equipment at rather high altitudes for the late nineteenth century. And weather data not previously accessible to earthbound men began to fill the meteorologists' record books.

Although Eddy was ostensibly a New York newspaperman, he continued to experiment with kites for weather and other purposes, including methods of mounting cameras on kites for aerial photography. He also experimented with effects of small perforations in kite surfaces to achieve better control. All fabric-covered kites have tiny perforations in the weave, and Eddy discovered that adding perforations of various sizes and shapes in strategic points along the surface would affect the stability of a bowed kite or enable the kite flier to control the direction in which the kite moved. At one time Eddy nearly outdid himself in an experiment to see how many kites he could fly in one train; after he added the eighteenth kite to the train, he quit because the line had obviously reached the limit of its strength. If there was one shortcoming of the Eddy kite, it was the tremendous lift produced by Eddy kites in trains. And on more than one occasion near the turn of the century, grown men were observed chasing runaway kite trains across the countryside, utilizing every available form of locomotion from steam train to horse and buggy in an effort to catch a drifting kite line.

By 1896, the U.S. Weather Bureau had switched to a modified Hargrave box kite for lifting meteorological instruments into the skies. But Eddy kites still were used on occasion, and as late as May, 1910, meteorologists at the Mount Weather, Virginia, station set an altitude record of 23,385 feet with a train of ten Eddy kites.

American enterprise in the use of kites for meteorological work was sparked by the conviction of two top officials of the U.S. Weather Bureau that kites were suitable devices for exploring the atmosphere. One was Willis L. Moore, who favored the use of kite trains in the early 1890s, and the other Charles F. Marvin, who directed the establishment of seventeen kite stations around the nation to be used regularly for weather observations. Marvin also designed a meteorograph as the basic instrument to be carried on kites. It was a device that automatically and simultaneously recorded barometric pressure, wind velocity, temperature and relative humidity.

Under Marvin's direction, the use of kites for weather observations was refined to an exact science. Every detail regarding kite design, materials used, launching and landing, sites for launching, and so on, was spelled out in reams of government instructions. The launch site, for example, was specified as a 40-acre square tract of land with open country to the east but with a small town approximately one kilometer to the west. The site had to be level, cleared of trees and stumps, and "surrounded by a strong fence to keep out livestock." The surrounding country had to be free of forested tracts, lakes, marshes, rivers, steam and electric railways, and high-tension power lines. It was Marvin's intention to locate sites away from objects that might, because of "influence on meteorological elements," result in "erroneous relations indicated between the surface and free-air conditions."

The government weather observers used three different sizes which were

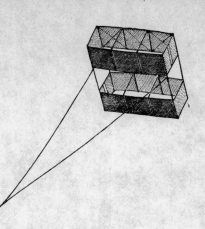

This is the prototype Lawrence Hargrave box, or cellular kite, which the Weather Bureau used extensively in its early weather research.

classified as high-wind kites, moderate-wind kites and light-wind kites. The 68-foot model illustrated in this book was known officially as the moderate-wind kite; the design of the other sizes was about the same, with modifications of dimensions. A moderate-wind kite was to be flown in winds of 12 to 30 miles per hour; the light-wind kite, designed for 8 to 10 mile-per-hour winds, required a lifting surface of 120 square feet and construction details scaled upward in proportion.

The dimensions of the moderate-wind kite used by the U.S. Weather Bureau until 1933 are as follows:

Length or distance fore and aft: 6 feet 8½ inches, or 204 cm.
Length or distance side to side: 6 feet 5½ inches, or 197 cm.
Depth or distance from top to bottom of cell: 2 feet 8½ inches, or 83 cm.

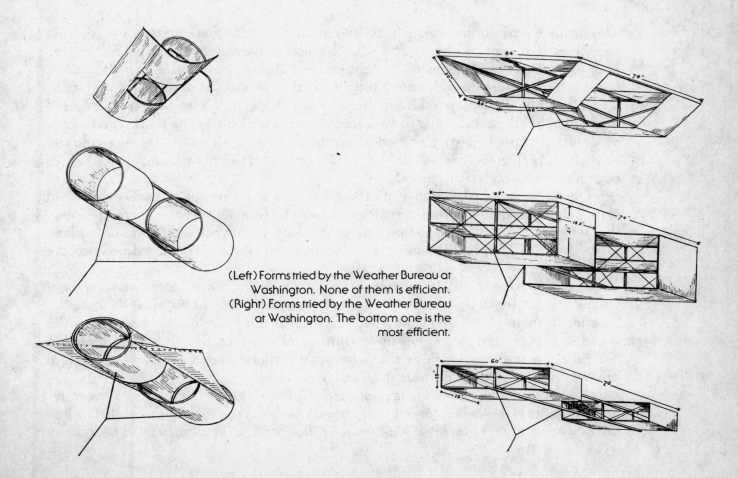

(Left) Forms tried by the Weather Bureau at Washington. None of them is efficient.
(Right) Forms tried by the Weather Bureau at Washington. The bottom one is the most efficient.

Weathermen watch as a Hargrave kite carries a weather instrument aloft, in the early 1900s, from a field near what is today Washington National Airport, which years later banned kite flying. (*National Oceanic and Atmospheric Administration*)

The lifting or sustaining surface is 68 square feet, or 6.3 square meters; the steering surface is 22.8 square feet, or 21.1 square meters; the weight is 8½ pounds, or 3.8 kilograms. Forty-one pieces of straight-grained spruce are required for the framework. Weather Bureau carpenters used 78 metal angles to fasten principal and intermediate joints. Coarse waxed linen thread and 175 feet of fine piano wire were used to supplement the reinforcing of metal angles and for bracing. The fabric surface was made of 13 yards of 26½-inch-wide Lonsdale cambric, although the rear cell and sometimes both cells were covered with black mercerized silk which is less likely to become waterlogged than cambric.

One detail of construction of Weather Bureau kites that sometimes is overlooked is that although the outside dimensions of both the front and rear cells are the same, the front cell is subdivided so that it actually consists of two cells. The middle plane in the front cell represents one major modification by the Weather Bureau of the original Hargrave box kite design.

The moderate-wind kite obviously is not a toy, despite its comparatively light weight. It requires a flying line with a test strength of at least 50 to 60 pounds; the Weather Bureau kite fliers used 300-pound-test piano wire for kite line. Since the Weather Bureau sent these kites up to altitudes of several miles, they were reeled in and out on electric-motor-driven winches, and elaborate precautions were taken to protect the kite handlers from static electricity shocks.

The official procedure for launching one of the kites— and two men were required for the task—called for one man to walk out from the reel house while holding the kite at an angle of about 45 degrees with the horizon, keeping a good tension on the line between himself and the reel. Marvin's manual explained: "When the head kite [they can be flown in trains] is to be launched in a moderate wind, it should be taken out about 60 meters to the leeward of the reel house and released, if possible, while the wind is fairly steady; in a light wind it should be taken out 100 meters or more and pulled up into the air by reeling in; if the wind is strong, it should be released while walking away from the reel and should be allowed to go out rapidly."

Actually, a reel house is not necessary. But two people still are needed to launch a 68-square-foot Weather Bureau kite; one holds the kite in the air while the second runs out about 150 feet of kite line. If the wind is favorable, the person holding the kite tosses it upward and in the direction it is to go, which should be directly in line with the wind. If properly constructed and launched, the kite should perform remarkably well. But if the kite darts or turns over after it has risen a short distance, the malfunction is a sign that the fabric surface material is not distributed properly or that there is a distortion in the framing. The kite should be reeled in carefully and examined before it crashes and has to be rebuilt anyway.

One common problem experienced by the Weather Bureau kite fliers was that the surface fabric would occasionally absorb moisture and shrink; the contraction of the surface fibers during shrinkage can be powerful enough to distort or even crush parts of the wooden frame of the kite.

After the U.S. Weather Bureau got into the use of meteorological kites with intense seriousness in the 1890s, the emphasis was shifted toward obtaining accurate and regular reports rather than making static electricity demonstrations or trying to

Landing a weather kite is a delicate operation as shown on this weather field in Drexel, Nebraska. (*National Oceanic and Atmospheric Administration*)

Except for its stripes, this is an exact duplicate of the U. S. Navy barrage kite. These kites were used for gathering weather data, and similar ones were used against Nazi plane invasions over London before the balloon barrages were developed. This kite was developed for the Navy by Harry Sauls.

set new altitude records. This required almost daily flights in all kinds of weather, and during the winter months the kite line had to be wiped free of ice and frost as it was reeled in. The line also had to be oiled regularly to prevent rust formation. Such housekeeping chores probably reduced the recreational pleasure associated with kite flying. But as the government later noted, such activities "served the nation well" in obtaining better weather data than was available in most other parts of the world.

A dynamometer was attached to the winch-driven reel to measure the pull on the kite line. By reading the pull in pounds on the dynamometer, the men operating the kite station could estimate when to add secondary kites and when to begin reeling in kites; increases in wind velocity or reeling in too rapidly could snap the main kite line by producing too much tension. Generally, the weathermen tried to limit the amount of pull to a little more than half the test strength of the piano wire, which meant they would quit adding secondary kites when the reading on the dynamometer reached 150 to 180 pounds of pull—but depending upon the number of kites already flying. If, for example, the pull of two kites was 150 pounds, the pull per kite would be about 75 pounds and adding a third would raise the tension to 225 pounds. But if a train of seven kites produced a total pull of 175 pounds, the average pull per kite would amount to 25 pounds and adding an eighth kite could be expected to increase the total pull to no more than 200 pounds. The same rule of thumb could be applied today for building trains of kites, assuming that the kite flier knows the test strength of his line and can make a fair estimate of the pull of the kites, with or without the aid of a dynamometer.

Still another lesson for today's kite fliers, but first documented by Weather Bureau men, is that building trains of kites is no guarantee that the kites will continue to move onward and upward, because there will be occasions when the best winds are close to the ground. The Weather Bureau kiters sometimes found that they were reeling out trains of kites that reached a level where there simply was not enough

If you don't trust your neighborhood weatherman, here's an NOAA blueprint whereby you can build your own kite—and create your own weather information center.

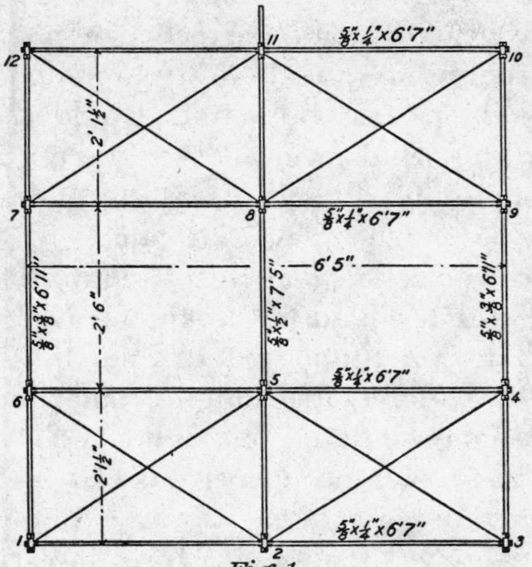
6'5"
2' 1½"
2' 6"
2'1½"

Fig.1.
front

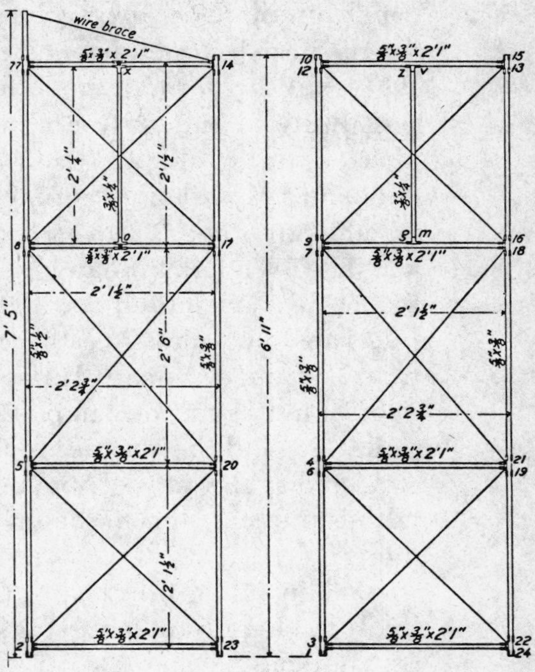
wire brace
7' 5"
6' 11"
2' 1½"
2' 2¾"
2'6"

Fig.2. center | *Fig.3.* ends

Kite Sticks, Clamps &c.

1	$\frac{5}{8}$"x$\frac{1}{2}$"x7'5" square edges.	48 Metal clamps – Fig.6.
5.	$\frac{5}{8}$"x$\frac{3}{8}$"x6'11" " "	30 " " " 7.
8.	$\frac{5}{8}$"x$\frac{1}{4}$"x6'7" rounded edges.	175 ft. No. piano wire
12.	$\frac{5}{8}$"x$\frac{3}{8}$"x2'1" tapering to $\frac{5}{8}$"x$\frac{1}{4}$" at ends.	13 yds. Lonsdale Cambric
8.	$\frac{3}{8}$"x$\frac{1}{4}$"x2'1" rounded edges.	26½" wide.
4.	$\frac{3}{8}$"x$\frac{1}{4}$"x3'2$\frac{3}{16}$" " "	
3.	$\frac{3}{8}$"x$\frac{1}{4}$"x2'$\frac{1}{4}$" " "	

CONSTRUCTION OF A WEATHER BUREAU KITE

In these early plans for building a weather kite, Figure 1 shows the front; Figure 2, the center; Figure 3, the ends; Figure 4, an isometric view; Figure 5, an isometric detail, with the metal clamps appearing in Figures 6 and 7. Figure 8 depicts a simple form of kite completed and the details of several parts appear in Figures 9, 10, and 11.

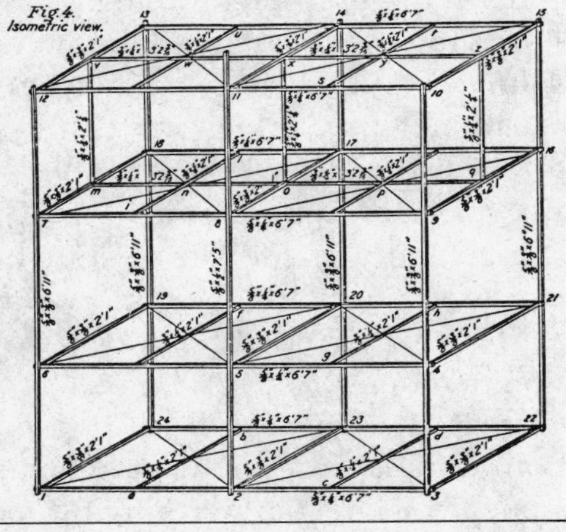
Fig.4.
Isometric view.

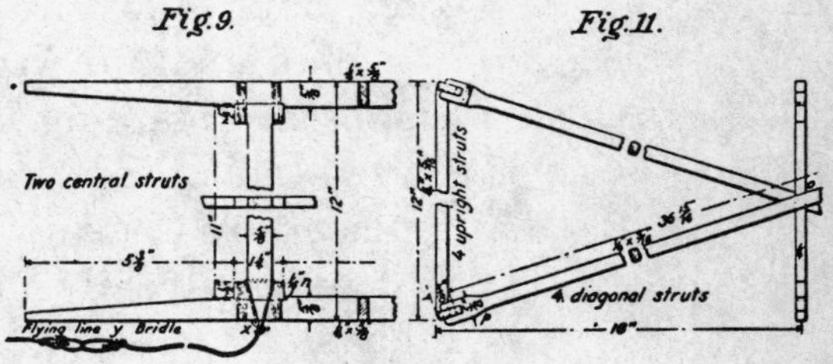
Fig.9.
Two central struts
Flying line y Bridle
Fig.11.
4 upright struts
4 diagonal struts

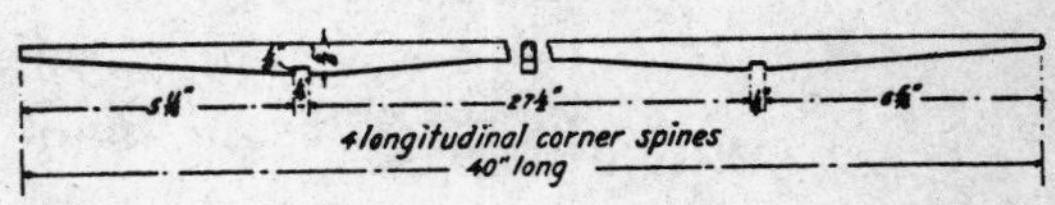
Fig.10.
4 longitudinal corner spines
40" long

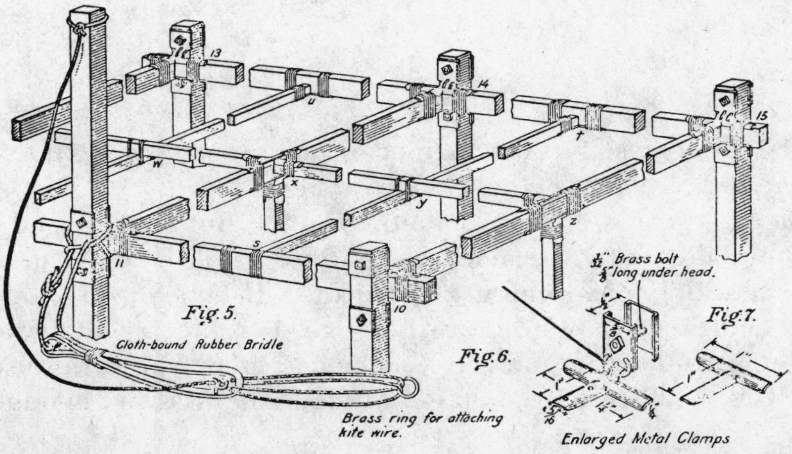
Fig.5.
Cloth-bound Rubber Bridle
Brass ring for attaching kite wire.
Brass bolt ¾" long under head.
Fig.6.
Fig.7.

Enlarged Metal Clamps

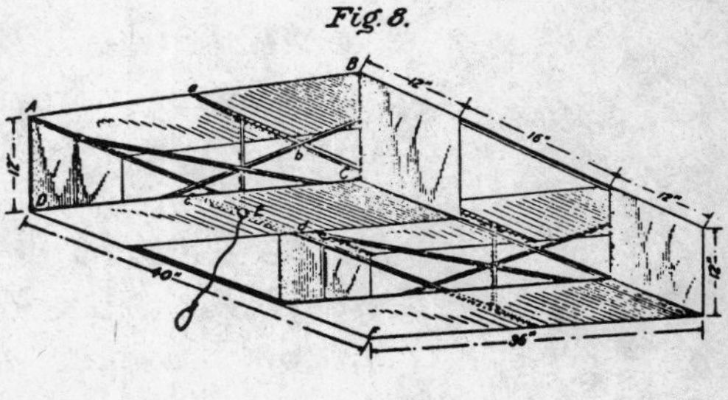
Fig.8.

wind to sustain a train. The kites just floated on the top of a lower level wind current like boxes drifting on a lake surface. The kite flier has the choice of reeling in carefully and reorganizing the train, waiting patiently for a change in the upper-level winds, or using such maneuvers as reeling in quickly to try to nudge the lead kite into a still higher altitude where the winds may be better. A hidden hazard is the possibility of suddenly finding a strong wind from another direction at a higher altitude; this could put an abrupt increase in pull on the kite line and whip the kites about in a 180-degree turn. So, the kiter who plays the game of flying trains of weather kites needs a good mixture of experience, patience, and intuition.

The Weather Bureau kite fliers further added to the knowledge of kite performance by developing correlations between surface winds and the movements of highs and lows across weather maps. They found, for example, that when the barometer is low and stationary, surface winds may be light, "and under such circumstances, one should resist the temptation to use large and many kites." If the barometer is quite low and the preceding fall was rapid, a sudden rise in wind velocity can be expected at altitudes of about 600 feet above the ground. During a period of rapidly falling pressure that is below normal, the winds may become too strong for kite flying.

When, on the other hand, the barometer has been low but is rising, the winds are likely to be uniform in direction and velocity, and abrupt changes are unlikely. After pressure has become high and stationary, light to moderate winds can be expected to a considerable height above the ground. And the average strength of the winds will depend upon the magnitude of the high-pressure cell and the location of its center with respect to the kite flier. However, the kite-flying weather observers found that getting a kite launched is the most difficult when high pressure is at its peak, and the kiter should wait until the barometer starts to drop again.

By the end of World War I, the airplane had pretty well replaced the kite as a means of obtaining weather information, although the U.S. Weather Bureau continued kite observations for an additional fifteen years. The airplane itself has been replaced by more sophisticated radiosonde balloons and rocket-launched satellites that transmit daily photos of weather conditions, which are in turn projected on television screens in millions of homes.

But there is no doubt that kites in their time "served the nation well" in obtaining weather information. And because the United States was willing to invest in the research and development of kites and kite-flying techniques to improve the service, every kite flier today has access to a wealth of information that otherwise might still remain undiscovered.

Military kites, like meteorological kites, remained in active service until replaced by the more sophisticated airplanes of the World War I era.

The American-born Samuel Franklin Cody, sometime called Buffalo Bill Cody after the famous American buffalo hunter, became a naturalized English citizen and was the maker of the first practical flying machine, a towed kite which he made in the British War Office Balloon and Kite Factory in Farnsborough. His military kite system could lift an observer equipped with camera, telescope and firearms to altitudes of as much as 3,500 feet. The Cody system included a telephone line so that the

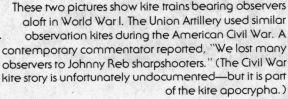

These two pictures show kite trains bearing observers aloft in World War I. The Union Artillery used similar observation kites during the American Civil War. A contemporary commentator reported, "We lost many observers to Johnny Reb sharpshooters." (The Civil War kite story is unfortunately undocumented—but it is part of the kite apocrypha.)

observer could report military activity to the ground, and the observer was able to travel up and down the kite line in a wicker basket trolley equipped with brakes. The system could be used by ships at sea as well as by ground forces and, after Cody patented the revolutionary man-carrying kites in 1901, the War Office adopted them in 1904. Mrs. Cody had such confidence in her husband's invention that she sometimes flew with him.

The Russians earlier had developed a method of towing torpedoes quickly and accurately toward targets, using twelve-foot kites. The pre-Soviet Russian military also tested man-lifting observation kites which, like Cody's system, were held aloft by a train of Hargrave-type box kites.

One of the more novel military adaptations of the kite was a German-designed man-lifting box kite that folded neatly into a package that could be stowed inside a submarine. When the submarine surfaced, the kite could be launched to fly an observer well above the surface of the ocean. The movement of the submarine provided enough breeze to lift the device and if the observer became an enemy target, the kite

In order to train antiaircraft crews in World War II, Commander Paul Garber, curator emeritus of the Smithsonian Institution, developed a target kite. This kite was inexpensive, maneuverable, and realistic—it looked like a Nazi plane, at least from a distance. The kite was five feet high and carried a controllable rudder. At a distance of 150 feet, the silhouette resembled an enemy plane in flight at a distance of about one mile. Although this kite was eventually replaced by radio-controlled gasoline-engine model planes, a Navy source says it is still practical for elementary training with small-caliber machine guns. (*Smithsonian Institution*)

Paul Garber's target kites are demonstrated at the Naval Air Station in Anacostia, in 1944. These are seven-footers—his first were five-footers. These kites were made highly maneuverable by installing in this essentially two-stick kite a keel, a rudder and twin flying lines.

could be quickly converted into either a glider or a parachute device—depending upon which model was used—and descend to water level.

Both war and weather demands have served as stimuli in accelerating the development of new kite designs and techniques throughout history. An important American contribution spawned by the sudden needs of World War II was the development of target kites for training antiaircraft crews. The responsibility for this project fell to Commander Paul E. Garber, a U.S. Navy officer who is mentioned earlier in this book.

Garber designed a five-foot diamond kite with a rudder that permitted line control of intricate airplanelike maneuvers; the kite could be made to dive, loop and spin figure-eight patterns. The Garber target kites were covered with a translucent blue cloth on which were stenciled silhouettes of enemy aircraft. When flown, the blue covering blended with the sky at a distance of 150 yards and only the airplane silhouette was distinguishable. Hundreds of thousands of such kites were used in training gunners, at a great saving to the U.S. government in money and manpower.

The box kite, sometimes called the Hargrave kite, was developed in the late nineteenth century by an Australian, Lawrence Hargrave, who was searching for a way to add stability to kites already in use for both military observation and weather studies. The aerodynamic details of this kite are described in Chapter Five. Hargrave described his kites as "cellular" and appearing like "pieces of honeycomb on the ends of a stick," which was quite accurate; the early models were designed as large boxes filled with smaller boxes. Many of his contemporaries in those days referred to box kites as "Hargraves."

The Hargrave kites not only found enthusiastic response among military leaders and weather observers, but also led almost directly to the development of powered flight. Orville and Wilbur Wright flew Hargrave kites as gliders at Kitty Hawk, North Carolina, before they tried such modifications as adding a gasoline-engine-powered propeller to produce a controlled airflow over the wing surfaces of the box kites. Meanwhile, another pair of brothers on the other side of the Atlantic, Gabriel and Charles Voisin, were similarly inspired to invent the airplane by being carried aloft in a Hargrave box kite during a windstorm. The Voisins did not receive as much publicity as the Wright brothers, but they did become the first professional manufacturers of aircraft in the world by producing biplanes which were essentially Hargrave kites powered by gasoline engines.

Eventually, the airplane replaced the Hargrave box kite as the most efficient chassis for both military observation and weather studies—until the arrival of the

This is the exquisite moment . . . the beginning of powered flight. The date is December 17, 1903. The place is Kitty Hawk, North Carolina—where the kite became an airplane. (*Library of Congress Collection*)

January 13, 1943. **The Montreal Standard** published this picture showing downed airmen on a rubber raft flying a box kite. The box kite acted as an antenna for the small distress transmitter and radio receiver. This kite antenna was rarely used because the box kite structure was too difficult to set in stormy weather, when it was most often needed. The kite antenna came back into use when the nonrigid, easily assembled Rogallo kite was born.

space age, that is. But the Hargrave kite itself had replaced the earlier Eddy, or bow, kite, described earlier, which for several years had dominated the field of "working" kites.

But what about some of the other major advances in man's progress into the technical world. Radio, TV? Yes. Marconi's first antenna was sent up on a kite in 1901. What is little known is the earlier work on wireless radio by an American, Dr. Mahlon Loomis, who first used kites to raise aerials and transmit signals through the air.

From the long-forgotten *Literary Digest* of July 29, 1922 (price 10 cents), comes this enlightening story, which in turn quotes from the *New York Evening Mail*, also long gone:

It appears that the pioneer experiments were made with kites, let up from mountain peaks eighteen or twenty miles apart, each kite having attached to its underside a piece of fine copper wire gauze about fifteen inches square, connected with the wire, 600 feet in length, which served at once as kite string and aerial. An electric apparatus was used, and connection was made with the ground by laying in a wet place a coil of wire, one end of which was secured to the binding-post of a galvanometer. There was precisely the same electrical equipment connection with each kite, and signals were tested by observations of the deflection or movement of the galvanometer needle, the two stations being used alternately as transmitting and receiving stations.

This demonstration in 1866 from two peaks in the Blue Ridges in Virginia was called aerial telegraphy by Dr. Loomis, who failed to gain financial support for his far-out instruments of communication which were obviously ahead of their time. Money was hard to raise at the time because of "the panic of 1869 and the Chicago fire in 1871," according to his notes.

However, recently Loomis' place in radio has finally been recognized. In 1965 Senator Byrd of Virginia introduced a resolution to the U.S. Senate which cited Dr. Loomis as the inventor of radio telegraphy. This retroactive honor made him inventor of radio two years before Guglielmo Marconi was born. Dr. Loomis ended his days not as a radio or electrical experimenter. He finished his life as a dentist.

When Leonardo da Vinci submitted his secret of bridge building to Count Sforza he failed to include his use of kites to span rivers and gorges. It wasn't until many centuries later that kites were used to fly the first line across a gorge. One of the more dramatic examples of this in comparatively modern days was the flight of the first line across the Niagara Gorge, which resulted in the building of the first of the great suspension bridges. Homan Walsh was one of a number of kids who came out to the starting site of the bridge on a beautiful fall day in 1848. The Army engineers could not carry a line across the turbulent gorge via boat. A ten-dollar prize was offered by Chief Engineer T. G. Hulett to anyone who could fly a strand of line 800 feet across the river gorge to the Canadian side. Young Walsh's kite was the only one that made it from a field of twenty kids. His line landed clean across on the Canadian side and was hauled in carrying a thicker line, which in turn hauled in a still thicker line and finally a wire cable across the gorge. Architect Edward Wellman Serrell rightly gave the kite credit for the building of the bridge.

Without question, the designs of Eddy and Hargrave and others—including the most recent contribution to kite history, the nonrigid kite of Francis Rogallo described in Chapter Five—all fit into the recurrent pattern of toys that can serve mankind in peace and war.

4 ODD USES OF KITES

One of the most potent put-downs is the phrase "Go fly a kite." This expression conjures up the image of a ne'er-do-well who engages in trivial matters such as flying kites. The contrary is the truth, despite examples such as:

1. A banker who built a kite from bad checks;
2. A telephone company executive who flies kites from the window of his office to relax him in tense moments.
3. A businessman who travels a great deal and flies his kite on the road before contacting his next customer.
4. An Alcoholic Anonymous who flies a kite whenever the urge for a martini hits him.
5. The minister who flies prayers on his kite.

What better use of kited checks than to make a kite of them! This one-of-a-kind box kite was made for Philadelphia banker Edward A. Aff by his friend George R. Cook, III, president of the Princeton Bank and Trust Company in New Jersey.

One of the largest kites ever recorded was made by the French inventor Marcel Maillot. In 1883, he put together an octagonal kite that measured 32 feet across and had a surface of 775 square feet. In May, 1886, the kite lifted a 150-pound bag of sand 30 feet above the ground. The modern kite record for size is claimed by Bob Bartlett of Crete, Illinois, whose tetrahedral measures 83 feet long, has a total surface of 820 square feet of cloth and weighs 62 pounds. There is no record of Maillot's kite's weight.

The foregoing demonstrate that the kite is a fine substitute for the tranquilizer.

Not as well known, of course, as the previously discussed landmark kitings are such incidental events as Ben Franklin towing himself across a pond on his kite—not the same kite on which he discovered electricity. B. Franklin also used kites to tow himself on skates.

In parts of the Philippines the rice crops are protected from bird depredations by the use of large versions of bird kites, hawk shapes made of bamboo and paper. These bird kites are attached to the tops of supple poles erected in the fields and react as though handled by humans.

Well known for his electrical kite experiments, Benjamin Franklin was an even greater innovator of kite towing. He is shown here being towed across a lake by a kite "in an agreeable manner," while his son, who assisted him throughout the electrical experiments, here waits for Franklin with some dry clothes.

The Chinese, as well as the French, used kites to signal troop movements. The French flew what are now known as French military kites against the Germans in the Franco-Prussian War. They lost that war. They should have been fighting instead of flying kites if they expected to beat the Boche, according to contemporary thinkers.

The Chinese also used kites to fly fireworks over the heads of their enemies and scare them into thinking that the gods above were favoring the Chinese. Fireballs were also carried in this manner. The fuse was a fired punk that released the fireball from the kite when it burned through at a designated time.

In Portugal, fishermen went out to sea on sail and came back to their home ports on kites. Half an hour before returning to port, just as the wind died down, the fishermen would send up kites into an inshore current of air 500 feet above the sea. This took their boats right to their wharves.

In Connecticut Long Island Sound waters, Ben Kocivar (a brilliant writer, photographer, kite flier and sailor) and I improvised a catamaran rig which flew a combination of kites that towed his vessel into the middle of the sea. The kites were in tandem and random formation. They were controlled by pulleys attached to his mainsail post.

Master mariner Ben Kocivar and the author demonstrate the use of kites as sails to pull a catamaran. A military, sled and delta-wing kite were sent up to 20, 40 and 60 feet and managed to pull the boat at 1.5 knots in Long Island Sound. (*Ben Kocivar*)

People on the Delaware River "sailed" their sleds on the river 100 years ago. It's become a lost art, now being revived, for example, in Norwalk Harbor in southern Connecticut. On this river kite-drawn sleds were matched against sail sleds. As a witness and participant, I regret to report that the sail sleds outmatched the kite sleds.

In the days when there was good skating on the Delaware, the *Monthly Weather Review* of September, 1896, reported: "A sled is rigged up for the winter so as to be drawn by kites whenever there is unusually good skating on the Delaware."

Kites have been used in fields as scarecrows. In ancient China they were also used to signal field workers to assemble at the emperor's palace when the enemy was sighted.

In Jane Yolen's *The Emperor and the Kite*, a Chinese leader is imprisoned in a tower from which there seems no way for him to escape. But his darling little daughter flies a kite to her father in the tower. He cuts loose the kite, saves the rope, ties the rope to his prison bed, and slides down it to escape.

Kites are used today as an advertising medium. The large kite-manufacturing companies are now imprinting kites with all sorts of advertising messages. Hi-Fliers is probably the leader in this field, although the other companies listed in Appendix V will set up an ad campaign to fit any purpose.

The marriage of advertising and kites was actually a big business venture as early as 1906, when Samuel Perkins introduced his "Aerial Advertising Kites" at the Brockton Fair in Massachusetts. His clients included Coca Cola Company, A. S. Beck shoes and other popular products of the time still in existence today. Arthur Combs of Scituate, Massachusetts, was his partner in this venture.

No story of kite advertising is complete without Jim Moran's part in it. An inspired zany of a publicity man, he asked me to help him put together a kite that would carry three midgets on a flight along Fifth Avenue in New York City. These midgets would be raised from floor to floor and sing commercials into people's windows. The client was a candy manufacturer whose symbol was a trio of midgets enjoying a piece of candy.

For a month we worked on a huge kite in my apartment on Central Park West, across from the park. When we finished the kite it was so huge we couldn't get it out the door. So we sailed it out the window. We dragged it into the park where one of Moran's assistants had rounded up a number of newspapermen and photographers. Another assistant had the three trembling midgets in tow.

In full view of the newsmen and photographers, Moran directed the three midgets from Central Casting to get into a bosun's chair beneath the kite which was set up on a dolly that was to be rolled into the wind. The midgets whimpered at the moment of truth.

Persuasions, threats and promise of a bonus won over the midgets' fears. "Get into that chair, you cowardly little finks," he hissed. Moran is over six feet tall and almost as wide. The midgets put up no argument. A team of men began to wheel the dolly along a path. The midgets began to howl in fear when up came a policeman and ordered, "Halt."

All stopped dead in their tracks. The midgets dug their heels into the ground and cackled happily. "You are all under arrest," the cop stated. "You can't fly no midgets

An artist's rendition of press agent Jim Moran's midget-on-a-kite caper in Central Park, New York City, in 1951. In fact, the midgets never ascended and a park cop threatened to arrest Moran, thus stopping this use of kites as an advertising medium dead in its tracks. (*Jim Moran*)

in no Central Park in no kites, no time." Five negatives in one sentence, a grammatical feat unequaled in our time.

Despite Moran's arguments and the newsmen's pleas not to be a spoilsport, the cop was adamant. The only advice he could give was "Try Van Cortlandt Park."

In the confusion, the midgets escaped and Moran retreated in disgust. The great innovation in advertising and kite flying was forever gone.

It was only years later I learned from him that he had arranged for the phony arrest because he knew in his heart that the midgets would cop out. As it was, the arrest made as much news as the flight itself would have.

Another footnote to the history of the advertising profession is the attempt to set up an ad business by Harry Sauls, one of the great kite fliers of all times. Harry's company slogan was "Give 'Em the SKYSIGN." His customers included Silver Foam soap, 7-Up and Hearst's newspaper *The Examiner* of Los Angeles. One of Sauls's most spectacular banners was 24 feet high. Sauls's banners were set in nettings of No. 6 nylon cord. The letters were made of imported gauze of pure linen, "$1.00 per yard in quantity." The weight of a typical banner was about 50 pounds.

Sauls went broke in this business when the airplane and skywriters took over.

Harry Sauls, pioneer kite flier and creator of kite-flown advertising campaigns, with a Hargrave weather kite. (*Don Wellenkamp*)

Advertising has been part of the kite scene as far back as 1906 when Sam Perkins of Hingham, Massachusetts, introduced his "Aerial Advertising Kites" at the Brockton Fair. Some of his clients included Coca-Cola and Beck shoes. Harry Sauls also sent up 24-foot high banners, as shown, for 7-Up and Silver Foam soap. (*Harry Sauls*)

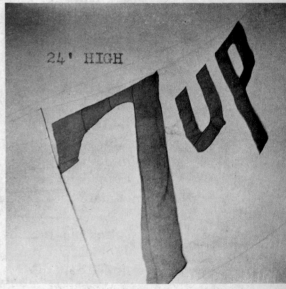

In 1972, The Tea Council used the classic Hi-Flier two-stick kites to promote their products. The event took place in Central Park with the author (left) and Mike Freedman (right) sending up 38 kites on one line. The stunt failed when the line broke.

In 1960, Ken Purdy, then the editor of *True* magazine, witnessed "kites as big as barndoors being flown seaward to rescue large boats simulating ships in distress. The jumbo kites were dropped so accurately, they effected rescues and created tow lines on sailing vessels a half mile off Compo Beach in Westport, Connecticut." I was also a witness to these simulated rescues by kites and, in fact, participated as technical adviser.

One of the most colorful and legendary characters in the history of kiting is Windwagon Smith, whose Conestoga wagon roamed or flew in the sea of grass on the plains of New Mexico. He is lost in the mist of time, and his name is unrecorded in history books. Nevertheless, I talked to people whose grandfathers had heard of him in their childhood. This was in Santa Fe in 1940 when making a Warner picture called "Sante Fe Trail," starring the late, great, romantic Errol Flynn. Windwagon Smith, according to local legend, was to come down from the Sangre de Cristo Mountains every hundred years in his kite-drawn covered wagon. We waited for him to arrive and give his blessings to the film, which told the story of the heroic mountain and plains men of the early nineteenth century.

Needless to say, Windwagon Smith failed to come in from the hills despite some inspired planning by the Warner Brothers publicity department. A local buffoon had volunteered to pull off the stunt with a covered wagon, which he planned to liberate from the Sante Fe Museum.

Windwagon Smith must have read about George Pocock, who early in the nineteenth century designed a special lightweight carriage to be drawn by kites on English roads. On January 8, 1822, Pocock gave his kite-drawn carriage its first road test.

The kites were foldable ones, with joints in the wings. The kites were manipulated by four lines which controlled their lateral as well as longitudinal angle to the wind. In this way the kites could be flown across the wind. They were flown in tandem.

Pocock called his carriage Char-volant from the French word for "kite," *cerf-*

volant. On his first test, his kite-drawn carriage traveled at speeds of 20 miles per hour and thus passed the horse-drawn carriage of the Duke of Gloucester. Conscious of this breach of manners, he slowed the Char-volant and let the nobleman pass him. The Duke's reaction to being outsped by a bunch of kites has not been recorded.

After giving a number of demonstrations, including one before George IV, Po-

In 1887, five ingenious kite enthusiasts of Terryville, Connecticut, built a giant kite that was reported to have towed them along a country road at 9 miles per hour. (The Sunday Republican, *Waterbury, Connecticut*)

Pocock's kite-powered carriage, the Char-volant, managed to do 25 miles per hour in 1825 but snagged its guidelines on tall trees.
(*Bettman Archives*)

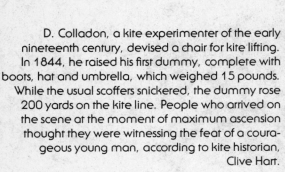

D. Colladon, a kite experimenter of the early nineteenth century, devised a chair for kite lifting. In 1844, he raised his first dummy, complete with boots, hat and umbrella, which weighed 15 pounds. While the usual scoffers snickered, the dummy rose 200 yards on the kite line. People who arrived on the scene at the moment of maximum ascension thought they were witnessing the feat of a courageous young man, according to kite historian, Clive Hart.

cock tried to make it commercial. But it never became a success. The most Pocock got out of it was free passage through tollgates.

The same George Pocock also took to the air by kite many times himself. He often attached chairs to giant kites and soared aloft to the complete consternation of his more staid British neighbors. They didn't particularly mind him risking his neck, but he also sent up his son and daughter.

In 1901 Almenia Rice, one of the loveliest trapeze artists of the day, attempted a kite flight. She or her agent hit upon a kite-flying stunt to call attention to her trapeze act, which was playing Boston. She had a giant box kite built and with proper fanfare hauled it to the top of the highest building, at that time approximately nine stories high. With several aides manipulating the giant two-celled kite, she seated herself in a sling attached to the spars and allowed herself to be flown off the building. The pretty girl, swinging beneath the giant kite, could be seen from all over Boston and by passengers and crewmen on ships entering and leaving the harbor. The kite was kept in the air for several hours before the girl finally was pulled safely back to the building and disembarked.

Another great English kite flier who contributed to the store of legends, lore and facts of kite flying was Lord Baden-Powell, who was an honored soldier and founder of the Boy Scout movement. Baden-Powell was a captain in the British Army in 1895 when he got wind of some of the experiments being conducted with man-carrying kites. He decided to see for himself whether this trick was feasible and had any practical use, so he hoisted his 150 pounds several hundred feet into the air on a number of occasions, using as many as five kites in tandem to achieve this feat. He is reported later to have used man-carrying kites for scouting purposes in Africa.

In the year 1405 Germany was using hot-air kite balloons which were dragon-shaped and hollow and carried lighted candles in their bellies. They were used as military standards, held aloft by horsemen.

The military use of kites by Samuel Franklin Cody has been described on pages 50–51. Cody also experimented with kite towing, and towed a "kite boat" across the

S. F. Cody and his novel kites. (a) Mr. Cody sending up the kite. (b) Mr. Cody in his kite-drawn boat. (c) Preparing the kite for its long flight. (d) Nearing the English coast.

English Channel. Later he attached an engine to a modified kite, called it a "power kite," and in it made the first short airplane flight in England. However, his kite was not box-shaped, although it was multicellular. All other experimenters in kite-airplanes had used the box kite. As a matter of fact the first airplanes were called "box kites." His kites were said to be the forerunner of the equipment used by the Royal Flying Corps in Aldershot, England, in 1904.

Albert Santos-Dumont, a wealthy Brazilian who lived in France, borrowed the Hargrave box kite idea to get his planes in the air as early as 1906, when he flew 25 meters to set a record.

In March, 1966, a spectacular photo of a ship at sea was made by Hank Van Meekeren, a professional photographer for the Holland-America Lines since 1956. At that time Hank—or the "Flying Dutchman," as he is called—attached a camera to a huge kite and went aboard the *Statendam*, to which he was assigned. With a bit of help from his wife, he built a photo-kite. The kite was a six-sided Blériot type of vehicle similar to the French military kite and was an adaptation of the powered kite that Louis Blériot flew across the English Channel.

At the bottom of the kite Hank suspended a piece of fishing rod to which he attached the camera. He launched the kite in the breeze as the ship traveled at 20 knots, going with the wind. A music-box-type mechanism tripped the camera shutter and he got a fine picture (bird's-eye view) of the *Statendam* under way. The picture was made 300 feet up. The camera was an old 2½ by 3¼ Zeiss with a Netter lens. *The New York Times* reproduced the picture.

This toy catamaran with its kite sail was built by Cap Herreshoff, according to the notes of the late F. Rankin Weisgerber, one of the great kite innovators. The kite sail was used 70 years ago and, according to witness Weisgerber, was capable of sailing 25 miles per hour.

Van Meekeren has tried to make pictures from kites in many foreign countries but is always balked by demands of police that he get an aerial photography license.

In Nassau, a new water sport has been developed—kite snorkeling—which is a boon to lazy swimmers. The principal equipment consists of kites and snorkels. Thus while peering into the blue-crystal world beneath the sea, the snorkeler hitches himself to prevailing trade winds via kites sailing high overhead. The more kites on your string, the faster you snorkel along.

Several more odd uses of kites are named by Clive Hart, distinguished Australian kite historian: (1) releasing pigeons from lofted baskets; (2) sending lifesaving equipment to stricken ships offshore; (3) carrying rocket flares; (4) passing contraband whiskey over the walls of cities; (5) sending surrender and safe passage documents over enemy lines (in American Civil War); (6) propaganda leaflets as in 5; (7) scaring partridges out of the brush.

But without a doubt the most ingenious use of a kite was demonstrated in a snowstorm in Aspen, Colorado, a few years ago when a skier who was experimenting with kites was felled and buried in a huge snowdrift. His rescuers covered every inch of the area where the drift had buried him but failed to find him. Finally one of his rescuers looked skyward and saw his kite aloft. They followed the kite line to the exact spot where the line entered the snowdrift. Sure enough, there was the kite skier, cold as mutton but alive, still clutching the kite line.

5 HOW EVER DO THEY FLY?

Several years ago, the small son of a West Coast aeronautical engineer announced that he no longer believed in Santa Claus because it would be impossible for an old gentleman burdened with a bag of toys, a sled and eight reindeer to fly through the air. However, the father restored the lad's faith by showing with charts, graphs and mathematical formulas that it would be possible, theoretically, for Santa to make his annual winter trip by air. All that would be needed really were the proper conditions of lift, drag and other aerodynamic factors.

Some veteran kite fliers will argue that given a strong enough line and a powerful wind, they could fly a manhole cover like a kite. Winds of hurricane or tornado fury, of course, have been known to lift automobiles, homes, trees and even railroad cars. At one of the breeziest spots on earth, Mount Washington, New Hampshire, stone buildings are anchored to the ground with heavy chains to keep them from blowing away in gusts that have been measured at over 200 miles per hour.

It is doubtful that any reader would consider flying a kite in a hurricane or any other winds packing enough force to cause property damage. A light breeze of only 4 or 5 miles per hour can be sufficient to get a kite into the sky. But the same aerodynamic factors needed to fly Santa Claus, a manhole cover or a jet plane are involved in getting a simple kite off the ground.

Although kites have been flown since prehistoric times, the question of just what made them fly was not considered on a scientific basis until the nineteenth century. The British scientist Sir George Cayley observed at that time that there were certain relationships between the shapes and sizes of bird wings and the ability of birds to fly; he also noted, importantly, that the angle at which the bird wing moved through the air had something to do with the bird's upward movement. Cayley built various kinds of kites and model wings, based on his bird studies, and tested their performance in air currents. Cayley's experiments eventually led to the development of the first gliders and the first known manned flight in gliders some fifty years before the Wright brothers' successful powered-flight experiments. From Cayley's studies came the term "lift," which he used to describe the effect of air pressure on an inclined plane surface, whether wing or kite, which helps it to rise upward.

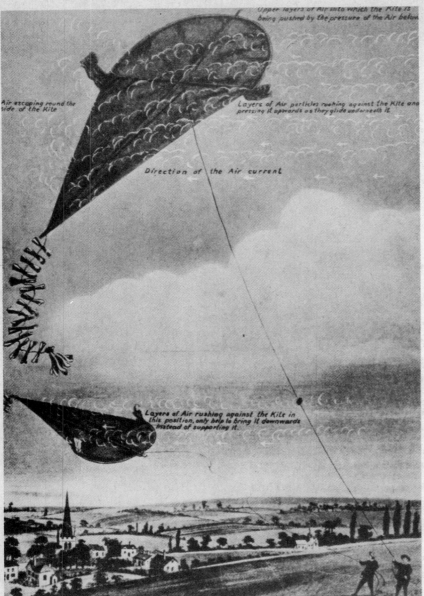

Upper layers of Air into which the Kite is
being pushed by the pressure of the Air below

Air escaping round the
side of the Kite

Layers of Air particles rushing against the Kite and
pressing it upwards as they glide underneath it

Direction of the Air current

Layers of Air rushing against the Kite in
this position, only help to bring it downwards
instead of supporting it.

The important thing in kite flying is that the line hold the kite against the air in a diagonal position. Then the rush of air against it acts like a wedge, tending to push the kite upward and backward. The line keeps the kite from going back, so it rises. (*New York Public Library Picture Collection*)

There are actually three different kinds of lift that can act on a kite to cause it to fly. The first kind can be demonstrated by playing the old game of sailing a deck of playing cards, one at a time, into an upturned hat. You will find that when you try to launch a card that is held parallel to the floor, or tilted slightly toward the floor, it is less likely to hit the target. The best success usually is achieved by holding the card so the leading edge is tilted slightly upward when it leaves the hand. The force of the air on the lower surface of the moving card will provide a bit of a lift. Although the air itself is still, there will be a relative motion of air against the undersurface of the card from the action of traveling from your hand to the hat. The lift effect is equivalent to what would be produced by a breeze traveling through the room at the same speed as that of the tossed card; at some point the force of the breeze against the bottom of the card would be sufficient to overcome the pull of gravity on the card.

A simple flat kite gets virtually all of its lift in this manner from the wind blowing against its lower surface when the kite is held at an angle that tilts the top upward. The kite thus gets its lift from the downward deflection of the air flowing toward it—whether the kite is held in the face of a natural wind or it is towed by its connecting line into calm air.

The paradoxical effect of a kite's lifting force being obtained from downward air deflection is based on Sir Isaac Newton's third law of motion, which states: to every action there is an equal and opposite reaction. When the momentum of the relative movement of air produces enough force to overcome the pull of gravity and the drag force, which tend to retard lift, the kite becomes airborne. Once airborne, the kite can continue to climb or be held at a fixed elevation as long as energy is expended by natural wind forces or by pulling or towing the line attached to the kite so that sufficient downward air deflection is maintained by the kite surface.

The second kind of lift is somewhat different, and requires a slight digression to explain it. In 1738 a Swiss mathematician named Daniel Bernoulli published a classic paper about the behavior of fluids (like water and air) in motion. One of Bernoulli's conclusions stated that fluids in motion exert less pressure on their surroundings the faster they move. If you pinch a hose, water will flow faster through the pinched section but at the same time will exert less pressure on the hose. Bernoulli's principle has been applied to the design of the airplane wing to produce the so-called airfoil shape.

This shape, a half-teardrop in cross section, has a curvature which causes the airflow over the top to travel faster than the airflow along the lower surface. This increase in the speed of the air above the wing produces a drop in pressure, which gives a lifting force to the air pressure on the wing's undersurface.

You can perform a simple experiment that demonstrates the lift exerted by air acting according to Bernoulli's principle. Hold a piece of ordinary 8½ × 11 inch paper by the corners of the short side. Hold it with your thumbs on top. Raise the paper to your lips and blow hard across the top. The rear end of the paper will lift up. The harder you blow, the greater the lift.

You can stimulate a nice argument among scientifically minded kiters as to exactly what application Bernoulli's principle has to a kite in flight. Probably, Bernoulli's principle has a negligible application to a flat kite flying at a low altitude, both because a flat kite lacks a significant airfoil curve and because any airfoil shape must be virtually flat to the wind—in effect, parallel to the ground—to work at all. But Bernoulli's principle probably does apply to many other types of kites, particularly to those whose covering bellies out to form a curved upper surface and which fly flat to the wind. At least one kite, the flexible Jalbert parafoil, gets almost all its lift from the application of Bernoulli's principle, since it is designed to have a cross section like that of an airplane wing.

There is a third way—admittedly, a minor one—in which kites can be lifted into the air: by updrafts, such as occur along the edges of mountains or inside the invisible vortex bubbles of heated air known as thermals. Sailplanes, vultures, hang gliders, eagles and skilled kite fliers all maneuver to take advantage of rising air whenever possible. Some idea of the lifting power that rising air possesses can be gleaned from the experience of Lieutenant Colonel William H. Rankin, a U.S. Marine pilot who bailed out of a disabled jet fighter over North Carolina in July, 1959. After a free fall of seven miles from an altitude of nearly 50,000 feet, Rankin's parachute opened as he passed through the upper cloud layer of a thunderstorm. The warm updrafts of the storm caught his chute like a kite and held the pilot high in the sky for nearly 40 minutes. As the storm abated, the chute was released from the lifting force of the rising tide of warm air and Rankin was lowered to the ground.

If lift were the only aerodynamic force acting on a kite, every kite would float overhead and stay there, restrained only by the pull of the line. But in fact, kites do not behave that way at all. Lift is in part counteracted by the weight of the kite and in part by the force known as drag—the resistance of the air to the motion of the kite both forward and backward. Drag affects all airborne objects, whether they be birds, jet aircraft, space capsules, or kites. When gravity and drag reach an equilibrium with the lifting forces, the kite stops moving upward and hovers in one spot, maintaining a constant angle with the ground. When drag and gravity forces become greater than the lifting force, the kite will drop back toward earth. But drag is not always the enemy of kite fliers. It is the drag of a kite tail, not its weight, that is the principal stabilizer of the flat kite everywhere.

The relationship of lift to drag usually is expressed in the form of a ratio, L/D. And although various subtle factors are involved in computing the efficiency of an

A kite-flying demonstration at the St. Louis Exhibition, 1904.

airfoil, such as a wing or a kite, a general rule of thumb is that the flyability of an airfoil is determined by the size of the L/D ratio. In other words, an airfoil with an L/D of 15/1 will be easier to fly than one with an L/D of 3/1. Since the L/D ratio also indicates the glide performance of an airfoil (a free floating kite with an L/D of 15/1 should coast 15 feet for every foot of altitude it drops if the wind movement suddenly stops), the lift-to-drag ratio is important in maneuvering a kite through gusts and shifts in air currents.

Although a kite of high efficiency, that is, one with a high lift-to-drag ratio, is needed to reach a high altitude, there are occasions when a kite of low efficiency is preferred. An example is the use of a kite to tow a boat across a lake, in which case the kite performs the function of a sail; a low L/D ratio would hold the kite at a low angle above the horizon and the wind energy would be converted to traction power. A kite with a low L/D ratio also is required when the goal of the maneuver is to get a line across a river or a canyon; a high-efficiency kite rising in a vertical manner would be useless for such a function.

The basic rules of aerodynamics for kite flying generally are described in terms of flat kites. However, a perfectly flat kite would lack stability if the covering material did not yield a bit to the pressure of air currents to form one or more slightly concave pockets. The billowing of the cover material offers some stability to a flat kite, but greater stability is built into the airfoil by adding a tail. The tail of a kite sometimes is called a keel, a more appropriate term because its function is like that of a ship's keel in providing resistance to the seemingly whimsical fluctuations of the fluid currents.

As described in the previous chapter, William A. Eddy discovered that tails were not essential to kites if they were designed with a bowed frame. Eddy's bow kite became popular because of its self-stabilizing design. By bowing the cross-stick, the kite automatically compensated for pressure changes caused by wind fluctuations; if the kite pitched in one direction, the increased pressure on either the top or bottom tended to correct the action. The spine of the Eddy kite functions as the keel, so that no tail is needed. And the covering material of the kite performs like the sides of a boat, in conjunction with the keel, in maintaining trim. Being shorter and wider than the traditional diamond or hexagonal flat kites, the Eddy design yields a more efficient L/D ratio—hence, a much better lift effect. Because of Eddy's interest in developing kite trains, the bow design enabled him to advance rapidly toward that goal.

Still another approach to the aerodynamics of kite flying was followed by the engineer Hargrave, who pioneered in the development of rubber-band-powered model airplanes in the 1880s. Like Cayley, Hargrave devoted much of his early research to the aerodynamics of flight by birds. He was particularly fascinated by Nature's design of the wings of birds that seemed to be able to cruise endlessly on air currents without flapping the wings. One of the results of his studies was the design of kites with two flat surfaces, one on either side of a wooden stick, or keel. Because the kite panels were set at an angle to the keel, the kites were called dihedral kites. The original dihedral kites, not surprisingly, resembled stick figure drawings of birds in flight, their wings held in position for soaring on updrafts. One of the early dihedral kites built by Hargrave had plane surfaces made of bird feathers. Hargrave observed that the dihedral designs gave his kites a unique kind of stability.

From various bird-wing configurations of dihedral surfaces, Hargrave advanced

The Giant Skyscraper. Eight box kites
secured together make a spectacular sight.
(*Ray Holland*)

toward kite designs in which the planes or panels of covering material intersected at right angles, resulting in vertical stabilizing surfaces between two superposed planes. The next step was the now popular box kites, which Hargrave preferred to call cellular kites. Some of the first box kites were indeed cellular rather than boxlike in appearance; they consisted of as many as sixteen small boxes fastened together in honeycomb fashion. He also experimented with box kites in which the surfaces were round rather than square. Still other Hargrave box kites had a basically square or rectangular design but the surfaces were rounded or cambered slightly, like the top surfaces of modern airplane wings. In addition, Hargrave designed and flew kites made with a covering surface of sheet tin rather than fabric or paper.

Hargrave's experiments contributed greatly to kite aerodynamics. His box kites had great efficiency and were stronger and more stable, especially in strong winds and poor weather, than the lighter kites that had been available previously. Their only disadvantage was that they were more difficult to get into the air during a mild breeze than the flat and bow kites. Hargrave's kite designs were adapted by meteorologists as a tool for studying and forecasting weather conditions. And the Wright brothers' kite glider, which preceded the first powered airplane flight by three years, was designed according to the principles developed by Hargrave.

There were experiments by Hargrave and the British military Captain B.F.S. Baden-Powell to develop nonrigid kites, or kites that did not require some kind of rigid framework in their structure. However, the first real success in producing a workable nonrigid kite was achieved by the American aeronautical engineer Francis Rogallo. While working with flexible wing designs in 1945, the National Aeronautics and Space Administration scientist began exploring the idea that an airplane wing could be packaged and deployed like a parachute. Previous uses of flexible materials in aerodynamic surfaces, Rogallo recounted some years later, had included parachutes, kites, boat sails, and windmills. And although the thin cantilever wings of modern high-speed airplanes are not completely rigid, they are elastic rather than flexible. They could not be folded up like a balloon or parachute.

"Although the chances of attaining any degree of success in such an endeavor appeared at the outset to be slight," said Rogallo, "it was possible to do a lot of exploratory work in the evenings and on weekends at little expense and without any special equipment. In the beginning, the aeroflexible lifting surface was called a kite because, of the three experimental methods used—testing in a homemade wind tunnel, free flying as hand-launched gliders, and tethered outdoor flying as kites— the kite appeared to be the nearest to a useful marketable application."

In November, 1948, Gertrude and Francis Rogallo filed an application for a U.S. patent on the device which was called a "Flexible Kite," even though it had applicability to all heavier-than-air flying machines. The patent was issued in March, 1951, and stated that while only one form of the kite had been shown insofar as configuration was concerned, other forms were entirely possible. "Probably our only precedent as to aeroflexible structure was the parachute," Rogallo recalled. "Our first models were made of cloth and looked something like parachutes because of the number and length of the shroud lines. And although we soon changed to plastic materials, the structure remained the same for several years.

"We attached threads to them at various points and towed them about the living room. When we found a promising configuration, we built a larger model of cloth and took it to an open field on the shore of Hampton Roads, Virginia, for a trial. If it didn't fly, we thought of a way to improve it, took it home for modifications, then returned to the open field for another trial. In order to pursue our experiments at night, we installed a 36-inch fan in our home so we could test kites in the doorway between two rooms. Our efforts were not in vain, for after many attempts we succeeded in making one of our kites fly. Many shapes and materials were tested in our homemade wind tunnel and in flight until we had developed several thoroughly satisfactory models.

"The shape of the flexible kite's lifting surface is not like that of a parachute but

As early as 1962 a **Science Newsletter** was announcing that "a $1.00 toy will help make possible a multimillion-dollar manned spacecraft to land on solid ground." It referred, of course, to Francis Rogallo's nonrigid kite shown here with the inventor himself.

is more nearly like that of a highly cambered supersonic wing. A very simple model can be made of a one-foot-square sheet of paper or plastic, with one of the diagonals serving as a centerline. A tail can be attached at a single point on the centerline or at the juncture of a pair of lines attached to the trailing edge, about midway between the centerline and the tips. The basic flexible kite has four shroud lines, similar to those used on parachutes, with two on each side, holding the surface area in a lobe or inverted bucket shape. By attaching additional shroud lines along the centerline diagonal, the surface can be formed into a double lobe or several lobes. A 25-inch kite may have 14 shroud lines altogether, and a 50-inch kite 28 shroud lines. But starting with the basic design, area and shroud lines can be added with almost no limit.

"Tests of the early configurations showed that some form of stabilizer was needed. At first we used long ribbonlike tails such as are commonly used on rigid kites. But later we adopted miniature tow targets that serve not only as stabilizers in flight but also as storage or carrying cases for the kites and flight line when not in use.

"While nonrigid, nonreinforced lifting surfaces are preferred in the design of flexible kites, the use of reinforcements can reduce the number of bridle lines needed, particularly in the larger versions that could be adapted for military or other purposes. However, the reinforcements can consist of hollow fabric tubes which are open at the front ends and closed at the rear ends so as to be inflatable by the oncoming wind and thereby maintained in shape.

"Since the early experimental days, manned flexible-wing aircraft have been towed by cars, boats and aircraft. They have been flown down gentle hills, they have been 'jumped' from aircraft, and powered versions have been taken off and flown under their own power.

"These kites can be flown either on a single line like a conventional kite or on a double line for precision control and acrobatic maneuvering—the high aerodynamic performance and crash resistance make the flexible kite ideal for acrobatics. Rigged for two-control operation, it can be made to dive, loop, do figure-eights, land and take off, and do other interesting maneuvers, either solo or in formation. Although it is waterproof, and unbreakable, the material will wear out with repeated hard crashes or rough handling. But generally, you can roll them up and even sit on them without causing damage to the kites.

"Among the variations in design for military and other purposes are a six-string model, which was evolved to reduce the number and length of shroud lines and to reduce the time required to attach them, and a four-string model, the result of further efforts to reduce the number and length of harness lines. A change in configuration of the surface also was found to eliminate the need for a tail, although this design was found to be more sensitive to atmospheric disturbances and other flight factors. If a load is attached to the loops in place of the flight line, the tailless kite can be converted into a glider.

"Control of the glider model is relatively simple. If the line to the right tip is shortened, the glider will turn to the right. If the rear line is shortened relative to the front lines, the glider will trim at a higher level of attack. An L/D of more than 6/1 is attainable with a glider of this design.

"The glider model could be scaled upward to carry people or cargo loads. Such a glider could be towed into the air by an automobile, boat, airplane or powered winch, or it could be launched from a tower or any high point of ground, or it could be dropped from an aircraft. One might even be able to soar with such a device. Propulsion could be added, using either propellers or jet engines. The device might be used as the lifting component of a flying automobile or as an auxiliary wing for an airplane. The possibilities of its use in both war and peace are numerous."

The flexible-wing concept, according to Rogallo, may be as old as the pterodactyl. And it was given serious consideration by Leonardo da Vinci. But modern airplane design followed the rigid-wing concepts, utilizing the experiences of man in building roof trusses and bridges, and box kites and gliders. With the entry of the United States into the space race, following the successful Soviet launching of Sputnik I, NASA officials took a more serious look at Rogallo's experience with his patented "Flexikite" and decided that the two-lobe, single-curvature, suspended-load model should be investigated as a possible reentry glider for space capsules. It also was demonstrated as a wing for powered aircraft and an air-drop glider, both radio controlled, as well as for the recovery of rocket boosters.

Because of the versatility of the flexible-wing design, there is no single model that is "best" for all possible applications. In wind tunnel tests at the NASA Langley Research Center, various Rogallo kite designs were shown to cover a lift-drag spectrum ranging from that of slightly gliding parachutes, with an L/D of about 1/1, up to the level of high-efficiency conventional rigid wings, with an L/D of over 30/1. They have been tested with payloads of up to 15,000 pounds. Used as personal portable gliders, they have been used in ridge-soaring flights of over 60 minutes' duration. Several different army ground vehicles, including a jeep and a sled loaded with cargo, were converted to towed gliders by the attachment of simple flexible wings. The military advantage of such devices is that aerial towing of vehicles or heavy weapons can enable a strike force to move equipment and supplies by literally jumping over bridges, tunnels, overpasses, narrow roads, or other possible surface restrictions. Large surfaces are needed, of course, to lift large loads; a 4,000-square-foot wing was developed to deliver a load of about 6,000 pounds.

Thomas H. Purcell, Jr., who helped develop the first man-carrying flexible wings, adapted the Rogallo concept to the design of a flying boat equipped with a flexible wing that can be folded down inside the hull by turning a crank inside the cockpit. Others have studied applications of the flexible wing in the development of flying automobiles; flying sports cars have been in use for several years, but the pioneering designs were based on the use of rigid wings.

Rogallo flexible-wing models have been built with surface materials of cloth, sheet aluminum, and several plastic materials; the surface can be transparent or coated with a variety of materials, such as a radar-reflecting paint. They are adaptable to a wide range of flying conditions, including travel through sonic and thermal barriers. Among suggested uses for the future are flexible wings that can be packed into the fuselage of an aircraft and deployed to gently lower the airplane to the ground like a glider if the aircraft lost power while in flight.

Among other modern investigators of the aerodynamics of kite flying is Robert H. Gonter, who has developed a digital computer program for calculating the performance of kites. Using the facilities of the Research Computing Center of the University of Massachusetts, Gonter determined optimum performance characteristics for flat kites, Eddy kites and airfoil kites. He also calculated effects on performance of

Top secret until released for this book, these six photographs show the progress of the nonrigid kite as a working tool for the military as well as for industry. (*Ryan Aeronautics-6*)

Short takeoffs and landings make this "flying Jeep" ideal as a utility cargo vehicle servicing remote, rough areas where limited airstrips are available.

The prototype of the world's first manned test bed which was successfully flown in 1961 to demonstrate functional and aerodynamic characteristics. Upon completion of this flight test program, the test bed was presented to the army, which cooperated with NASA in successful completion of the extensive wind-tunnel testing to confirm and correlate data obtained in actual test flights.

This flex-wing air cargo glider is towed behind a helicopter to increase cargo capacity.

The Precision Drop Glider is designed to carry large quantities of priority cargo into areas of limited landing space. The PDG can "home" on a portable ground beacon, or be remotely controlled to a pinpoint landing by launch aircraft or an operator on the ground. It is dropped from fixed-wing aircraft or helicopters.

The Towed Universal Glider (TUG) is designed to carry 4,000-pound payloads, the largest ever carried by flex-wing vehicles. TUGs would enable helicopter squadrons to move into forward bases and establish supply dumps, thus helping to solve logistic problems complicated by dense terrain.

The Flex Bee Surveillance Drone is a lightweight, highly mobile experimental reconnaissance vehicle used in the military for launching from forward areas and bringing back intelligence photos of enemy targets that cannot be seen from the launch site.

kites of different weights according to different kite-string angles as fixed by the bridle. His calculations, for example, indicated that a weightless flat kite flies at the highest angle of all three types and does so at a kite-string angle fixed by the bridle of 90 degrees; his computer-plotted graphs also show the decrease in angle associated with increased weight of the kite. An Eddy kite, by comparison, has an equilibrium string angle of about 64 degrees and is relatively insensitive to the angle fixed by the bridle between 90 and 105 degrees, while the weightless airfoil kite has a string angle of almost 80 degrees when the angle fixed by the bridle is near 100 degrees.

Gonter's program is based on the premise that kites with a higher L/D ratio will fly at a higher angle. Thus, "the measure of performance is the angle the kite string makes with the horizontal; the larger the angle, the better the performance." Gonter also has used the computer to calculate the relation of string tension to equilibrium angles for the three types of kites. His studies show that a weightless flat kite has very small pull at its high angle. And when the "weight is increased, the equilibrium string angle is lower but the string tension is much higher." The performance of the Eddy kite is similar in that respect, with string tension increasing with increased weight, "but with only small changes in tension for large changes in angles of attachment." But Gonter found that the airfoil kite has opposite characteristics, with string tension decreasing as the weight increases.

Gonter's work helps confirm the aerodynamic concepts of kite equilibrium in flight. When the wind speed increases, the force against a conventional kite surface increases and both the lift and drag components increase. The lift component will temporarily exceed the weight of the kite and the vertical component of the pull. As the kite rises in response to the added lift component, against a fixed length of line and fixed bridle, it will be restrained from flying outward but the angle with the horizontal will increase. The kite will then offer less resistance to the wind, and equilibrium will be restored at a new altitude and angle to the horizontal.

If the reverse wind action occurs, the lift will decrease to less than the opposing forces of kite and string weight and string tension, and the kite will drop. As the kite drops, the angle with the horizontal decreases. The kite then will offer more resistance to the wind, and while large lift and drag components are produced, there will be more drag than lift. But the kite will seek a position of equilibrium again at a lower altitude and smaller angle with the horizontal. Similar changes in equilibrium can be effected by controlling the tension on the line; reducing the tension on the line can reduce the lift and relative wind, whereas increasing the tension by pulling on the line will increase the lift and relative wind.

As indicated by Gonter's computations, the design of the bridle is an important factor in kite performance. Proper design and location of the pivot point and the bridle contribute to kite stability. He found, for example, that performance of an airfoil kite should improve if the bridle attachment angle is closer to 100 degrees, or 10 degrees greater than the bridle angle attachment recommended for flat kites, although the bridle attachment angle for an Eddy kite could vary somewhat without affecting performance significantly.

Gonter also has contributed some important studies on the drag forces of kite string on the height and position of the kite, the singing or Aeolian tones produced by wind vibrating a kite string, and a method of computing the position of a kite that cannot be observed because of clouds or other visual obstacles. Working with

20-pound-test nylon net twine, Gonter determined that the wind force perpendicular to a kite string can produce a drag component that is equivalent to from 20 to 40 times the weight of the kite string. Although kite fliers generally have assumed that the force of wind against the line is almost nonexistent, Gonter's calculations suggest that the drag factor is significant enough to be included in careful studies of kite performance. The studies also indicate that the drag factor produced by wind blowing against the kite line increases with the altitude of the kite. His paper on the Aeolian vibrations of kite strings offers further evidence of the effects of wind pressure on kite lines, since wind velocity and string diameter are key factors in the production of the tones.

The introduction of wind tunnels, computers, new synthetic materials and new

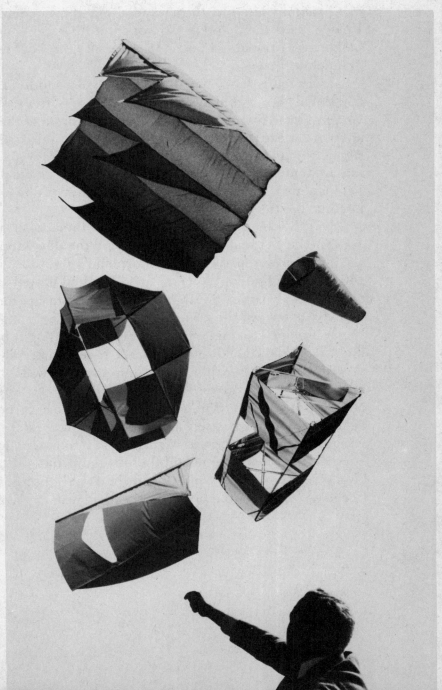

Aerodynamics in action: classic rigid and nonrigid kite designs for today include the Jalbert Parafoil (top); a spectacular winged box kite (left center); a maneuverable tethered airframe box kite that uses a double line to loop, spin, stall and more (right center); the Allison flexible kite, a variation of the sled (bottom). A ''flight tube'' helps control the parafoil. (*Courtesy The Kite Factory, Seattle, Washington*)

scientific knowledge into the ancient art of kite flying has helped rejuvenate interest in the sport. A generation ago, one might have wondered, "What can there be that is new about flying a kite?" But the recent work by Rogallo, Gonter and others has greatly advanced kite technology and suggests that the final paragraph on kite aerodynamics will never be written as long as man continues his search for better kites and new ways to utilize them.

Rogallo had taught me the use of the most scientific and sophisticated kite conceived in the long history of flying instruments. Gonter taught me that nimbleness in kite flying was more important than arcane knowledge.

In a meadow near my daughter's home in Massachusetts, Gonter and I held a shoot-out, he with a simple flat-bowed kite, I with a huge French military kite mounted to an 80-pound-test line on a 10.0 reel. My son-in-law, David Stemple, associate director of the Computer Center, acted as referee.

I shot my kite into the air and climbed over some hundred-foot trees over which I played and gamboled as Gonter carefully eased out his kite near my position, just looking for company. I began to show off in front of my daughter, her friends and my grandchildren.

I was really fancy dancing when all of a sudden a gust of wind tightened my line and down went my heavy kite into a copse of trees. I was humiliated, but sportsman Gonter began to maneuver his line under mine to thus lift me out of the trees where another breeze would set me free. Patiently and skillfully he performed this delicate separation and set me free. To free himself from my hug of death, he withdrew his kite from my line and went on his way, only to have my kite dive down once more as I impatiently fast-reeled it and thus created a downward pressure that crashed the kite into the trees.

It is still there, a monument to man's impatience and his pride.

The kite's great contribution was in the development of the airplane. Sir George Cayley is now regarded as the airplane's basic originator. As discussed earlier, in 1804 he built five-foot-long gliders, "the first proper successful airplanes," according to Charles H. Gibbs-Smith, aeronautical historian for the Science Museum in London. A kite formed the glider's wing.

A biplane kite and a buzzard taught the Wright brothers how to control airplane flight. "The Wright brothers didn't invent the rudder, the wing or the engine," according to Paul Garber, "but their airplane was controlled in all three axes, yaw, pitch and roll," and roll they learned from the kite. Wrote Wilbur Wright: "My observations of the flight of buzzards led me to believe that they regain lateral balance when partly overturned by a gust of wind, by the torsion of the tips of their wings." When the buzzard is gusted out of horizontal position, it pulls down the rear edge of its dropped wing and thereby gains more lift. This "roll" control seemed to be the secret of flight control, and the Wright brothers began to construct a biplane kite to demonstrate the principle they had just discovered.

6 HOW TO MAKE AND FLY SOME DAZZLING KITES

By now, you will be ready and eager, we hope, to try making or even designing some kites of your own. This chapter, prepared under the supervision of technical adviser Caleb Crowell, shows you how to do this. It contains a discussion and listing of kite-building materials and tools, followed by a detailed series of plans and directions for constructing more than two dozen different kites. First, however, a few general observations.

Once you have selected a particular kite design, you can follow its plan literally. Or you can modify the dimensions, within limits, so long as you do not change the proportions. Beginning with the basic two-stick kite, for example, the ratio between the height and width should be 6 to 5. If the height is 36 inches, the width should be 30 inches. If you make the height 48 inches, then the width will be 40 inches; a smaller size would be in the proportion of 24 inches of height to 20 inches of width, and so on.

There are certain important constraints you should keep in mind whenever you build a kite. One is the weight factor. Always use the lightest but strongest materials available. And remember that, paradoxically, a big kite with a large lifting surface may fly more easily in a light wind than a kite of the same design that has less weight but also less surface material. A Hargrave weather kite with 120 square feet of lifting surface, for example, is easier to fly in a wind of 8 to 10 miles per hour than a kite of the same design with only 68 square feet of surface; but the smaller kite flies better in a moderate wind of 12 to 30 miles per hour.

A second set of reins on your creativity is the laws of aerodynamics. Despite the apparently infinite variety of kite designs and patterns, just about all kites fall into three basic types—the flat kite, the box kite, and the flexible kite. All flyable kites are simply variations of these basic designs. And for nearly the entire history of kites, stretching over perhaps five thousand years of time, there was only one type of kite in use: the flat kite and its primary variation, the bowed kite.

This bit of information is important to remember when building kites from kits or from raw materials, or when designing a new variation, because any individual touches that you might add to a basic kite pattern will have to conform to the aerodynamic limitations of the existing types. This advice is not intended to discourage

The inventive Leo Eustis of West Newton, Massachusetts, shows his kite spaceship as a lesson in redundancy: he's reinvented the airship. This one is 14 feet long, 8 feet wide at wingspread. It is completely collapsible to fit into a corrugated box 6 feet long and about 8 inches square. Eustis believes that under proper conditions the kite, made of soft pine and polyester crepe cloth in varied colors, can explore the fringes of space. Incidentally, he recommends the following conditions for a flight into space: wind velocity 25 miles per hour; preferably an easterly wind. (*Leo Eustis*)

any imaginative kite flier, and if some innovative kite builder comes up with a fourth basic type of kite he will certainly be treated as a hero by millions of kite fliers around the world. But it should be noted that, with the exception of journalist William Eddy's reworking of the Malay bowed kite that now bears his name, the only radically new ideas in kite designs in recent generations were developed by aerodynamic scientists. Lawrence Hargrave, inventor of the box kite, was trained as an engineer and contributed numerous scientific articles to professional journals during the nearly twenty years that he devoted to the development of the box kite concept. The flexible kite designs of Francis Rogallo also evolved not from a sudden brainstorm but from years of patient scientific research.

But enough about limitations. Kites are meant to lift your spirit, not to confine it. Select your materials, choose your design, and go build a kite.

MATERIALS AND TOOLS

As you start work on a kite, give some thought to what you're going to build it out of and what tools you're going to use. Different materials have different characteristics, and a material that is suitable for one kind of kite may be next to useless for another. If you try to make an Indian fighter kite out of the sturdy dowels and coarse-weave cloth that are fine for a big delta wing, you'll end up with a structure possessing the grace of an airborne gorilla. On the other hand, if you try to make a flexible Rogallo kite out of the ultrathin plastic sheeting that works so well with a fighter kite, you'll have an object that the wind crumples in midair like a fist. The description of kite materials that follows should help give you some idea of the virtues and deficiencies of common materials used in making kites.

Coverings

Paper, cloth, or plastic—these are the three standard coverings for a kite. Which one you choose depends in part on the size of the kite and in part on other characteristics to be discussed. Paper, the childhood standby, makes an excellent covering for all but the largest kites. Its obvious defects are that it tears easily and that it dissolves in a rainstorm. The standard remedy for the latter defect is, of course, not to fly a paper kite in a rainstorm. The former defect can be alleviated, if not cured, by reinforcing all edges. Running tape along the edges is the quickest and easiest way. Folding and glueing the paper edges over an outlining string is more elegant and stronger, but also more time-consuming. Either way if handled with care, a reinforced paper kite can last for several years. Those rips that do occur can be mended with tape with little or no impairment of the kite's flying characteristics.

Almost any kind of paper can be used for some kind of kite, if you take into account its peculiarities. Newspapers, for example, can't withstand a pull, so they have to be carefully reinforced and not put under too much tension. Rice paper is strong but heavy, and makes a strong, heavy kite. Most tissue paper tears easily, so avoid it for all but the smallest kites. There is one exception: the extra-heavy grade of tissue paper often found in Oriental stores or five-and-dime stores. One type is generally known as Madras tissue. It's striped in various colors, and makes an attractive, decorative kite. Of all papers, it's close to the best compromise for a light but strong kite material.

Cloth is another standard kite covering. Ordinary muslin is a fine fabric for the larger kites. Silk is an old favorite, although it tends to be hard to work with and expensive, and it's not as light as you might think. Beware of cheap synthetics in loose weaves that may stretch out of shape. A new favorite of many kite enthusiasts is nylon Ripstop, also called Zephyrlite or spinnaker cloth, a lightweight (1 ounce or less to the square yard) strong cloth that can make just about any kind of kite. The newest modifications of this cloth don't even need hemming!

Except for the new Ripstop, the edges of cloth usually need some kind of reinforcing to prevent rips or unraveling. Hemming is fine if the edge is straight; otherwise an overcast or staying stitch will have to be used. The edges of older types of nylon Ripstop can be protected by a third method: melting. You can both cut Ripstop and melt the cut edges with a pencil-type soldering iron. Experiment with a scrap before you try it out on a kite, however!

Plastic is the third type of kite covering. Polyethylene—the plastic that garbage and garment bags are made from— is widely used in commercial kites, but it tends to stretch and does not take glue well. More useful is Mylar polyester, a plastic sheeting made by Du Pont in a range of thicknesses. It is either clear or aluminized; in the latter case it looks like aluminum foil. Half-mil Mylar (one half of 1/1000 of an inch), about the thickness of the cellophane wrapping of a cigarette package, is a fine kite material: tough, strong, light. If you can't get it at a store that specializes in selling plastics to artists and craftsmen, or if there is no such store near you, go to a sporting goods or camping store and ask for a Space Rescue Blanket. You'll get a Mylar sheet about 56 by 84 inches, silver on one side and copper-colored on the other, ideal for making small to medium-sized kites. Goodyear's Pliobond glue (glues are discussed later) can be used on it, as can all the standard tapes. If you reinforce the edges with tape, you'll have a virtually untearable kite. Heavier Mylar is good for large kites, particularly box kites and flexible Rogallo kites.

A new plastic material, Du Pont's Tyvek, has come to the fore in recent years. A form of spun polyethylene, it has some of the characteristics of cloth, some of paper, and some of plastic. It is light, needs little reinforcing along the edges, and can be glued with ordinary white glue. It can be ordered from the L. G. Striegel Mfg. Co., 1223 Arcade Avenue, Louisville, Kentucky 40215.

Sticks

All kites except the very modern flexible types use sticks of some kind as framing material to give the kite its shape. Wood slats are perhaps the commonest type of stick. Spruce, white pine, or other strong light wood is fine. Look out for yellow pine or fir, which tend to snap easily. Balsa is useless. If it has to take any strain whatever, it snaps. Hardwoods, oak or ash, for example, are heavier than pine and spruce, but their extra strength may not compensate for their increased weight. Hardwood dowels, however, are widely used for many kinds of kite. The commonly used ones range in size from ⅛ inch to 5/16 or even ⅜ inch in diameter. Maple and birch are both good dowel woods.

Bamboo and rattan are two useful materials for flexible sticks. Bamboo is the toughest and springiest of natural materials; rattan is equally tough and even lighter than bamboo. It is also less springy and more pliable. You can get bamboo strips from a bamboo roll-type window shade. Laminate them by glueing strips together, one on top of another, for extra strength. Or get a bamboo pole, split it lengthwise into sticks, and sandpaper into the size you want. The shiny outside of the bamboo is the strongest part. Don't slice or sand it off. As for rattan, the most useful size is a quarter inch in diameter. Use it for curved or bowed frame members.

Fiber glass rods (also called GPO, for glass polyester) are moderately heavy but unbelievably strong and resilient. Beware of trying to shape them, however. If you try to sandpaper a fiber glass rod, for example, tiny fibers and slivers of glass can get in your hands, your clothes, even the air you breathe.

Glue

For wood, a white glue (like Elmer's) is strong, springy, and waterproof enough for most kite-building uses. (When you glue two pieces of wood together, incidentally, first apply glue, then wrap the joint tightly with heavy thread or string, and finally spread a second layer of glue over the thread.) White glue can also be used on the heavier grades of paper. For lighter paper, like the Madras tissue previously recommended, rubber cement or plastic cement like Du Pont's Duco is preferable, since the water content of white glue tends to wrinkle tissue.

In addition to white glue and rubber cement, a glue called Pliobond, manufactured by Goodyear, is a tough and versatile adhesive with characteristics resembling a very strong rubber cement. So-called five-minute epoxy glues make very strong wood joints.

Tape

Tape is the kite maker's standby for constructing, reinforcing, and repairing paper and plastic kites. The clear and the cloudy tapes are both useful; the ordinary Scotch brands you find in stationery stores are perfect for most uses where they are not required to withstand strain. Where a stronger tape is needed, use one of the so-called fiber tapes or strapping tapes, with fibers running along its length and sometimes across it as well. For cloth kites, there are certain iron-on cloth tapes available in five-and-dime stores. They are heavy, however, even heavier than strapping tape, so don't load a kite down with lots of iron-on tape connections.

Line

Last of the kite materials is line, or string, or thread—used for framing a kite, for making its bridle, and for flying. Don't skimp on good line if you want your kites to fly well. Heavy wrapping twine, for example, is useless because of its weight, and ordinary string is so fuzzy that it catches the wind and adds tremendous drag to the kite.

For very light kites, use thread, but fairly heavy thread. Carpet thread, or the thread size referred to as 12/4, is ideal for most purposes. Or use a nylon monofilament line. You can get it in a sporting goods store, where different strengths of monofilament are sold as fishing line. Twisted nylon string can withstand medium to high pulls; so can braided Dacron. A visit to a fishing store or sporting goods store will provide you with many different varieties of kite line. And as a bonus, fishing line is rated according to the strength of the pull required to break it. A 28-pound-test line, which can withstand pulls up to 28 pounds, is a fine weight for a medium-sized kite. A large kite—one the size of a man (or a large boy)—may need a line in the 80-pound-test range. As for a really giant kite, you're on your own.

Tools

Fortunately, you don't need many tools to build kites. You should have scissors and a sharp, pointed knife of the kind model-makers use. Draftsman's tools for drawing the kite include compass, pencils, and rulers—a 12-inch one and a good, straight, preferably metal yardstick. A saw is necessary if you're going to work with wood, and a small C clamp is useful to hold sticks in place during glueing. If you work with cloth, a sewing machine is almost a necessity, particularly with slippery-surfaced cloth like nylon Ripstop. And whittling bamboo to shape is most easily done with a linoleum knife, which has a curved blade like a sickle.

THE BERMUDA CHILDREN'S KITE

To get you started right away, here's a little kite that's both easy to construct and a surprisingly good flier. Children on the island of Bermuda make it. It is one of the easiest kites in this world to build. The other kites in this book must be built from

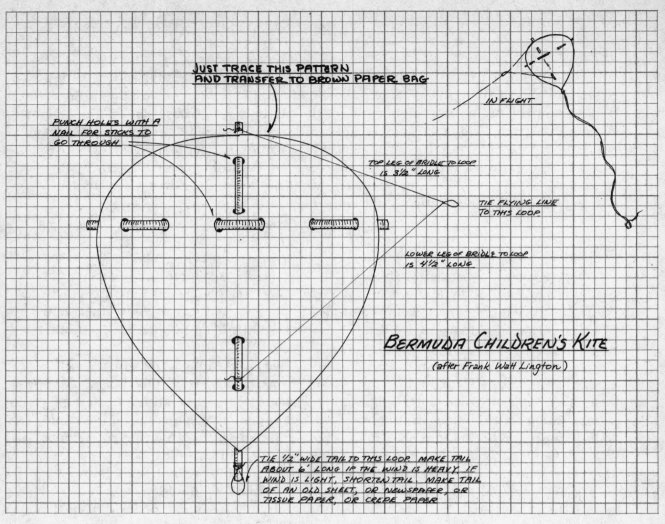

JUST TRACE THIS PATTERN
AND TRANSFER TO BROWN PAPER BAG

IN FLIGHT

PUNCH HOLES WITH A
NAIL FOR STICKS TO
GO THROUGH

TOP LEG OF BRIDLE TO LOOP
IS 3½" LONG

TIE FLYING LINE
TO THIS LOOP

LOWER LEG OF BRIDLE TO LOOP
IS 4½" LONG

BERMUDA CHILDREN'S KITE

(after Frank Watt Lington)

TIE ½" WIDE TAIL TO THIS LOOP. MAKE TAIL
ABOUT 6' LONG IF THE WIND IS HEAVY. IF
WIND IS LIGHT, SHORTEN TAIL. MAKE TAIL
OF AN OLD SHEET, OR NEWSPAPER, OR
TISSUE PAPER, OR CREPE PAPER

plans; this one need only be traced, since the accompanying drawing is actual size. Thanks go to Mr. Frank Wattlington, who depicts this kite in his booklet *Bermuda Kites, How To Make—and Fly Them.*

Materials

brown paper bag or brown wrapping paper
reed stems, or twigs, or strips from a packing crate, or bamboo barbecue skewers, or any wood that is light in weight; about 1/16 inch in diameter is fine
thread, and a nail to punch holes
strips of paper or cloth ½ inch wide and 6 feet long

Tips on Construction

Trace the kite and transfer to the back of a paper bag. Follow the directions on the drawing.

Variations

How can you vary something this simple? Make it bigger—or make it smaller. See if you can use this design to come up with a duplicate of the first kite, which was probably just a leaf. Use a large leaf instead of paper. The rib of the leaf serves as an upright stick so you need only find a twig to use as a crosspiece. See what you can improvise as a tail—perhaps wisps of braided grass. Even if your variation never gets off the ground, it should give you a new respect for that unknown East Asian genius who, thousands of years ago, constructed the first kite.

Flying the Bermuda Children's Kite

To fly the Bermuda children's kite, follow the directions given at the end of this chapter. If you don't get a perfect flier right off, maybe there's not enough wind. But if the wind is OK and you still have trouble with the kite, experiment with two things, the tail and the bridle. The tail may be too short, in which case the kite will twist and turn in every direction, or it may be too long, weighting the kite down.

The other, more delicate type of adjustment is made on the bridle. If the upper leg of the bridle string—the part above the loop— is too long, the kite will pull hard but won't rise in the air. If it's too short, the kite will tend to flip over toward you and dive headfirst into the wind. You should experiment with different adjustments of the bridle string until you become familiar with what different positions do to your kite's prowess as a flier. You'll find, interestingly enough, that the best position in a light wind may not be the best in a heavy wind.

THE BASIC TWO-STICK KITE

This is the classic kite design, the anonymously created shape that has been flown for generations and has withstood the test of time. It really needs no introduction.

Materials

1 flat stick ½ × ⅜ × 36 inches
1 flat stick ½ × ⅜ × 30 inches
1 sheet of light paper or light plastic, 30 × 36 inches
length of string, about 20 feet
glue

Tips on Construction

Cut a notch in each end of both flat sticks, deep enough to hold a width of string firmly. Wrap a few turns of string firmly around the sticks just below each notch and cover with glue, to prevent splitting. Place the 30-inch stick horizontally across the 36-inch stick at a point 7 inches below the top of the longer stick. The shorter stick should extend about 15 inches in either direction from the point where it crosses the longer stick. Tie the sticks firmly at that point with a short piece of string, and cover the tied string with glue. This is the frame of the kite.

Next, run a length of string around the perimeter of the kite frame, beginning at the top of the cross. The string should run through each of the notched ends of the

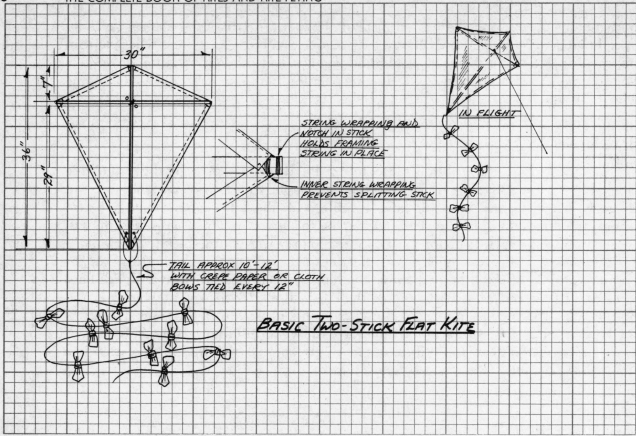

STRING WRAPPING AND NOTCH IN STICK HOLDS FRAMING STRING IN PLACE

INNER STRING WRAPPING PREVENTS SPLITTING STICK

IN FLIGHT

30"

7"

36"

28"

TAIL APPROX 10'-12' WITH CREPE PAPER OR CLOTH BOWS TIED EVERY 12"

BASIC TWO-STICK FLAT KITE

sticks to form an outline of the kite. Be sure the string is fairly taut but not tight enough to warp the shape of the sticks. Tie a small piece of string around the outside of each stick end after the framing string is in place.

Place the frame over the sheet of kite surface material and cut the paper or plastic with a margin of ½ to ¾ inch around the framing string. The additional material is needed as a flap to cover the framing string. However, the surfacing material should be trimmed around the notched ends so they remain exposed at the tips.

Spread glue or paste along the flaps and fold them over the framing string. After the framing string is completely enclosed, except for the tips of the sticks, let the glue dry.

You can fly this kite without a bridle, simply by punching two holes through the covering where the sticks cross and tying your flying line there. Look at the diagram to see where to make the holes. The kite will be steadier, however, if you use a bridle. Attach a string to the two notched ends of the short stick, running across the kite at the point where the sticks cross, so that the string has about 6 inches of slack. Then attach a second string running the length of the kite. Tie it to the notched ends of the long stick so that it also has about 6 inches of slack at the intersection of the sticks and can be tied to the cross string length of string at that point. The two strings, with lines running to the four corners of the kite, will form the bridle. The kite line will be attached to the bridle at the point where the bridle strings cross and are tied together.

Add a tail at the bottom of the kite, using scraps of cloth or similar light materials tied to a string. The tail can be lengthened, if needed, by adding more scraps of cloth, depending upon how much length and weight are needed to achieve good kite performance and stability in the available winds of the day.

Variations

Since the flat kite with a tail is the oldest type of kite, it may be imagined that it has numberless variants. A few are shown in the next section of this chapter, including ones with more than two sticks. Follow the plans for them, or try your luck with a design of your own.

Flying the Basic Two-Stick Flat Kite

The two-stick kite is a kite with considerable drag. Don't expect it to soar overhead. Its tendency is to fly outward, not upward. So be sure you have plenty of space in which to fly it, free of power lines and trees and not over any roads or highways.

If your kite doesn't perform quite as well as you might wish, experiment with the bridle and the tail, as suggested in the description of the Bermuda children's kite. A simple test for the bridle is as follows. Let the kite dangle from the flying line. The bridle should hold it so that the spine of the kite is inclined at about a 15-degree angle above the horizontal. From this point, the bridle can be adjusted for best performance.

Junius Bradshaw's "Perfect" Two-Stick Kite

Despite the variety of kites being flown today— delta wings, parafoils, sleds, and whatnots—the homely two-stick kite still has its partisans who consider it the best of all kites. One partisan is Junius Bradshaw, master kite maker and flier from rural Carrsville, Virginia. Junius considers his variant of the two-sticker to be the "perfect" kite. Until April, 1975, he had little chance to demonstrate his powers outside the Carrsville area. But on April 26, 1975, he hit it in a big way. He made his first trip to New York City to demonstrate his "perfect kite," high over Central Park's Sheep Meadow, while more than a thousand persons, including TV cameramen and press photographers, looked on.

Junius is a foreman for Union Camp Corporation in Franklin, Virginia. In 1974, the company's employee magazine came to the attention of the New York City Police Athletic League, and they asked if Junius would be willing to assist in the running of its 1975 annual kite-flying contest. I was asked to be judge—nine years after I had been chased by the cops in the park for kite flying!

How perfect is Junius' "perfect" kite? He has put one literally a mile high, out of sight, and it would have gone higher if he had had more string on it. I find a single fault with the "perfect" kite—it is not instantly assembled, today's criterion for kite flying.

Junius' "perfect" kite does not differ greatly from the basic two-sticker just described. It is slightly smaller, measuring 34 inches long by 28 inches wide. It is made of brown paper (like that used for grocery bags), with ribs of white oak that have a cross section of ³⁄₁₆ inch for winds less than 10 mph and only ¼ inch for winds more than 10 mph. But the crossing point of the sticks is proportionally lower; the

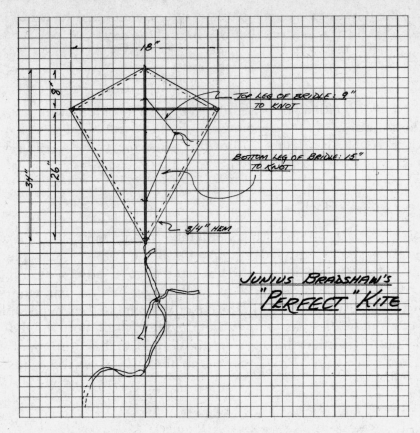

kite measures 8 inches above the crossing point and only 26 inches below it. The ribs are lashed together where they cross each other.

The bridle for Junius' kite is carefully positioned. He pierces the paper 2 inches above and 18 inches below the crossing point of his kite sticks, and ties two 18-inch strings, one through each hole to the vertical rib. He then knots the two strings together so that the knot is 5 or 6 inches above a point one third the distance from the top to the bottom hole. The flying line is then tied at the knot.

Junius makes his kite tail, 8 feet or more, from 3- to 4-inch-wide strips of old bed sheet. He cuts one strip of cloth into pieces 8 to 10 inches long, then ties them at 3-foot intervals to the main length of tail. The exact tail length is variable, depending on wind conditions: Junius suggests starting with at least 8 feet (you can always cut some off if it's too heavy).

ADDITIONAL FLAT KITES

Once you have built, flown, and mastered the classic flat two-stick kite, you will easily be able to build dozens of other kites constructed on the same principles. Here are five to stretch your imagination. Each is, or has been in the past, a classic in its own right. The arch-top kite is one of the oldest European designs, dating back to the 1600s and before. The three-stick, or "barn-door," kite is another old design, at one time immensely popular in the United States and still widely flown throughout the Caribbean and Latin America. The diamond kite is a favorite in Puerto Rico, where it is used as a fighting kite. The snake is a favorite in Cambodia, and the centipede is a design masterpiece from China and Japan. (Both of the latter kites have been called "dragon" kites; they are referred to here by their alternate names to prevent confusion.) The kites are presented in an order in which the function of the tail is increasingly important; with the centipede, the tail itself consists of a series of kites strung out one after another, so that it could be said that the tail *is* the kite!

Since you have (presumably) already experimented with the two-stick flat kite, these additional flat kites are described in less detail than the two-sticker.

Arch-Top Kite

The arch-top kite is very similar to the two-stick kite, except for the replacement of the cross-stick with a curved stick at the top of the kite. If a wood slat is used, you may have to impose the curved shape on it by warping the slat around a curved form. Make the form by driving nails halfway into a board along a line that has the same curve that you want the wood to take. Pour boiling water onto a 26-inch wood slat measuring ⅜ × ⅛ inches and gradually warp it to shape around the nails. You may have to repeat the application of boiling water a number of times before the arch takes a good, permanent set. If you don't want to mess with boiling water, use quarter-inch rattan instead of wood for the top. You won't even need to warp the

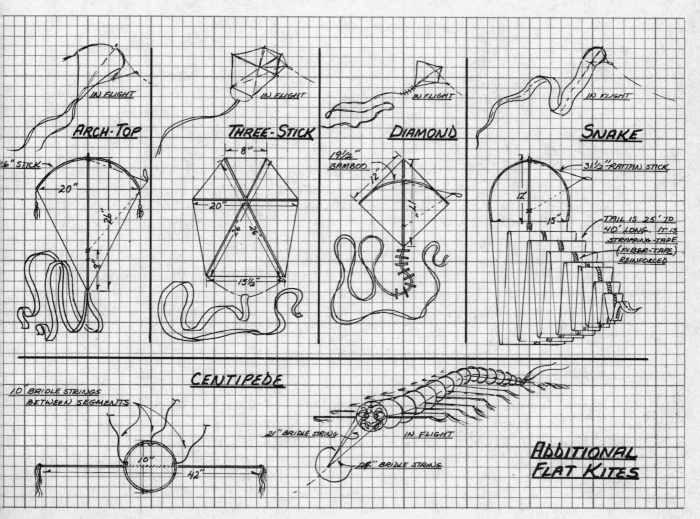

rattan around a form. Just bend it to the shape you want. Hold the shape with a string tied to the ends of the arch.

When you have made your arch, construct your kite the same general way you made a two-stick kite, tying the arch to the end of a vertical spine as shown and outlining the bottom edges of the kite with string before covering it with light paper or cloth. The drawing suggests two decorative additions: short tassels hanging from the ends of the arch and a double tail of crepe paper rather than a single tail composed of a series of small bows.

Bridle and fly like the two-sticker. For a two-leg bridle, tie one end of the bridle to the point where the arch and spine join, and the other end 8 inches up from the point where the tail starts.

Three-Stick Kite

Constructed as shown, with three sticks instead of two. Frame with string and cover like a two-sticker. The tail is not attached directly to the kite; it hangs from a loop of string that swings between the two sticks at the rear of the kite. Construct a three-leg or even a five-leg bridle. Tie the legs of the bridle to the crossing point of the sticks and to the ends of the two sticks at the front of the kite. Fly like a two-sticker.

Diamond Kite

Cut out a square of heavy tissue paper, newspaper, or half-mil Mylar one foot on a side. Reinforce edges with tape, and frame with a light vertical strip of bamboo and a cross-stick of bamboo that is bent into a bowed curve as shown in the drawing. This cross-stick should be springy enough to hold the paper taut, but light enough to bend when given light pressure from the fingertips. When bent, the bend should be exactly symmetrical. The tail should be very long and very narrow, perhaps 15 to 20 feet long but only ½ inch wide, made of either Mylar, tissue paper, or crepe paper. Paste a few cross-strips of paper or Mylar across the tail right below the kite, as shown. Bridle with a two-leg bridle tied at the crossing point of bow and spine and at a point 4 inches up from the pointed base.

When you fly this kite, fly it with repeated short jerks on the line. You will find that this action sends it snaking through the sky in the direction its nose is pointing. To make it change direction, rapidly relax the line. The kite will flutter this way and that until you are ready to send it off in a new direction with another series of rapid jerks.

Cambodian Snake Kite

Here the tail wags the dog—or kite. The kite itself is a relatively small, arch-top shape supporting a wide, tapering tail that flows from 25 to 40 feet beyond the kite. The tail must be made of a material light enough for the wind to support. Tissue paper and half-mil Mylar are both good materials. Anything else drags down the kite. Quarter-inch rattan or bamboo is an ideal material for the kite frame. Use a two-leg bridle. Reinforce with strapping tape (fiber tape) across the bottom of the kite face, where the tail begins, and by running a strip of tape the full length of the tail down its center.

Centipede Kite

The centipede kite is essentially a set of ten to fifty flat circular kites that fly in a series, one circle behind another. Each circle has a pair of balancing "legs" that helps keep it steady in much the same way that a tightrope walker uses a long horizontal pole.

To construct one of the units that make up this kite, bend and glue a thin, narrow strip of bamboo into a circle. The circle shown uses a 33-inch strip to make a 10-inch-diameter circle. Cover with light paper, light plastic, or light cloth—the lighter the better. Cut out three small semicircles at the top and the two sides for the strings that hold the kite together. Reinforce around these semicircles as necessary, to prevent rips. Finally, glue a 42-inch-long light strip of bamboo or dowel across the circle and decorate the ends with fringes of light material. Construct as many of these units as you wish your kite to have. You can make them all the same size, or decrease gradually in size from front to back.

Run three sets of strings through the semicircular cutouts, one on top and one on each side, as shown in the diagram. Tie all the segments together, 10 inches apart. Use very strong string—the pull of this kite is much stronger than you might expect. A 20-segment centipede kite has almost as much surface as a two-stick kite 5 feet high and 5 feet wide. The segments will be exactly parallel to each other. Finally, add a three-leg bridle to the front segment. The two side strings should each be 24 inches long. The top string should be somewhat shorter—21 inches or so. This bridle will cause each individual segment of the kite to slant forward in flight at the correct angle for maximum lift. Decorative touches include adding a couple of paper streamers at the rear and painting the first segment to represent a fearsome face.

Don't expect the centipede to fly high. It flies as much like a banner as like a kite. You'll probably need the help of a friend to get it off the ground. But once airborne, it wriggles and shimmers through the air with an unbelievably fluid, lifelike motion. Some kite fliers attach a centipede to the line of a kite with great lifting power, and send the two high overhead.

Handkerchief Kite

As a postscript and farewell to the flat-kite-with-a-tail concept, here is a description of how to build a kite in the exact words of one of the greatest experts on the subject. The description is so simple and elegant that it needs no illustration, and the kite it describes is a true classic: the most famous ever built.

Make a small Cross of two light strips of Cedar, the Arms so long as to reach to the four Corners of a large thin Silk Handkerchief when extended; tie the Corners of the Handkerchief to the Extremities of the Cross, so you have the Body of a Kite; which being properly accommodated with a Tail, Loop and String, will rise in the Air.

Thank you, Dr. Franklin.

THE BOWED, MALAY, OR EDDY KITE

This kite looks like a wide, tailless version of the ordinary two-stick kite. In fact, it is an adaptation of the two-sticker inspired by the distinctive kites flown in Malaysia and Indonesia. The Indonesian kites were built of palm fronds or other large tropical leaves in a framework of bamboo; vines were used for kite lines. The earliest European explorers who traveled to the island areas south of the Chinese mainland saw the green kites in the skies and occasionally found a wet kite frame floating in the offshore waters. But it was many years before traders and missionaries gained the confidence of the local people and learned the history of their kites. And many more years elapsed before the techniques of building tailless kites reached Europe and America. The secret, discovered by William Eddy, was a simple one—bowing the cross-stick back—but no one in Europe had thought of it.

As discussed earlier, the U.S. Weather Bureau used the Eddy kite; Eddy had, incidentally, introduced a new system of flying kites in trains that was utilized by weather observers for many years. Earlier kite fliers had built trains by attaching one kite's line to the framework of a lower kite. But Eddy found that a more effective system was to attach the end of an individual kite line to another kite line. And the development of the Eddy kite apparently made this system more feasible.

The catch to the trick of flying kites in trains, of course, is that each kite adds to the total lifting surface of the train and increases the pull on the kite line. Eventually, a point is reached at which the strain on the basic kite line is too great and the line breaks. Eddy himself had several such experiences with breakaway kite trains and on one occasion saw a train of his kites break loose and drift from New Jersey across New York Harbor and into the suburbs beyond the city; Eddy retrieved the kites, but only after a chase across the countryside by boat, train and horse.

When you build a bowed kite according to the instructions in this chapter, you will note the basic similarity between the bowed and simple flat kite designs. But before flying, the horizontal cross-stick of the Eddy kite is bowed backward. This bow, or bend, produces a sort of pocket in the inner surface of the kite covering material. When a gust of wind hits the surface and threatens to twist the kite around, the surface on the other side of the bow reacts with a compensating effect to neutralize the push of the wind. This aerodynamic compensator is what gives the bowed kite a much greater stability in the air than is possible with a simple flat kite.

Materials

2 flat sticks, ½ × ⅜ × 42 inches
1 sheet of light paper or cloth, 42 × 42 inches
length of string, about 18 to 20 feet
glue and/or needle and thread

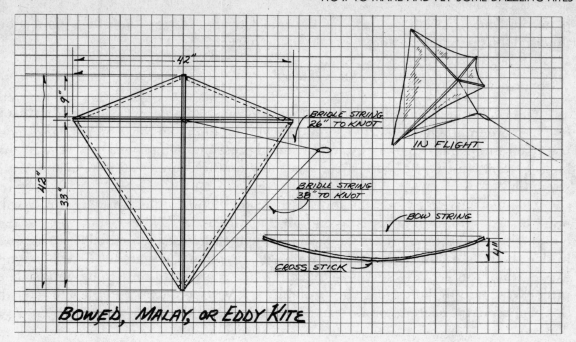

BRIDLE STRING 26" TO KNOT

IN FLIGHT

BRIDLE STRING 38" TO KNOT

BOW STRING

CROSS STICK

BOWED, MALAY, OR EDDY KITE

Tips on Construction

Start by cutting a notch in both ends of each of the sticks; make the notches wide and deep enough to accommodate the string that will be threaded through the notches.

Place one stick across the other at a point about 9 inches from the top of the second. Tie them together at that point and cover the tied string with glue to prevent slippage. Wind a length of string around the perimeter of the kite's outline, feeding it through each of the notches; tie short pieces of string over the notched ends to keep the framing string from slipping out of the notches.

Cut the covering material along the outline of the framing string, adding a margin of ½ to ¾ inch to be folded over the framing string. If paper is used, the flaps can be coated with glue and folded over the string; if cloth is used, the flaps can be stitched down over the framing string.

After the covering has been completed, attach the bridle. Cut a piece of string about 75 inches long. Pierce the kite covering at the point where the vertical and horizontal sticks cross and tie one end of the string around the crossing. Tie the other end to the bottom of the kite. Then make a loop in the bridle for your flying line. The knot of the bridle should be located so that the top leg of the bridle is 26 inches long and the bottom leg is 38 inches long. The precise point of attachment can later be altered as needed to improve kite performance by lengthening or shortening one of the legs of the bridle.

It should be noted that the bowed Eddy kite requires no tail for stability in the air. Before flying, the horizontal stick is bowed back about 4 inches and tied in this position, as shown in the diagram. This bow, representing about 10 percent of the width of the airfoil, provides a dihedral effect. This means that rather than presenting a flat surface to the wind, the bowed kite has two planes facing somewhat toward each other across a small angle. Wind currents that hit one dihedral plane surface of the bowed kite are less likely to affect the kite's stability because the facing dihedral plane will move to compensate for the effect of the gust on the other plane; the dihedral thus provides an aerodynamic balancing act.

Variations

The Eddy kite is one of those kites that can be varied greatly in size. Eddy kites 8 feet or more in height are fairly common. If you build one of these giants, be sure to use spars strong enough to withstand the wind pressure. You may have to glue one or more laminations on the cross-stick, especially on the center position, for this extra strength.

You may wish to try one variation in the construction of this kite that was developed by Eddy himself. This is to cut out a medium-sized, kite-shaped vent at the crossing point of the sticks. This hole should be the same shape as the kite itself, and in size should measure about 12 inches in each direction. Contrary to what you might expect, this vent actually serves to make the kite more stable in strong winds. The principle of adding holes to a kite to stabilize it will be encountered again later in this chapter in the sections on Korean fighting kites and sled kites.

Flying the Bowed Kite

The first step in flying the bowed kite is to bow it. Tie a string between the ends of the cross-stick so that the stick bends back with an arch of about 4 inches above the crossing point (see diagram). Then tie your flying line to the loop in the bridle and send the kite on up.

You'll need a good strong line to fly an Eddy kite. It can pull terrifically hard, as might be expected from a kite that was once used to lift meteorological instruments into the clouds. But unlike the two-stick flat kite, the Eddy also frequently soars overhead with a very light pull. One of the distinctive characteristics of the kite, in fact, is the alternation between heavy and light pulls as the kite changes its flying angle. When you finally bring your kite back down, take the bowstring off so that the crossbar doesn't warp permanently.

THE KOREAN FIGHTING KITE

One of the commonest, and oldest, kite shapes in China and Japan is a simple rectangle framed with crisscrossing strips of light bamboo. Combine this design with a tied-back bow like that on the Eddy kite plus a circular vent in the center, and you have the simple, elegant fighting kite of Korea. When properly made, this kite is maneuverable, moving in the direction its top is pointed as long as there is tension on the line. Relaxation of the line tends to make the kite shift its position, and pulling on the string makes it move steadily again. Many Koreans use a kite reel rather than manipulating the kite by hand. Contests are held in which kites whose lines are covered with ground glass try to cut each other out of the air. Two fighting kites will dive at each other, duck, dart to left and right until the more skillful kite manipulator slices through his opponent's string and cuts his opponent out of the sky.

The design for this kite was provided by a former colleague of mine at Hill and

Knowlton, Inc., which put up with this sort of moonlighting because of an enlightened policy that encouraged madness. Victor Chong Seung Han, a handsome, talented public relation staffer; his father, Korean ambassador stationed in Vienna, Austria; and his beautiful mother, a Ph.D. in anthropology, made up this team of designers and fighters whose kite is herewith demonstrated. Among them, they have 118 years of kite-fighting experience!

This kite is made in the traditional manner, using overcooked and mashed rice for paste. The short-grain rice used in much Japanese cooking is better for this purpose than long-grain rice.

Materials

rice paper (can be purchased in many art supply stores or in the Chinatowns around the nation)

thin and narrowly split bamboo (a bamboo window shade may be used as a source of bamboo)

cooked rice

string (fishing tackle, light gauge, is excellent, though not traditional)

Tips on Construction

Cut the rice paper to 25 × 31 inches. This will allow for a ½-inch paper hem around the kite. Cut out a circle in the center with a radius of 4 inches.

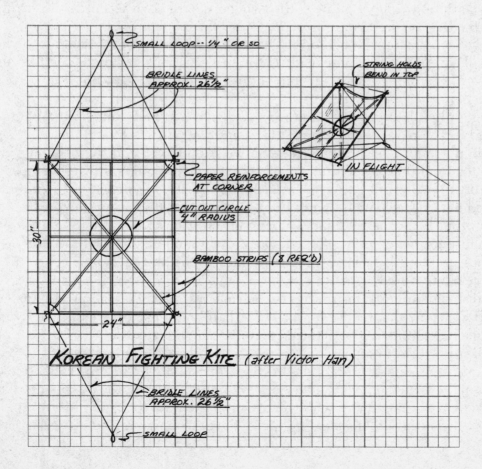

KOREAN FIGHTING KITE (after Victor Han)

Form the border of the kite with two 30-inch and two 24-inch bamboo strips. Secure the corners of the border of bamboo by tying them together tightly with string. Attach a piece of string to the ends of the bamboo strip along the top of the kite. Be sure the string is attached securely and tightly. It will be used to bend the bamboo back in a bow. Attach bridle lines to the four corners of the frame as shown on the diagram.

Using the cooked rice as paste, glue the bamboo border onto the rice paper. Then glue the six crosspieces into place. Let dry. Rice will dry in about half an hour.

Using rice paste again, reinforce the corners by covering the bamboo at the corners with two or three extra pieces of rice paper. The kite is now complete.

Variations

This traditional kite will not stand much variation. You may wish to make a slightly smaller version, in which case you should build the kite to the following measures. Size, 14 × 18 inches. Central hole, 6 inches in diameter. Omit the bottom stick and the two side sticks of the kite frame (keeping the four cross-sticks and the stick at the top). Use a lighter-weight paper—Madras-type tissue is fine. Fly with a three-leg bridle attached to the top corners and to a point on the vertical central stick halfway between the hole and the bottom.

Flying the Korean Fighting Kite

To start, tie your flying line to the two loops of the two sets of bridle strings. This should be done on the same side of the kite as the bamboo.

Bow back the top of the kite 2 to 4 inches. Use the string along the top to hold the bow in place. Your kite is now ready to fly. Because of its weight, it needs a fairly stiff breeze—a little more wind than conventional American kites. But it will fly through hurricanes.

You will probably have trouble flying this kite at first. Remember, its's a fighter kite, and therefore maneuverable. This means that you will fly it right into the ground if you aren't careful. To get used to it, have a friend hold it upright, facing you. Walk off about a hundred feet of line, walking into the wind, of course. Then, as you give *gentle* tugs on the line, have your friend let go. Coax the kite up in the air with repeated gentle tugs. When your kite is well above the ground, experiment to see what pulling in on the line and slacking off on it do to the kite. See what happens with light tugs, heavy pulls, and fast hand-over-hand taking in of the line. Alternate with repeated rapid slacking off on the line, You'll find that pulls cause the kite to move, slacking off causes it to stop or change its direction. *Important:* if you find yourself about to get into trouble (which means, usually, diving the kite into the ground), *slack off the line. Don't pull it!* A half-hour or so of practice, and you'll find yourself a newfound master of the art of flying a maneuverable kite.

A last tip: bridling is crucial on this kite. If the kite tends to curve toward one side in its flight, one or both of the bridle strings on that side are probably too short. Lengthen the string, or shorten the corresponding string on the other side. If the kite doesn't seem to want to rise in the air at all, shorten the two top bridle strings. And if the kite is too flippy and unsteady, shorten the two bottom bridle strings.

THE INDIAN FIGHTING KITE

The two preceding kites—the Eddy and the Korean fighter—introduced you to the principle of the tailless, bowed kite. The Korean also introduced you to the maneuverable fighting kite. The Indian fighter kite and the simplified version that follows are also bowed kites, but with a difference. Whereas the Eddy-type bow is held back in flight by a bowstring, the bow-back of the Indian fighter and its relatives is formed by the pressure of the wind against the face of the kite. Thus, when the kite line is held steady against the wind, the wings of the kite arch back and the kite is stable. If the line is pulled, the stability of the kite is maintained and the kite moves in the direction that its nose is pointed. But the kite is only conditionally stable: slacking off on the line permits the bamboo crosspiece to spring back to its normal position, and the kite flutters, spins or changes direction. Pull again, and the stability is restored; the kite starts off in a new track.

The Indian fighter is one of the most extraordinary of all kites. Unlike the strong-pulling Korean fighter, it is light, weighing less than an ounce, and can fly in almost no wind at all. An Indian fighter will dance high in the sky when other kites can't even get off the ground. It is the fastest moving of all kites, as fast as many birds in its flight, and able to reverse direction faster than any bird. You can spin it like a pinwheel, dive it toward the ground at close to 30 miles per hour, then, when it is knee-high, reverse it within its own length to dart overhead again. Some kite-flying fanatics, once they have mastered the Indian fighter, simply refuse to fly anything else.

Unfortunately, the kite is quite difficult to build. The sticks are not merely lengths of bamboo; they are carefully tapered and smoothed to exacting specifications. Don't even attempt the job unless you are prepared to bring patience and craftsmanship to it. And it is strongly urged that you first build and learn to fly the simplified fighter kite that is described after this one before you tackle an Indian kite. Then, when you're ready, come back to the following set of directions.

Materials

heavy tissue paper, such as Madras paper, or ½-mil Mylar plastic sheeting 34 × 23½ inches

2 bamboo sticks, 23½ inches and 33½ inches long, ⅛ inch thick, and 3/16 inch wide

2 slivers of bamboo, 4 inches long and about the width and thickness of a flat toothpick

tape (if Mylar is used)

sandpaper

Tips on Construction

Split out bamboo sticks from a bamboo pole that is at least one inch or more in diameter.

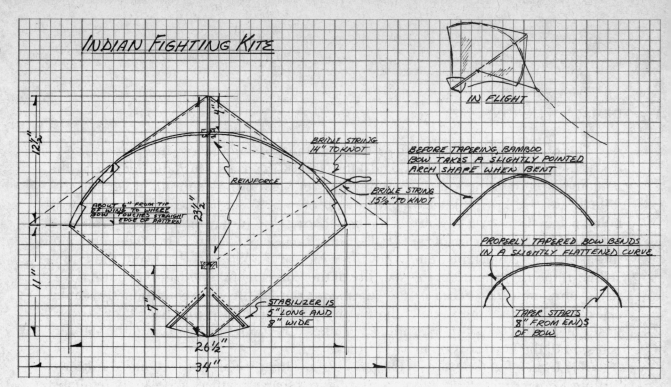

Cut and sandpaper the sticks until they are the dimensions listed above. Do not work on the hard, shiny side of the bamboo; leave that untouched except for smoothing down the knots that occur every foot or so.

Taper the longer stick of bamboo as shown in the diagram, again without disturbing the shiny surface. Ends will be about 1/16 inch around, slightly wider than thick. In cross section, the stick should be rounded like a dowel, except for the flat shiny surface. The basic test, however, is feel and appearance when flexed. Flex must be exactly symmetrical; feel should be delicately springy, not hard, not soft.

Cut out the kite pattern to the shape shown by dotted lines: a diamond with extended "ears" at wingtips. Don't cut the bow shape yet. Reinforce the pattern's edges with tape or with edges folded and glued over string. Then lay the tapered bow, with tips flexed 26½ inches apart, on the surface of the kite as shown. Cut kite (cutting off the "ears") to conform to the shape of this bamboo bow.

Where the bow touches the edges of the pattern, glue or tape it as shown, with the shiny side of the bamboo on the inside of the curve. Reinforce with extra tape at tips and where bow arcs away from kite edge. Do *not* glue any part of the bow where it crosses the surface of the kite.

Glue the spine down on the length of the kite body. The spine should pass under the bow. Add two small strips of strapping tape—one beneath the crossing of spine and bow and one 7 inches up from the base—before glueing spine down. Kite material should be held stretched taut, almost like a drumhead, by the spine and bow.

Add a small "fishtail" stabilizer, 5 inches long and 8 inches wide, to the *front* of the kite. Glue bamboo strips onto the back of the kite, extending onto the stabilizer. Bridle kite as shown. Reinforce with strapping tape at both tips of spine.

Variations

The Indian fighting kite has many small variations in outline and dimensions throughout India and Southeast Asia, particularly in Thailand. A variant made of rice paper also crops up in Japan, where it is known as the Nagasaki kite or *hata*, from the Japanese word for flag. The Nagasaki kite in outline appears somewhat like a cross between the Indian fighter and the Eddy kite, and it lacks the fishtail stabilizer of the Indian. The curve of the bow is also shallower than that of the Indian. No matter what the shape, however, the kite is rarely much larger than the size described here. An increase in size makes the kite sluggish, slow moving, with the feel of a plowhorse instead of a dragonfly.

Flying the Indian Fighting Kite

To fly this kite, first bow the *spine* backward slightly, so it holds a very slight arch like a swan diver. Then launch and fly it as described in the section on the Korean fighting kite. Remember, however, that this is a very different kite, with practically no pull and requiring the lightest line to fly it.

If the kite tends to curve to one side, slightly bend the tip of the bow on that side toward you, up out of the flat plane of the kite. Do this carefully—you don't want to snap a carefully worked-on bow.

If you want to steady the kite, so that it flies without maneuvering, add a crepe-paper tail streamer about 10 to 15 feet long.

THE SIMPLIFIED INDIAN FIGHTER

In New York City's Central Park, a dedicated group of fighter-kite buffs has experimented for a number of years with the contours and proportions of the Indian fighter kite. One of them, a gentleman named Al Berman, has developed a shape of such mathematical simplicity that the basic pattern can be cut with two strokes of a razor blade. With the substitution of simple, untapered dowels for tapered bamboo sticks (a substitution that won't work if you're building the true Indian fighter), you can construct a kite with characteristics amazingly close to an Indian kite. This is one of the easiest kites in the book to build, yet one of the most rewarding to fly.

Materials

2 hardwood dowels, ⅛ inch in diameter, one 18¼ inches long and the other 30 inches long
1 piece of heavy tissue paper
2 slivers of bamboo (from bamboo skewers) 4 inches long
clear tape and strapping tape
rubber cement

Tips on Construction

As a glance at the diagram will show, the basic shape of the simplified fighter is a diamond formed by two equilateral triangles, base to base, with a right-angle triangle glued on at the end. First cut out this diamond shape from the paper. Then cut out the triangular stabilizer and glue it to the diamond. Reinforce the kite all around the edges with clear tape. (You'll have a lighter kite if only half the standard tape width of ½ inch goes onto the kite, and you cut the rest off. A taped border of ¼ inch is sufficient to prevent most rips.)

Next, bend the longer of the two dowels and glue it along the leading edges of the kite, as shown in the diagram. Hold it in place with four pieces of tape. If the curve of the bow is not absolutely symmetrical, you may be able to mold the dowel to the proper curve with slight bends at appropriate spots along its length. Be careful not to snap the dowel while doing this, however.

Add strapping-tape reinforcements to the places where the bridle strings will go through the paper. Glue the spine to the kite body. It should pass beneath the bow, next to the paper. The spine and bow should between them hold the paper taut, with no bagging or wrinkling.

Bridle the kite as shown. The end of the top bridle leg ties around both the spine and the bow. As a finishing touch, glue the two slivers of bamboo to the stabilizer to give it the required stiffness. Reinforce the kite with tape at the tip of its nose and its tail.

Variations

This kite is itself a variation on the Indian kite. You might try to make a bow out of bamboo, as Berman himself does for this kite, tapered somewhat at the ends. It's good practice for making a real Indian fighter, and it will make the kite a faster mover than is possible with a hardwood dowel bow.

Flying the Simplified Indian Fighter

For flying, follow the general directions given earlier for flying the Korean and Indian fighter kites. You should be pleasantly surprised at how easy this kite is to fly once you get the hang of it, yet how responsive it is to your control. It does not maneuver quite as rapidly or tightly as a real Indian fighter, but it is the nearest thing to it you are likely to come across.

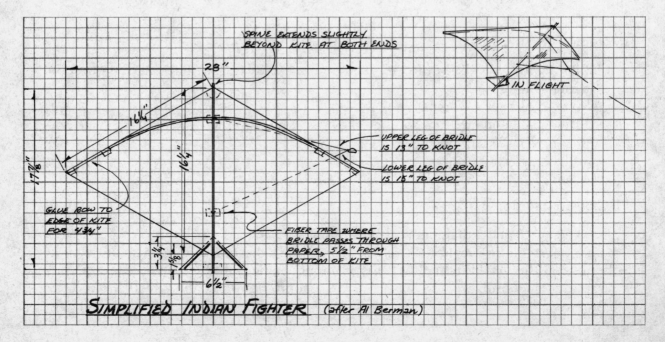

SIMPLIFIED INDIAN FIGHTER (after Al Berman)

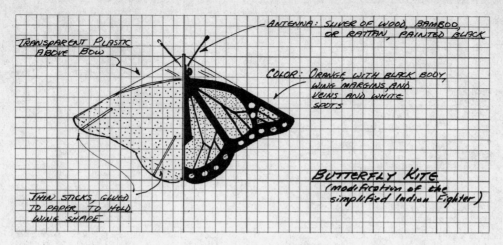

The Butterfly Kite

This is a further variation on the simplified Indian fighter kite. A slight change in the shape of the trailing edge of the simplified Indian fighter, and you have the basis for an attractive and realistic butterfly created especially for this book by its technical consultant, Caleb Crowell. The diagram shows how: the basic two-triangle shape is cut with two extra lobes added to the rear edge and stiffened with light slivers of wood, bamboo or rattan. If orange tissue paper is used, decorate with black Magic Marker and use drops of household bleach to bleach out the white spots. The result: a monarch butterfly that will flit about the sky like the real thing. For extra realism, replace the paper above the bow (which makes the front edge of the butterfly's wings) with a piece of transparent, nonstretch plastic like clear half-mil Mylar. If you can't get Mylar, try taping or glueing together pieces of cellophane from the outside of cigarette packs, reinforcing the edges with more tape.

THE PAPAGAIO

From the beaches of Rio de Janeiro comes the Papagaio (the name means "parrot"), the traditional bird kite of Brazil. It is maneuverable, and cuts a dashing figure as it flutters in the air above a beach. Really good fliers of this kite can dive a Papagaio at a handkerchief on the sand and pick it up, using fishhooks attached to the tail tip. The Papagaio is one of those kites that everybody wants to try his hand at flying.

Materials

light cloth, 55 × 33 inches
three ⅜ inch dowels, 27¼ inches long
nail, at least 1½ inches long
epoxy glue
strong thread

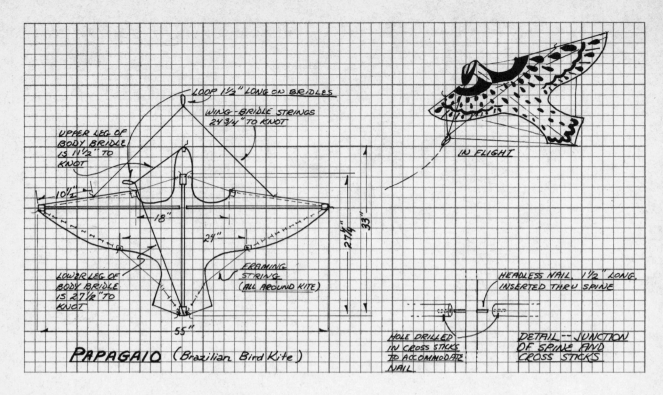

LOOP 1½" LONG ON BRIDLES

WING-BRIDLE STRINGS 24¾" TO KNOT

UPPER LEG OF BODY BRIDLE IS 11½" TO KNOT

10½"

18"

24"

33"

27¼"

LOWER LEG OF BODY BRIDLE IS 27½" TO KNOT

FRAMING STRING (ALL AROUND KITE)

55"

HEADLESS NAIL 1½" LONG, INSERTED THRU SPINE

HOLE DRILLED IN CROSS STICKS TO ACCOMMODATE NAIL

DETAIL -- JUNCTION OF SPINE AND CROSS STICKS

PAPAGAIO (Brazilian Bird Kite)

IN FLIGHT

Tips on Construction

Cut cloth to bird shape shown in diagram. Allow for hem on leading edge of wings. Sew on pockets to hold the sticks.

Add framing string as shown. The string goes inside the hem in the leading edge of the kite; it should be knotted firmly wherever it meets a cloth pocket. It should also be knotted to a reinforcement at every point where it enters the kite cloth, except at the tail. Note that the framing strings at the rear of the wings and the tail are stitched loosely in and out of the cloth material. Use an overcast stitch on unhemmed cloth edges to prevent fraying. This completes the kite's covering.

Insert the spine into its cloth pockets. Calculate the point on the spine where the two wing bars will meet it, and mark that point. Drill a hole through the spine at the marked point. The hole should be the same diameter as the 1½-inch nail.

Use a hacksaw to cut the head and point off the nail and smooth the cut edges with a file. Pass the nail through the spine, center it, and glue it in place.

Drill a hole in the end of both of the wing dowels. The hole should be the same diameter as the nail and the same depth as the length of the nail on one side of the spine—a maximum of ½ inch. Now slip the wing dowels into their pockets and onto the nail crosspiece. If the kite has been well made, everything except the head and the trailing edges of wing and tail will be held taut.

Add two bridles as shown. The wing bridles are attached to the hem strings on the leading edge of the wings, 10½ inches in from the wingtips. The body bridle attaches to the tail pocket and to a reinforcement patch at the tip of the bird's head. Decorate boldly with dye or marker pen.

Variations

Most Papagaios look pretty much the same, with minor variations in decoration and weight of cloth. A few are made with the meeting point of wing dowels and spine about 2 or 3 inches lower than on the design given here. This causes the wing dowels to point upward in a shallow V, since the wing pockets remain in the same place. The nail also has to be bent slightly at each end for it to fit into the angled wing dowels.

Flying the Papagaio

Assemble all dowels. Tie a string to both bridle loops, and launch your kite. Fly it much the same way you would fly a fighter kite. A Papagaio at first has an odd, springy sort of feel, since the wing bridles are attached to a taut string, not to a stiff spar. You'll get used to this after a while.

The Papagaio does not usually fly very high, and it needs a fairly strong string to fly it. In addition, it performs best in the strong breezes of a beach. If you want to steady its flight, bow its wings slightly backward with a string the way you would if it were an Eddy kite.

When you're through, untie the bridle string, remove the cross-sticks, and roll the whole kite up like an umbrella. This is the first kite in this chapter with the virtue of collapsibility. A Papagaio takes up virtually no space between flights.

THE COMPOUND BIRD KITE

Kites fly. So do birds, and they did it first. Partly in admiration, partly in envy, kite fliers of many lands have developed kites that look like birds and sometimes even fly like them. The Chinese construct a number of birdlike kites, some of which flutter their wings or wag their tails. The Maoris of New Zealand used to fly giant long-winged bird kites. The previous section of this chapter showed you how to make a Papagaio, the traditional bird kite of Brazil. And in this section, you can learn how to make the compound bird kite developed by Caleb Crowell.

As its name implies, the compound bird kite is actually made up of two separate elements that are joined to each other. The main piece is the body, built on the same general plan as the Indian fighter kite, with a head added at one end and a tail at the other. The other piece is the wings, which are constructed separately from the body. The two portions of the kite are thus free to move separately from one another. The result can be quite startling: a kite that looks like a bird, is almost as maneuverable as a fighter kite, and can even be made to flap its wings as it hovers overhead or dashes in pursuit of one of its steadier brothers.

Materials

¼-inch rattan sticks in the following lengths: 6, 11, 19, 26, 28, 30, and another 30 inches

two pieces of thin, clear half-mil Mylar or white nylon Ripstop, 28 × 22 inches and 47 × 11 inches

strong line, transparent tape, strapping tape, and Pliobond glue

Tips on Construction

First make the bird's body. Take the 26-inch piece of rattan, mark the halfway point, bow it, and tie the ends so that the bow tips are exactly 22 inches apart. Next cut out the pattern of the bird's body, following the plans and dimensions of the drawing. Then prepare the remainder of the sticks that go on the body to hold its shape. Split the 19-inch length of rattan lengthwise into halves (easier to do than it sounds, if you have a sharp knife and work carefully). Cut one of the halves into two pieces, one 12 inches and the other 7 inches. Split the 7-inch piece lengthwise. You should now have:

one half-round length of rattan, 19 inches
one half-round length of rattan, 12 inches
two quarter-round lengths of rattan, 7 inches

Tape and glue the rattan bows to the edges of the bird's body and tail. The center portions, where they cross the bird's body, are unglued. You may find that the bows tend to bulge slightly outside the outline of the body. Use tape to hold them in, and their natural springiness will help keep the kite material smooth and unwrinkled.

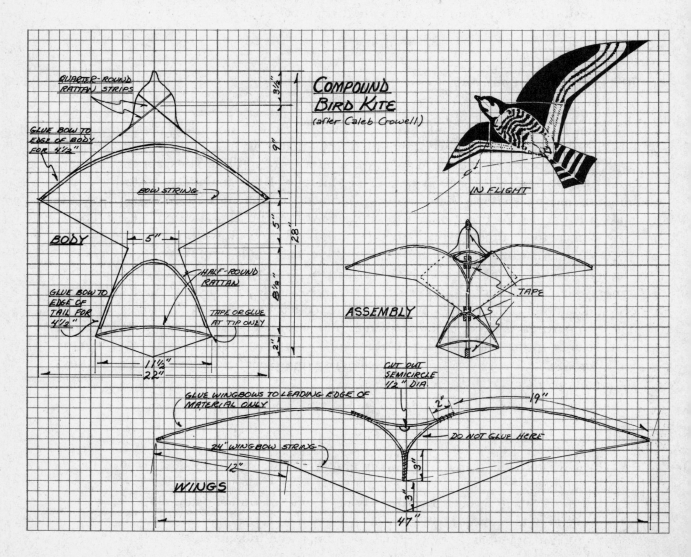

Trim the quarter-round sticks so they lie flat, and glue them in an X pattern to stiffen the head.

Next, make the wings. Bind and glue the ends of the two 30-inch sticks together for a distance of exactly 3 inches.

Then measure 19 inches from the free ends of the two sticks and mark them both at that point. Take the 11-inch stick and bind and glue it to the other two, forming a crosspiece and forcing the longer sticks apart in a Y shape. The ends of the 11-inch crosspiece should touch the marks you made on the longer sticks. The crosspiece should be bound and glued to the longer sticks for 2 inches at each end. While the glue is drying, you may have to adjust the glued joints to make sure that the rattan wing-bows will bend in the same plane. A little foresight helps—check for the natural bend of the rattan pieces before you bind them into the wing frame form.

Run two strings between the rattan wingtips and the bound base of the wings. The strings will impose a curve on the wings. Make the distance between each wingtip and wing base exactly 24 inches. You may have to bend or mold one or both of the rattan wing-bows with your fingers to make the curves symmetrical. Then cut a piece of material to follow the approximate curve of the wing-bows. The rear of the wing pattern should follow the line of the strings for 12 inches from the wingtips, then converge toward a point 3 inches below the base of the frame. Cut a small, shallow semicircle a half-inch or so in diameter at the center of the leading edge of the wing pattern. Once everything is in the best symmetry possible, glue the leading edge of the rattan wing-bows to the leading edge of the cutout wing pattern. Do *not* glue that portion of the wing-bow frame that forms a Y below the leading edges.

One last step before final assembly. If you are making the kite of Mylar, run clear tape along all unglued edges of both wings and body. This reinforces it and prevents rips.

Now assemble the two parts. Place the wings on the body and use two pieces of strapping tape (one at the front, passing under the wing-bows, and one at the rear) to tape them in place. Notice that it is the material of the wings that is taped to the material of the body. The framework is not taped.

Next put in the spine of your bird—the 28-inch length of rattan. Insert it as shown in the *assembly* portion of the diagram, passing under all the rattan bows of the body, wings and tail. Use strapping tape to hold the spine in place at the beak and tail ends. Then tie the crosspiece of the wings, the bound end of the wing-bows, and the smaller tail-bow to the spine. Tie lightly—you aren't trying to make a solid joint, only to keep the members from flopping around when the kite is in the air.

The body bow and the top bow of the tail are not yet tied to the spine. These two ties will be made with the ends of your bridle string. Take a 36-inch length of strong string. Pass one end through a hole in the material and tie securely to the crossing point of spine and body bow. Pass the other end of the string through a second hole and tie securely to the crossing of the larger tail bow and spine. Tie a loop in the bridle. The knot of the loop should fall at a point 14 inches from the tail bow and 11½ inches from the body bow. Your bird is now complete, ready for trial flight and/or decoration.

The shape of the bird appears marred by that unbirdlike expanse of diamond-shaped body. Decoration of the kite with markers will take care of that problem, camouflaging the diamond so that it disappears in the air. The head is white, outlined in black; the body below the head is orange striped with black. The tail and wings are white, striped with black. Legs are yellow. All else is left white (or clear).

What kind of bird is this? It's a Central American bat falcon, if anybody asks.

Variations

You may want to modify this basic design. Go ahead, but here are a couple of warnings and suggestions.

Changing the dimensions affects the flight characteristics. A smaller kite is stiff, hard to control. A bigger one tends to be floppy or almost too steady for easy maneuvering. The key structure in this regard is the wing-bow crosspiece. The longer it is, or the more of its length bound to the bows, the stiffer the wings will be.

A bird isn't the only shape you can make with this basic design. A few modifications, and you can make an angel. And you might want to experiment with bamboo or 3/32-inch fiber glass rods as construction materials instead of rattan. Don't use hardwood dowels; they'll snap.

Flying the Compound Bird Kite

In maneuverability and flight characteristics, this kite resembles a fighter kite, so the flying directions given in the sections on fighter kites apply here as well. The kite will not fly by itself; it requires constant attention. Your attention—and skill—will be rewarded by a kite that will dart from side to side, circle, flap its wings, dive, chase other kites, attack vicious dogs, and so forth. Only practice can make perfect, but here are the flying principles: Pulling in on the line causes the kite to move in the direction it is pointed. If it happens to be upside down, pulling in on the line will make it dive. Right side up, it will rise. Pointed left, it moves left. And so on. Slacking off on the line will make the kite waver, change direction, etc. Finally, regular rhythmic tugs will make the kite flap its wings.

You'll have to teach yourself how to fly the kite. No book can do it for you. One good way to learn is to let the kite out moderately high, perhaps 200 or 300 feet, and then experiment to see what various kinds of pulls and slacking off of the string will cause the kite to do.

No matter how hard you try, it is very unlikely that you will make your kite absolutely perfect. Both man and rattan are fallible. Here's how to make minor adjustments that affect flying characteristics:

1. Make the *front* leg of the bridle a bit shorter. This increases the ability of the kite to spin or change direction.
2. Make the *rear* leg of the bridle a bit shorter. This makes the kite steadier, less prone to turn. Warning—take your pick of this one or number 1, above. You can't do both.
3. Bend the tail backward. This increases the ability of the kite to spin when you slack off on the line, and enables it to change direction when you want it to—for instance, when coming out of a dive. In fact, you should do this anyway, before you fly.
4. Your kite may tend to circle or spin to one side when you pull on the line. To correct this, notice which side it spins toward. Bend the body bow or wing

bow on that side toward you, up from the plane of the rest of the kite. Or bend the bow on the other side backward. Or both.

5. Adjust the position of the wings. Since they are only held on with tape, this is easy enough to do. Rip off the tape—be careful not to rip the kite—move the wings to the new position—and tape again. Moving the wings to left or right can correct an undesirable spin that is otherwise hard to cure. Moving them backward or forward affects the steadiness of the kite in the air. Experiment!

6. Your kite may be slightly head-heavy, particularly if the wings are moved forward. To correct, add a little weight at the tip of the tail. A small lump of modeling clay is fine. Inelegant, of course, but it works.

7. To steady the kite, add a kite tail. Crepe-paper streamers taped to the tail will do fine, and they're attractive, too.

THE BOX KITE

At about the same time that Eddy was developing the modern bowed kite in the United States, Hargrave was working on the other side of the world, in Australia, on the box kite.

As described earlier, Hargrave's first kites were designed more like gliders than like the box kite which evolved from his experiments; they merely consisted of two small flat kite surfaces joined at an angle on a kite keel. He finally settled upon a design resembling two open boxes connected by a keel. And he did not call the device a box kite, but used instead the somewhat more accurate term of cellular kite. In fact, some of his kites consisted of many boxes fastened together to resemble a honeycomb. He also found that the cells did not have to be square but could be round or even triangular in shape.

The U.S. Weather Bureau found the Hargrave box kite an ideal device during the turn of the century for lifting instruments, and eventually operated 17 weather observation stations that sent up box kites to great heights each day. Even in the first decades after invention of the airplane, a train of Weather Bureau box kites carrying instruments aloft could obtain better data than was possible with an observer flying in an open cockpit biplane. And as noted earlier, kite trains were able to reach altitudes exceeded today only by jet planes with pressurized cabins. (The all-time kite altitude record, set in Europe, was about 32,000 feet.) A typical Weather Bureau box kite used 68 square feet of lifting surface and developed so much pull in a good wind that it had to be tethered with powerful steel piano wire and reeled in and out with an electric-powered winch. A special weather recording instrument called a meteorograph was developed for use in box kites. A medium-sized Weather Bureau kite was built on a framework of 41 pieces of wood, held together with 78 metal brackets and 175 feet of piano wire around the joints. It stood 7 feet 5 inches in height but weighed only a few pounds, and it flew like a glider. In fact, Orville and Wilbur Wright discovered one day at Kitty Hawk, North Carolina, that one of the kites could easily lift a man off the ground. They tinkered with several improvements, including the addition of a rudder plus an engine and propeller to generate wind over the kite surfaces. And in 1903, about ten years after Hargrave invented his box kite, the Wright brothers had converted the box kite into the world's first airplane.

You don't need to build a giant kite or an airplane to fly a box kite, of course. The plans that follow are sufficient to build a sturdy, dependable basic box kite.

Materials

4 sticks ¼ × ⅜ × 40 inches
4 sticks ¼ × ½ × 17 inches
2 sheets of paper, or light cloth, or heavy-gauge Mylar, 51 inches long and 12 inches wide
short length of string for bracing
glue

Tips on Construction

This simple box kite will have 12-inch-wide cells. So, first lay the two sheets of cloth or paper side by side and mark four 12-inch intervals on the covering material. At the end of each strip will be an extra 3-inch flap.

Next, take the shorter (17-inch) sticks and cut ¼-inch notches at each end. Also make ½-inch-wide cuts ⅛ inch deep at the center of each 17-inch stick; make the cuts so that each pair will fit snugly together to form an X pattern. A bit of simple geometry will show that 17 inches is approximately the length of the diagonal of a square that is 12 inches on a side; they should, therefore, be measured and notched carefully to fit at the corners of the kite cells as framing braces. Tie and glue each pair of cross-sticks together in an X shape.

Now, place each of the longer (40-inch) sticks across the sheets of covering material so that each stick covers one of the 12-inch interval marks. The paper or cloth strips should, of course, be laid parallel and separated so that there is a space of 16 inches between the two strips. Spread a neat line of glue between the narrow edge of each of the sticks and the inside of the covering material, along the 12-inch interval marks.

When the sticks and covering material are firmly glued, spread glue on the *outside* of the three-inch flap. You should at this point have a 12-inch flap at one end of the strip of covering material and a 3-inch flap at the other end; fold the 12-inch flap over so that it just covers the 3-inch flap, and glue the two flaps together. You should at this stage of the project have the equivalent of two 48-inch tubes of material with sticks at 12-inch intervals.

After the long sticks are firmly attached to the covering material and the glue has dried, insert the cross-sticks at positions that are in the middle of each cell. When the cross-sticks are properly inserted and fitted together at the center cuts (to form an X shape), each strip of covering material will take the shape of a cell or box that is 12 inches on a side.

Attach four bridle lines to the long sticks on one side of the box kite. One pair of bridle lines, about 30 inches long, should be fastened to the bottom ends of the two sticks; the second pair of bridle lines, slightly shorter—perhaps 25 inches long—should be attached to the long sticks at the center of the upper cell or box, at the location of the bracing sticks. The loose ends of the attached bridle lines can be tied in a knot with the end of the kite line. Or, better yet, tie all four of the bridle line ends

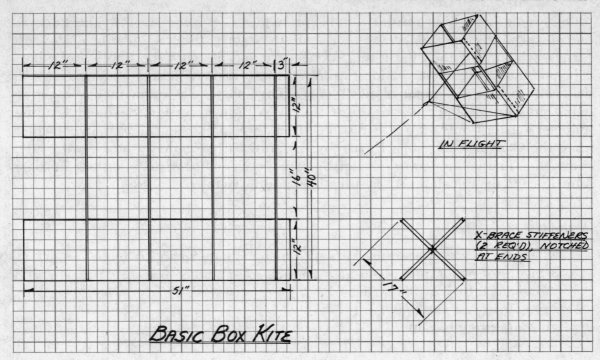

12"   12"   12"   12"   12"   3"

12"

16"   40"

12"

51"

IN FLIGHT

X-BRACE STIFFENERS
(2 REQ'D), NOTCHED
AT ENDS

17"

BASIC BOX KITE

to a small metal ring. The ring can be tied directly to the kite line or clipped to a fishing line swivel tied at the end of the line.

Variations

The box kite is susceptible of almost as many variations as the flat kite. Two of them, the triangular box kite with wings and the tetrahedral kite, are described in the following sections of this chapter. In addition, box kites can be joined together side by side (see page 72) to create contraptions of immense complexity and lifting power. The only limitations are the strength of the kite sticks and bracing, the tensile strength of the string, and your own imagination.

Flying the Basic Box Kite

The box kite requires a good, steady breeze to hold it up, but once flying it is amazingly steady. At low angles, it pulls hard, but when flying high it seems to float effortlessly with a minimal pull on the line.

A simple change in bridling can make a considerable change in the flight characteristics of the box kite. If you eliminate the bridle strings on one of the sticks, the box kite will fly "on edge," like a three-dimensional diamond instead of a three-dimensional square. When edge-flown, a box kite has somewhat less lift but even more stability than the same kite flown flat with a four-leg bridle.

THE TRIANGULAR BOX KITE WITH WINGS

The Hargrave box kite took the kite world by storm. For several decades after Hargrave perfected his cellular kite, enthusiasts experimented with all sorts of three-dimensional kites built on the cellular principle. One of the most successful was developed in the first decade of the twentieth century: the triangular box kite with wings, which combined the lifting surface of a flat kite with the stability of a box. This kite had two classic versions. An American version, patented by Silas Conyne, had cells that were not braced by stiffeners. Their shape was maintained in flight by wind pressure on the flat vanes of the wing. A French version, developed by the pioneer aviator Louis Blériot, had stiff cells and was proportionally somewhat wider than the Conyne kite. From its use by the army, it has come to be known as the French military kite. Today the distinction between the two types has become blurred with the development of still other varieties of the basic design.

Materials

4 hardwood dowels or spruce sticks, 3/16 inch in diameter and 26 inches long
3 pieces of paper, one piece 27 × 26 inches, one piece 9½ × 19½ inches, and
    one piece 10¼ × 19½ inches
strong thread or kite line
glue and strapping tape

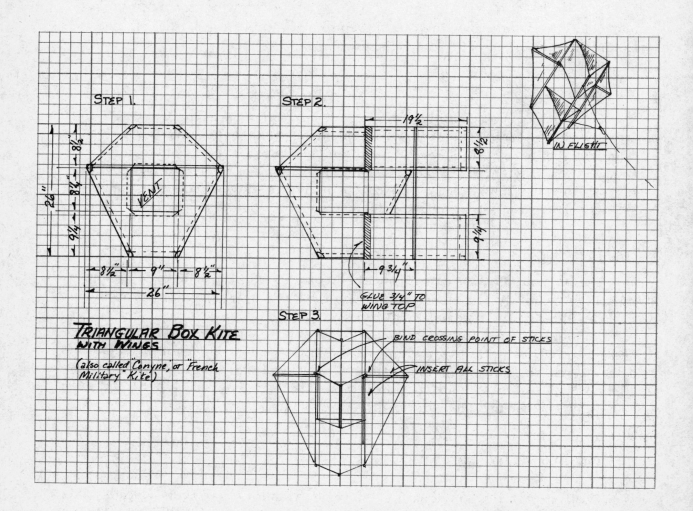

Tips on Construction

Cut out the pattern shown in Step 1 of the diagram. Fold over ½-inch hems all around the outside and the vent. Glue hems over strong thread or light kite line. Strong reinforcement of the outside edges is important in this kite. Then glue one of the sticks across the widest part of the kite surface as shown.

Cut out the two strips of paper 19½ inches long. Fold and glue the hems of the long edges over strong thread. Hems should be ½ inch wide.

Glue ¾ inch of the end of each strip to the top surface pattern as shown in Step 2 of the diagram, with the larger strip to the rear of the kite. Strips must go on straight, with no crookedness permitted. Place a dowel across the exact center of these two strips and glue it in place.

Fold the two strips over and glue edges on the other side of the vent. Insert the last two sticks in the corners of the cells and glue in place. Bind the two crossing points of the kite sticks with strong thread and a dab of glue. Bridle as shown in the "in flight" picture of the diagram. Your kite is now ready to fly.

Variations

This is a fairly small, lightweight version of the Conyne kite. You may wish to make it larger and cover it with cloth. You can also add a stiffener across the rear cell. Be careful of one rule of proportion in this kite, if you choose to vary its shape. If the wing area is too large in relation to the area of the side walls of the cells, the kite will lose stability. As a rule of thumb, the total wing area should be less than the total area of the side panels.

If you wish, you can add stiffeners to the cells of the kite, but instead of being X-shaped like stiffeners of a box kite, they should be Y-shaped.

Flying the Triangular Box Kite with Wings

Bridle the kite as shown in the drawing. Launch and fly like a box kite. You should find that the kite flies somewhat like an edge-flown box kite, but with slightly more lift, less pull, and greater steadiness.

THE TETRAHEDRAL KITE

The early years of the twentieth century were a golden era for experiments with three-dimensional, rigid kites such as the box kite and the Conyne kite. There was a purpose behind this kite-building mania. Most of the experimenters were looking for a design that was strong enough and light enough to support a heavier-than-air flying machine—an airplane, in short. Among the researchers was Alexander Graham Bell, already famous as the inventor of the telephone, who developed the tetrahedral kite described in this section.

Imagine a tripod whose legs touch the corners of a triangle. The figure you have imagined is called a tetrahedron, and it is theoretically the strongest, most rigid symmetrical structure that can exist in nature. Cover any two sides of the tetrahedron with material, and you have the basic cellular structure that Bell used in his kites.

"Passing over in silence multitudinous experiments in kite construction carried on in my Nova Scotia laboratory, I come to another conspicuous point of advance . . . another milestone of progress—the adoption of the triangular construction **in every direction** (longitudinally as well as transversely); and the clear realization of the fundamental importance of the skeleton of a tetrahedron, especially the regular tetrahedron, as an element of the structure of framework of a kite or flying machine.

"When a tetrahedral frame is provided with aero-surfaces of silk or other material suitably arranged, it becomes a tetrahedral kite, or kite having the form of a tetrahedron.

"A framework formed upon this model of six equal rods fastened together at the ends constitutes a tetrahedral cell possessing the qualities of strength and lightness in an extraordinary degree.

"It is not simply braced in two directions in space like a triangle, but in three directions like a solid. If I may coin a word, it possesses '**three-dimensional**' strength; not 'two-dimensional' strength like a triangle, or 'one-dimensional' strength like a rod. It is the skeleton of the solid, not of a surface or a line.

"It is astonishing how solid such a framework appears even when composed of very light and fragile material; and compound structures formed by fastening these tetrahedral frames together at the corners so as to form the skeleton of a regular tetrahedron on a larger scale possess equal solidity.

"I believe that in the form of structure now attained the properties of strength, lightness and steady flight have been united in a remarkable degree."

ALEXANDER GRAHAM BELL

Ingenious tinkerer and scientist Alexander Graham Bell sends off one of his tetrahedral compound kites which developed into the type of flying form the Wright brothers were testing.

In the summer of 1907, four years after the Wright Brothers' historic success with powered flight, experiments with tetrahedral kites still continued. (*National Geographic Society*)

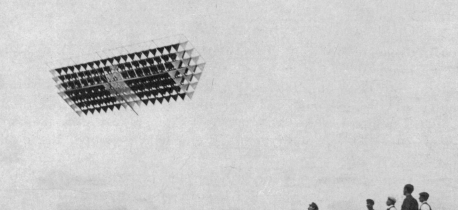

Contemporary designs for tetrahedral kites make use of today's durable plastic materials . . . and fly beautifully. (*Synestructics, Inc.*)

Using a tetrahedral cell to construct a kite has a number of advantages. The cells are rigid, and don't need extra bracing to maintain their shape. The kite itself is exceptionally strong and stable. You can build kites of almost any size simply by connecting tetrahedrons together, and you don't need to use thicker sticks as the kite grows bigger. Bell himself built gargantuan, man-carrying kites made of thousands of interlocked tetrahedral cells.

The kite does have disadvantages. It takes six sticks to brace a pair of triangular wings, and so the kite is not particularly efficient in the small, one-cell size. And it is difficult to construct a large, many-celled tetrahedral kite that will have the necessary rigid corners and yet will knock down for easy transportation.

Today, the tetrahedral kite is something of an anomaly. More recent kite designs stress portability, flexibility, shapes that conform to wind pressure, and little or no bracing. Thus, modern kites are in almost every respect the structural opposites of the strong, unyielding tetrahedral kite. Nevertheless, the tetrahedral kite remains an engineering marvel, the most advanced design in the box kite family. And in flight, a multicelled tetrahedral kite is one of the most splendid sights aloft, a pyramid of wings, with the same appearance of poised grace and strength possessed by a suspension bridge or the branches of an oak in winter.

The ensuing description of the tetrahedral kite will show you how to build a kite with only one tetrahedral cell. After that, you're on your own as far as building a multicelled kite is concerned. To beat Bell, you'll have to figure out a way of joining more than 3,393 cells together!

Materials

7 hardwood dowels ⅛-inch diameter and 18 inches long
light cloth, or half-mil Mylar, or strong tissue paper
glue

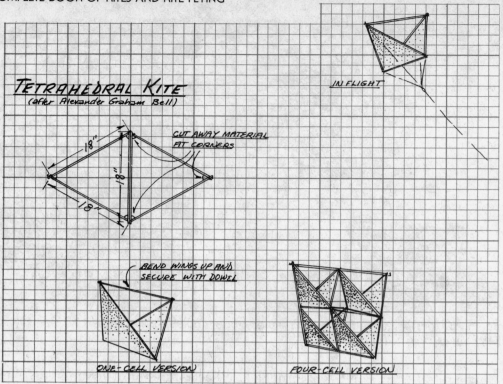

TETRAHEDRAL KITE
(after Alexander Graham Bell)

IN FLIGHT

CUT AWAY MATERIAL AT CORNERS

18"

18"

18"

BEND WINGS UP AND SECURE WITH DOWEL

ONE-CELL VERSION

FOUR-CELL VERSION

Tips on Construction

Make two separate triangles from six of the dowels. Notch the ends of the dowels slightly, so they fit together and lie flat. Lash and glue the corners together, overlapping the ends of the sticks about ¼ inch. Try not to use too much glue and thread when you lash the corners together. The joints must be strong and rigid, but not bulky with glue and thread.

Place the triangles side by side, and trim off any overlap at the corners that prevents a close fit of the two triangles. Then cut a ½-inch-wide, 17-inch-long piece of your covering material and glue it onto the two adjacent sides of the triangles, so that it holds the triangles together and serves as a hinge. Then cover the triangles with your material, making sure that the material is smooth and unwrinkled but taking equal care to make sure that the dowels do not curve out of shape. Trim a small bit of the material away at each corner.

Finally, bend the wings of the kite upward into a V shape, and hold them in position using the seventh dowel as a spreader. Lash the ends of the dowel to the upraised corners of the triangles to hold the assembly rigid. Your tetrahedral kite is ready to bridle and fly.

You can make a simple bridle for the kite by merely tying a 36-inch length of kite line to both ends of the central double spine. Holding the bridle near the center, let the kite hang like an upside-down V. Find the point at which the spine hangs parallel to the floor. Then move two inches toward either end and tie a small loop at that point. You should have a bridle with one leg of roughly 16 inches and the other leg 20 inches. You may, if you wish, make the bridle stronger and the kite steadier by running two additional lines from the other two corners to the loop in the line, as long as you do not alter the loop's position.

Variations

The principal variation of the tetrahedral kite is, of course, the addition of cells. The inset drawing shows a four-cell kite; you can make a sixteen-cell kite by first constructing 4 four-cell kites and then joining them together. Your main problem will be to find a method of making strong joints that will also permit the kite to be disassembled for portability. If portability is not an issue, of course, the problem is greatly simplified.

Flying the Tetrahedral Kite

Until you get the hang of it, you may wish to have a friend help you launch the tetrahedral kite by tossing it gently into the air as you stand about a hundred feet away pulling in the line. As soon as the kite gains sufficient altitude, you can start letting the line back out again.

Tetrahedral kites fly well in both moderate and heavy breezes. Be careful of one thing—if your kite suddenly tends to plunge forward in a nosedive when it reaches a critical angle above the ground, check both the bridle and the double spine. The upper leg of the bridle may need to be lengthened (or the lower leg shortened), or the spines may be curving inward because of too-taut kite construction.

When you have finished flying, unleash the spreader dowel. The kite will then lie flat, and will be easily transportable from place to place for subsequent flights.

THE DELTA WING

The delta-wing kite is the best-known of the modern innovations in kite design, principally because it has proved susceptible of so many commercial variations. If you buy a roll-up plastic kite that has a keel and that needs only the insertion of a dowel crosspiece to be ready to fly, you have what is basically a delta wing, even if it doesn't have the triangular shape of the original delta.

Deltas are easy to build, easy to fly, and look beautiful when airborne. That keel at the bottom gives them superb stability, so they don't need a tail. They tend to soar high overhead with a calm, deliberate motion, adjusting to wind currents and gusts with the ease of eagles. And you can make them out of almost any kind of plastic or cloth—even a coarsely textured weave if you make the kite big enough. In all, the delta-wing is probably the closest thing to a foolproof kite ever invented.

Materials

two ¼-inch hardwood dowels 36 inches long
one ¼-inch hardwood dowel 29 inches long
one ¼-inch or ⅜-inch hardwood dowel 24½ inches long
plastic sheeting or cloth 65½ × 29 inches
tape and glue (if plastic sheeting is used)
6 grommets or eyelets
2 drapery hooks

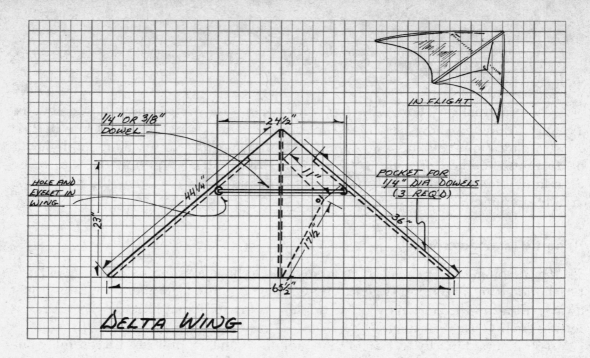

118

DELTA WING

Tips on Construction

The delta wing is simply a triangle of cloth or plastic, stiffened by four dowels and with a keel underneath it. There are, however, a few quirks in its construction that may not be evident from a quick look at the plans.

Construct the kite out of two pieces of material: the wing and the keel. To attach the one to the other, fold and crease the wing along the center line from top to bottom. Sandwich the long edge of the keel inside the fold. You now have three thicknesses of material. Stitch or glue the three thicknesses together for the length of the kite, about ⅜ inch from the crease. The keel is now attached to the body. In addition, you have a pocket between the crease and the stitches for the insertion of the 29-inch dowel that will form the spine of the kite.

The spine and the side dowels are held in place by sewn cloth pockets if the kite is cloth, and by glue and tape if the kite is plastic. Close off the ends of the pockets so the dowels are attached as permanent parts of the kite. The 24½-inch cross-stick, however, is not a permanent part of the kite. It is added just before flying.

Eyelets in the wing material plus drapery hooks attached to the end of the cross-stick are a good method for convenient attachment and detachment of the cross-stick. (Remember, you do *not* want a rigid joint between cross-stick and wing-sticks. The flexibility of the delta wing comes from a flexible cross-stick joint.) An alternative method is to sew leather pockets for the cross-stick, as in the description of the next kite in this book.

Variations

Because the delta wing can be made of so many different materials—nylon sailcloth, dress-weight cotton, half-mil Mylar, polyethylene bagging—it can be beautifully decorated and patterned in a variety of ways. Its shape, too, can be varied to imitate sting rays, eagles, hawks, bats or various abstract forms. A glance at a commercial kite display should stimulate your imagination. Only the basic flat kite with a tail is susceptible of more variation than the delta wing. For details of one variant, see the Pilch kite described next.

Flying the Delta Wing

The delta-wing kite practically flies itself: tie the string to the keel and away we go, assuming that the breeze is strong enough. Since it tends to soar, the pull is surprisingly light, but you'll still need a reasonably strong line to withstand sudden gusts. You'll probably find that the farther back you attach the flying line, the steadier the kite is but the harder it pulls. Experiment to see what positions suit your flying style under different wind conditions.

A MODIFIED DELTA WING

From Nottinghamshire, England, comes this graceful variation on the delta-wing kite, created by Mr. G. H. Pilch and included in this book with his generous permission. At first glance, it may not look like a delta wing—where is the classic triangle shape? Nevertheless, the Pilch version of the delta kite uses the delta's basic construction principles: fore-and-aft dowels used as stiffeners, a detachable cross-spar, and a triangular keel. It's a good example of the possibilities inherent in this way of constructing a kite.

Materials

> six ¼-inch dowels: one 40 inches long; two 30½ inches long; three 24 inches long
> plastic sheeting or cloth at least 65 × 40 inches
> leather strip, 12 inches × 1½ inches
> glue and tape (if plastic sheeting is used)

Tips on Construction

Since this kite is made in four pieces, you may wish to make a full-size paper pattern, following the dimensions of the plan as shown. Use the pattern to cut out one body, two wings, and one keel from your kite material.

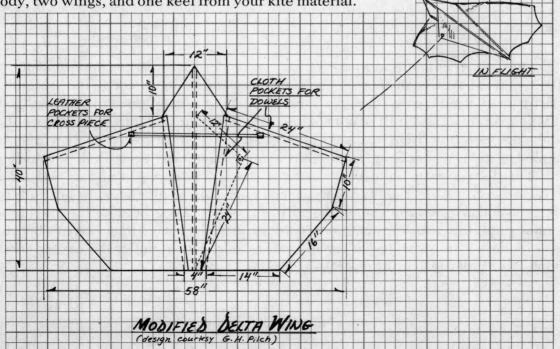

MODIFIED DELTA WING
(design courtesy G. H. Pilch)

Fold the body along the center line from top to bottom. Place the long edge of the keel inside the fold and stitch or glue everything together about ⅜ inch from the edge of the fold. The keel is now attached to the body and you have a pocket for insertion of one of the dowels.

Turn over the leading edge of each wing approximately ¾ inch and stitch a hem approximately ⅜ inch from the edge of the fold. This forms pockets for two more dowels.

Place wings on body, overlapping 1 inch, then stitch together, using two rows of stitches about ⅜ inch apart. This forms pockets for the last two lengthwise dowels.

Cut the leather strip into 3 pieces; 5 inches, 5 inches, and 2 inches long. Sew the longer strips onto the wings to form pockets for the insertion of the cross dowel, as shown on the diagram. The small piece of leather's stitched, folded, onto the point of the keel. Pierce a hole for the flying line through the leather reinforcement of the keel.

Insert your dowels and your kite is ready to fly. Incidentally, if you can't find a 40-inch dowel for the spine of the kite, you can make a perfectly good substitute by planning or whittling down a 40-inch length of quarter-round molding.

Variations

You may wish to take advantage of the four-piece construction of the kite by making wings, body and keel out of different colored pieces of cloth or plastic. It will make a boldly colorful kite, showing up at great distances. You may also want to add a short tail—not that the kite needs it, but simply for looks.

Flying the Pilch Kite

Since the Pilch kite is a variant of the delta wing, it needs no separate set of flying instructions. Just use a line strong enough to hold it down when the wind is high!

THE SLED

One of the simplest and most elegant of modern kites is the sled, invented in 1950 by W. M. Allison of Dayton, Ohio, and popularized by another Ohio kite enthusiast named Frank Scott. It's a good example of the principle mentioned earlier in this chapter, that most truly original kites have been the creations of people familiar with engineering and aeronautical design: Scott is a model airplane hobbyist and son of the late great Walter Scott, a kite innovator for whom the "Scott Sled" was named.

The sled is easy to build, tricky to fly. It likes to float on top of a light wind or soar heavenward on a thermal. Try to fly it on a gusty day or in a heavy wind, and it is likely to collapse and drop out of the air like a stone. This is because the kite has no lateral stiffening, a feature that permits it to curve to adapt to light breezes but that also renders it sensitive to eddies and crosswinds. Flown under the proper conditions, it is a delicate, darting insect of a kite.

Materials

lightweight plastic sheeting or cloth, 36 × 40 inches
three ⅛-inch hardwood dowels, 36 inches long
tape
2 eyelets or 4 gummed reinforcements (optional)
light swivel hook (optional)

Tips on Construction

Follow the plan strictly, and you won't go wrong. But change it even a little, and you'll have to live with the consequences. The dimensions of the sled have been carefully worked out, and any major tinkering or alteration, unless you really know what you're doing, typically results in a kite that won't fly. Here are a few suggestions on the construction.

First cut out the outside shape of the kite, then tape on the three dowels, and last cut out the triangular vent (see diagram left). If you cut out the vent before you attach the dowels, you may experience a little trouble in getting the covering flat and unwrinkled. And when you cut out the vent, round the corners a trifle or place tape at the corners to prevent a rip from starting.

You can use regular Scotch tape to secure the dowels to the lengthwise covering. At the ends of the dowels, however, it's best to use strapping tape to prevent the dowels from poking through.

The eyelets or gummed reinforcements are to prevent the bridle string from ripping through the plastic sheeting. If you don't have either, simply reinforce the

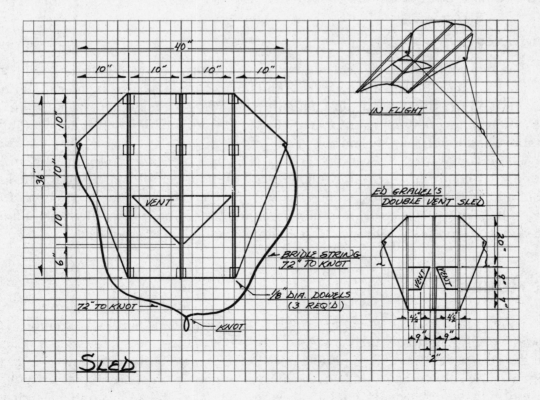

wingtips with strapping tape, punch a hole in each of the wingtips, and tie the bridle line through the holes.

A tip on tying the bridle: make it up before attaching it to the kite. Measure out about 155 inches of bridle line. Double it, and tie a 2-inch overhand knotted loop in the center. Then measure both legs of your bridle-to-be exactly 72 inches from the knot at the end of the loop. Mark with a pen. After you have made your marks, tie the two ends of the bridle to the wings of the kite, making sure that the 72-inch marks are located exactly where the bridle strings meet the kite.

Variations

As metioned, the sled is a design that cannot stand much modification. Some commercial versions lack the triangular vent, and you can spark a lively debate among sled enthusiasts on the subject of just how necessary that vent is. One different vent shape, developed by Mr. Ed Grauel, is shown on the plans. But aside from the presence or absence of a vent, the principal variations are in the material out of which the sled is made. Light, flat pine or spruce sticks about ⅛ inch thick and ⅜ inch wide can be used instead of dowels. Where covering material is concerned, the directions previously given suggest plastic sheeting, but light cloth is as good. Paper can be used, but it's a trifle less flexible and therefore less suitable. Incidentally, this is one of the few kites that can be made out of light plastic garment bags, if you aren't too concerned about how long the kite will last.

For decoration, you might like to make the lateral wings a different color, or even a different material, from the main body of the kite. If you like to paint faces on kites, let the vent represent a grinning mouth.

Flying a Sled

The two problems in flying a sled involve getting it above the ground wind and preventing lateral collapse if turbulence hits it. Let it out as fast as you can, with as little pull on the line as you can maintain but without unrestricted slack. It will fly best when you work it up to an angle of 45 degrees or more. Below that angle, it pulls, wobbles, and is very hard to control.

There is one trick you can use to help prevent a sled from folding up in midair under gusty conditions. Tape a 13-inch length of light, flexible rattan across the kite, about an inch below the top. A one-inch-wide strip of cardboard will do if you don't have rattan. But this is really a form of cheating: once you master the trick of flying the sled, you won't need any aids to keep it soaring high over your head.

THE KEELED SLED

Some kite designs seem to contain the germ for countless variations and modifications. There are today dozens of different kinds of box kites. Other designs stand alone as classics that are perfect from the start: no modification is as good as the original. The Allison-Scott sled once seemed to be one of the latter type. Instructions for building a sled usually contain a warning to the effect that both design and dimensions should not be tampered with. And along comes Harry Sauls of Miami Beach to demonstrate a successful and ingenious modification that he calls the "American sportsman" kite. Basically, it is a sled with a keel added, in the style of a delta wing, plus a slightly more complex bridling arrangement and a series of vents in place of the single vent of the sled. The result is a kite that combines the delicacy of the Allison-Scott sled with something of the steadinesss of a delta wing. The addition of a keel in particular goes a long way toward overcoming the sled's principal weakness: its tendency to lateral collapse. The version shown here is the large size in square footage, between three and four times the size of the sled described in the previous section. So don't try to fly it on a light line!

Materials

2 pieces of lightweight cloth or plastic sheeting to make panels 5 feet 6 inches × 5 feet 8 inches and 5 feet 8 inches × 1 foot 4 inches

five 5/16-inch dowels: one 5 feet 9⅞ inches long; two 5 feet 8 inches long; and two 1 foot 7 inches long

tape (if plastic sheeting is used)

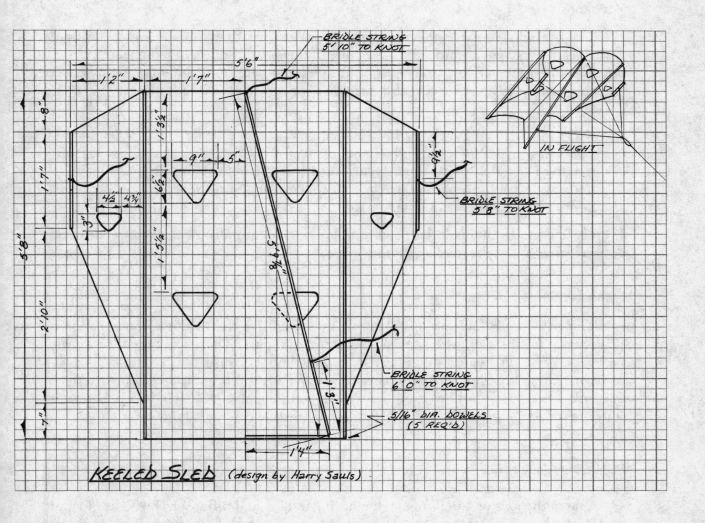

KEELED SLED (design by Harry Sauls)

Tips on Construction

If you have made a regular sled, you shouldn't have any trouble with this design. If you haven't, it may help for you to go back and look over the sled instructions before tackling the keeled sled. In addition, be careful of the following points:

1. Your local lumber supplier may not have dowels that are almost 6 feet long. Consider using quarter-round molding or any of the other substitutes discussed at the beginning of this chapter.
2. If you are making the kite out of plastic sheeting, use tape to hold the dowels in place. If you are making it out of cloth, you may wish to sew pockets and cross tabs to slip the dowels into.
3. There is a dowel along the bottom of the keel, but no dowel at the top where the keel joins the main body of the kite.
4. Elastic shock absorbers can be added at the ends of the two bridle strings that attach to the keel. The kite will fly without them, although they are useful in taking up stress if the kite gets hit by a sudden gust.
5. As with the regular sled, make up the bridle before attaching it to the kite.

Variations

The keeled sled exists in a number of smaller sizes than the one just described. If you want to try your hand at building one of the smaller ones, here are some of the critical dimensions. Use these plans, a little mathematics and some common sense, and you'll produce a very acceptable version of one of Sauls's smaller kites.

length: 4 feet; width: 3 feet 9½ inches
width of panels: 9½ inches and 13¾ inches
width of vents: 3½ inches and 6½ inches
length of dowels: 13¾ inches, 4 feet, and 4 feet 1¼ inches
length of bridle strings: 4 feet, 4 feet, 4 feet 2 inches, and 4 feet 4 inches
depth of keel at rear: 11 inches

If the kite is made out of cloth or colored plastic, an extremely attractive effect can be gotten by having each panel a different color.

Flying the Keeled Sled

The keeled sled, as you might guess, flies a lot like the keelless version. If you have mastered the sled, the keeled sled should be easy. There are two differences, however. First, the keeled sled is a steadier kite, both because of its keel and because of its rounded M shape in flight as contrasted with the regular sled's inverted U. Second, the keeled sled has a much heavier pull, especially at low levels before it lofts overhead. As previously suggested, use a line that can withstand strong tugs.

FOLDED PAPER KITES

One of the joys of kite flying is the finding of new and different as well as old and traditional kites. And one of the greatest of the new finds is the paper kite—not the traditional paper kite mounted on sticks, but the folded paper kite that has no wooden or other stiffening materials to hold it rigid. It is the father and mother of the nonrigid kite and even precedes Francis Rogallo's flexible kite, which startled the flying world when it was introduced to demonstrate the fact that kites, or for that matter aircraft, could be built without rigid trusses or framework because a flexible airfoil can adapt to the changing whims of the winds.

Such a paper kite is the chiringa, a popular toy in places like Puerto Rico where every kid seems to know how to make one of scraps of paper and thread, even though he may never have heard of the science of aerodynamics.

I first witnessed these little kites in Central Park in New York City. The children made them of squares cut from newspapers or wrapping paper attached to lines of sewing thread. When I examined the kids' chiringas to see what sort of sticks or reinforcing materials were used, the children laughed. I had presumed that my Rogallo-designed flexible kite was the only nonrigid kite in the sky over Central Park, but I soon learned that the hordes of paper chiringas floating nearby also were flexible kites.

The city kids also taught me how to make a flexible paper kite out of materials that most people throw away. I was thus introduced to the concept of recycling by a bunch of youngsters who had never heard of ecology.

It was not until years later that I discovered an imaginative gentleman named Edwin Grauel of Rochester, New York, who made a specialty of designing and building these little wingers. With his technical knowledge, Ed experimented with different types of paper and applied aerodynamics to the design of these kites.

In fact, Ed has become an authority on flexible paper kites and sends them to his friends in all parts of the world. He has revealed some of his secrets on the pages of this book so that you, the reader, can share the fun of making the inexpensive kites for yourself and your friends. Two of these kites are patented: the Doodlebug, or Chiringa, by Rex Zachary of Mountain View, California, and the Chinchbug, or Flying Nun, by William Schaeffer of Rochester, New York.

Materials

> supply of 8½ × 11 inch or 9 × 12 inch lightweight construction paper
> crepe paper, cut into strips ½ inch × 10 feet
> scissors, paper punch, stapler, thread, paste (No. 6 only)

Tips on Construction

The construction of the first four of the six kites illustrated is fairly similar. A few simple folds, a few snips with the scissors, two holes punched at the sides for the bridle string and a third hole at the bottom for a string to hold the tail—and your kite is ready to fly. Kites 5 and 6—the Chinchbug and the Junebug—are slightly different in that they require no tail in light winds. You will notice that the designs are in many cases folded paper versions of familiar kites: the Eddy, the Scott sled, and even the French military.

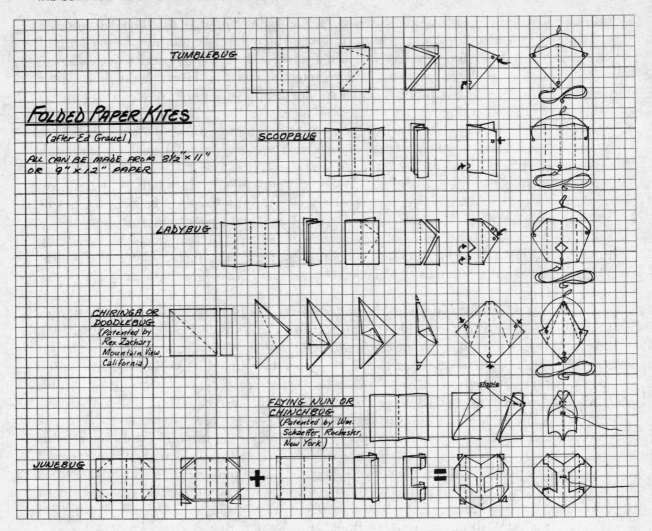

The following construction principles hold for all these little dingbats:

1. The central crease of the kite should always be toward you.
2. Make sure the bridle string is long enough—at least 15 inches—so that it extends beyond the top of the kite when the kite is lying flat.
3. The knot that forms the bridle loop must be centered exactly above the center crease, so the two sides of the bridle are exactly the same length.
4. Don't tie bridle and tail lines too tightly to the paper, or they will crumple it or cut into it. You might want to use gummed reinforcers, the kind you buy at a stationery store, to strengthen the paper at key points.
5. The tail is fastened to the kite by a short piece of thread. The tail itself should be one of the 10-foot lengths of crepe paper folded in half and tied in the middle, so that it forms two 5-foot lengths.

Variations

While it is recommended that these folded paper kites be made from 8½ × 11 inch or 9 × 12 inch paper, they fly very well in larger or smaller sizes. Experiment with different sizes from 6 inches to 20 inches and also with heavier and lighter paper. For example, the Scoopbug flies well when made with heavy construction paper or even brown paper from a paper bag. The Tumblebug, on the other hand, can be made of newsprint.

Flying Folded Paper Kites

Folded paper kites are tricky. They flip-flop every which way if you're not careful. Gusts of wind can send them spinning or turn them inside out. Your problems can be kept to a minimum, however, by careful construction, particularly in the placing of the bridle and the knot for the bridle loop, and in the use of extra tails if the wind rises much above eight to ten miles an hour. But these kites are so easy and quick to make that you can make a modification on the spot or even a new kite if for some reason one of them refuses to fly properly. If the idea of flying a folded piece of paper on a thread doesn't sound inspiring or up to the dignity of a kite enthusiast, judgment should be withheld until trial. These little kites do not have to yield anything to their big brothers in ease of launching or flying ability. In fact, initial reaction is usually one of amazement at how easily and steadily a piece of folded paper will fly.

THE FLEXIBLE KITE: PARA-WING

Para-Wing, Flex-Wing, Flexikite—these are all names for the remarkable kite invented by NASA engineer Francis Rogallo. At first sight, the simple version described here doesn't even look like a kite—a limp square of floppy plastic, a bridle composed of more than half a dozen shroud lines, and no sticks, dowels or other stiffeners to give it a permanent shape. If you lift it up, it just hangs droopily. If a child brought it to you as his own creation, you'd probably say, "That's very nice, dear," and throw it away when he wasn't looking. It looks like it will never fly.

But it does fly, and fly superbly. Its cousins, also designed by Rogallo, support flying machines, parachutists, hang gliders, and reentry space vehicles. In a breeze, the Flexikite assumes a double-arched configuration, like two wings, and heads up and out. Being flexible, it can adapt to changes in the wind. It is exceptionally stable, and gains both lift and efficiency from the fact that its flexible shape allows the wind to flow smoothly over it instead of breaking up into eddies and turbulence.

Materials

moderately heavy Mylar (about 3 mil) or other plastic sheeting
light flying line or heavy thread
tape

Tips on Construction

In essence, the flexible Para-Wing is constructed in much the same way as the folded paper kites just described. Take a square of material of the proper dimensions, fold it diagonally to make a central crease, attach shroud lines, and fly. But the

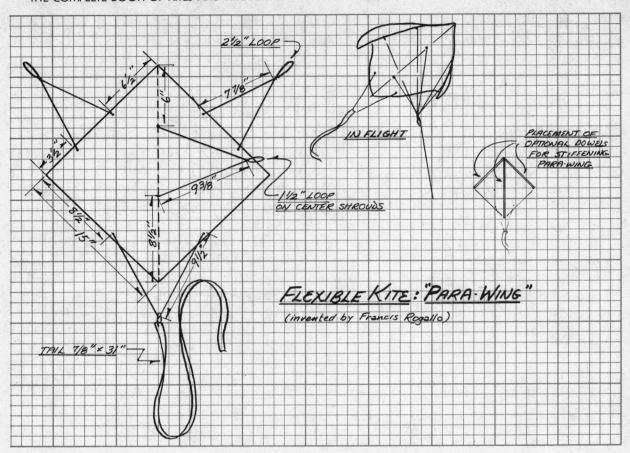

FLEXIBLE KITE: "PARA-WING"
(invented by Francis Rogallo)

dimensions are crucial here. A half-inch or so variation in one of the shroud lines can make the difference between a kite that soars and one that drops out of the air as soon as it gets off the ground. So follow the dimensions, and these tips, very carefully.

The diagonal crease should stay in the kite when flying, and the Mylar you choose for the kite must be heavy enough to hold the crease. Half-mil Mylar is too light. But Mylar is a plastic with a memory, and creases in it tend to disappear. So iron the crease in. Don't make the iron too hot. A setting for synthetics is about right. And place a scrap of brown wrapping paper between the iron and the Mylar when ironing. The heat plus the pressure of the iron will help the Mylar keep its set.

Tie the loops in the shroud lines *before* you attach the shrouds to the kite. That way you can measure each shroud line accurately as you attach it.

Variations

Fifteen inches on a side is not a very big kite. Can you make it bigger? And can you use other material, like light half-mil Mylar or light cloth? The answer is yes, but you may go through some frustrating experiments to get what you want.

First, a bigger kite means proportionately longer shroud lines. If you double the length of the kite, for example, you must double the length of each shroud line. So your first move has to be to go through the mathematics of making your shroud lines exactly proportional to the proposed increase in kite size. Next, of course, you build the kite.

But you don't stop there. A large flexible kite, particularly a cloth one, needs extra shroud lines to maintain its shape in flight. Lay the kite flat with the shroud lines arranged as in the plan. Now add two or three extra lines to each side and along the center crease. Simply attach them to the material of the kite and extend each one straight to the knot on its side. Tie at the knot. If you do this correctly, each set of shroud lines will be straight, none will be lax or floppy, and the loop knot will remain in the same position. (You don't need extra lines for the tail.)

There is another way to vary a Para-Wing if you wish to make it larger or if you wish to make it out of extra-light material. Instead of adding extra shroud lines, glue or tape three lightweight dowels to the kite: one along each edge and one down the center crease, as shown in the inset drawing. It's cheating, of course, since now the kite is not strictly flexible in all directions. But it's a form of cheating occasionally if reluctantly indulged in by Rogallo himself, since some of the Rogallo kites that support manned vehicles have similar stiffeners.

Flying the Para-Wing

To fly the Para-Wing, simply bring the three shroud line loops together, tie your flying line through them, and carefully let the kite out. Don't try running with it or giving it heavy yanks. The kite isn't responsive to that kind of treatment. If you play it out skillfully, it will move up and out, hanging gracefully in the sky, rolling and slipping in response to the wind.

THE FLEXIBLE KITE: PARAFOIL

A slice through an airplane wing reveals a distinctive shape: relatively flat on the bottom and curved on the top, with a blunt leading edge tapering to a sloping trailing edge. This shape is referred to as an airfoil, and it inspired an aeronautical engineer named Domina Jalbert to develop and patent a remarkable flexible kite. In cross section, Jalbert's kite is an airfoil like an airplane wing, but it maintains its shape by having its leading edge open like a windsock. The wind blows into the opening, inflating the kite into its airfoil shape. Below the kite are shroud lines like those of a parachute, which connect to the flying line. Hence the kite's name: parafoil, from parachute and airfoil. The kite can be made almost any size simply by sewing several airfoil cells side by side in a row. This produces a shape something like a flying air mattress, but one with remarkable lifting power. A parafoil will fly almost overhead in a strong gale; a light fabric model weighing 8 or 9 pounds can life a man high off the ground in winds of 30 mph. The small, four-cell parafoil described here won't lift you off the ground, but it will provide you with a considerable challenge to hold it down in a good breeze.

Materials

4 pieces of light nylon Ripstop, 7½ × 33 inches
4 pieces of nylon Ripstop, 7½ × 36 inches
5 strips of Ripstop, 34½ × 5½ inches

3 pieces of Ripstop, 14½ × 22 inches
3 pieces of Ripstop, 10 × 14 inches
6-pieces of shroud line, 80-lb. test, 28 inches long
6-foot drogue line
small ring or washer

Tips on Construction

Cut out five airfoil shapes like the one in the drawing from the 34½ × 5½ inch strips of material.

Cut out three triangular front shroud panels from the 10 × 14 inch strips of material and three rear shroud panels from the 14½ × 22 inch strips.

Sew the triangular shroud panels to three of the airfoil shapes as shown in the diagram. Notice that the shroud panels overlap somewhat, but the overlaps are not sewn to each other.

Sew the top panels (the 7½ × 33 inch panels) between the tops of the airfoil shapes and the bottom panels (7½ × 36 inches) between the bottoms of the airfoil shapes. The airfoils with the triangular shroud panels should be at the ends and in the middle. Then sew top and bottom panels together at the back. You should end up with a fabric kite consisting of four hollow cells.

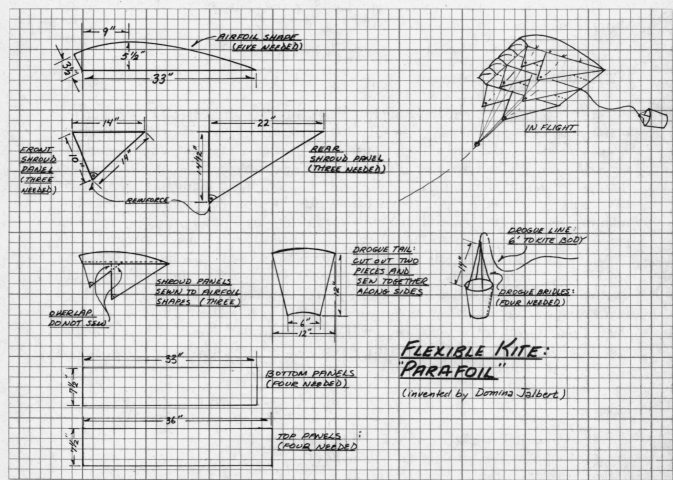

FLEXIBLE KITE: "PARAFOIL"
(invented by Domina Jalbert)

Reinforce the pointed tips of the triangular shroud line panels and attach the shroud lines to them. Tie the lines to a small ring. When you are ready to fly, all you have to do is tie the flying line to the ring.

As a last step, add a tail. You can use several long strips of Ripstop, or you can make the type of tail known as a drogue. From spare scraps of Ripstop, cut two shapes as shown. Sew to form a shape like a bucket with no bottom. Bridle as shown, and attach to the rear of the kite with a 6-foot line.

Variations

The parafoil is a fascinating but complicated kite to build. Because the kite has a scientifically exact shape, it is strongly suggested that you resist trying out variations until you have built and flown at least one successful version constructed along the lines just described. Then you can consider enlarging it by adding more side-to-side cells, lengthening it from front to rear, and adding more shroud panels below.

Flying the Parafoil

There is no particular trick to flying a parafoil—in any breeze strong enough to inflate the cells, the kite moves out and up. You probably will notice one unusual effect as you launch the kite. It pulls very hard at low levels. The pull slacks off as the kite rises and starts to fly flat to the wind. But as it swims overhead, the pull increases again. So don't try flying a parafoil with much less than an 80-pound-test line. In a strong wind a lighter line may snap like a thread.

HOW TO FLY A KITE

The simplest heavier-than-air flying vehicle is the kite. A kite is never absolutely inert and unflyable even if there is no wind. But it is important to know your friendly neighborhood winds and sites where they are most prominent. Hilltops, beaches, prairies, meadowlands (not in swamp areas) are most ideal. Thermal winds (hot air rising from the ground) can get kites off from a tennis court or backyard, though it may seem as though you're flying from the bottom of a well. Avoid areas with power lines and streets, or parking lots unless empty. These are some general guidelines.

The attitude of flight is simple: hold your kite by the bridle facing the wind. Watch the smoke from a factory chimney or the flapping of a flag. Or moisten your finger and determine whence comes the coolness. Pull the line into the wind.

It is not necessary to run into the wind to raise the kite. It is simpler to place the kite in an upright position, under a tree if there is little wind—there is always a breeze under a tree—and from a fifty-foot distance snap the line upward and pump it rapidly in short takes. Gently ease it away from the tree branches.

If you must run with a kite—and many kids insist on running—be sure that your forward path is free of obstacles.

The best kite launcher is the fishing rod and reel. I have hoisted kites on a two-knot breeze by whirling rod, reel and kite overhead and letting line out a little at a time until the kite enters a higher current of air and thus becomes airborne.

Al Hartig, the "Nantucket Kiteman," shows his one-man launching technique into the wind, with a hand reel, using his homemade delta wing. (*The New York Times*)

It is not necessary to own a wind meter. That's a little too much. But it is useful to know the Beaufort wind scale:

1 to 3 mph, lazy wind and smoke.
4 to 7 mph, tree leaves hum and rustle.
8 to 12 mph, flags fly, leaves dance.
13 to 18 mph, paper flies.
19 to 24 mph, trees sway, so do buildings.
25 to 31 mph, forget kites. Fly an anvil.

The big trick, really, is to get the kite off the ground. The ground winds are different from the upper winds. A little pumping, a little coaxing and a prayer will get you through most of the starting travail. The ecstasy of achieving flight is worth all the early troubles.

Although most kites are mass-produced, they have idiosyncrasies of their own or ones they pick up from the flier. Each needs to be individually handled, if not with love and affection, at least with a sure hand.

Here are some challenging situations and how to meet them with fortitude and élan:

1. Light breezes: Shorten tail or remove entirely. Extend top bridle line. Flatten bow as much as possible. Have a drink or get a lighter kite.
2. Power dives: Change bridle position upward. Pump line softly and try to establish a balance. Look for tears in kite.
3. Darting. Strengthen and lengthen tail. Lengthen bridle. Place a stabilizer patch or short tail on the side of the kite on which it darts.
4. Roller coasting: Lengthen bridle line. Tie flying line higher on bridle.

Here's some advice from expert Al Hartig, great kiteman of Nantucket. He says:

"Most people think that you must run with a kite to make it fly, but you simply put your back to the wind and hold the kite up. Any decent kite will fly out of your hand. At the most you might have to let out about 50 feet of line and . . . let someone hold it up . . ." And then snap it out of your partner's hand. Your partner should stand in back of the kite, not in front of it, I must add to Hartig's simple advice.

Further on, Hartig, with whom I flew his early kites in Central Park in New York, admits, "The only time I run is in under four miles an hour winds. I run to get it up at fifty feet, then spend another twenty minutes nursing it up another hundred feet."

Each kite has its flight peculiarities. Hence, in the sections on making kites, the instructions on how to fly individual kites.

This is the classic position of a kite flier and partner launching a keel Hi-Flier kite into the wind. (*Hi-Flier Kite Company*)

7 DROPNIKS AND OTHER FUN IN THE AIR

Among the many thousands of people, young and old, who fly kites there is a "fraternity within a fraternity" that has a strange devotion to dropping things from great heights. While most are dedicated kite fliers too, much of their interest in kites results from their being an excellent means of trundling objects aloft to be dropped.

With all the many titles we seem able to supply for people who engage in various activities such as "philatelist" for the stamp collector, "spelunker" or "speleologist" for the explorer of caves, and "deltiologist" for those who collect postcards, no one has come up with a fancy one for those who drop things from kites.

Admittedly there isn't too much demand for such a title, but a very simple and descriptive one has been originated. They are called "dropniks"—and with the current tendency to slangily add the letters "nik" to just about everything (beginning with the once-used "beatnik"), it is not surprising.

It has taken about a thousand years to get a kite flier to admit he flies kites, so it isn't to be wondered at that dropniks don't go around telling anyone about their strange hang-up of getting kicks from seeing inanimate objects come tumbling down from the sky. Therefore, the society is a rather secret one, activities and names gathered with some difficulty but real nevertheless.

To enhance the pleasures of kite flying a number of gadgets and gimmicks have been added to the flier's techniques, repertoire and inventory. For example, the late great kiter Frank Weisgerber devised simple "messengers" to send up the line. He made these from a square piece of stiff paper in whose center a hole had been punched. This square placed over the kite cord is carried up to the kite by the action of the wind.

David Omick, an eighteen-year-old high school graduate with a brilliant flair for the scientific, has a devotion to dropping model parachute jumpers from kites and has invented ingenious deployment systems and release mechanisms to do so. The excuse David gives is that he intends to perfect better deployment of parachutes with an eye to certainty and safety, and this may be true, but he has a lot more fun doing his research than a scientist is really entitled to.

Betrayal of what some people refer to as the "fun of little boys" is more than obvious in this young dropnik's activities, since he goes to great lengths to mold realistic faces on his miniature skydivers and equip them with crash helmets, goggles and boots, a sort of aerial GI Joe. Some dropniks would settle for a flat-faced expressionless object for such use, but the affection that David has for his courageous little jumpers precludes such indifference. And courageous the little guys are.

It isn't known for sure just who the first major dropnik was, but Tony (The Kiteman) Ziegler, a Michigan kite flier of considerable fame, got the first publicity as a contemporary and for good reason. Tony doesn't fool around with little parachute jumpers but has one about half the size of a man, actually a very large doll, which he drops from a huge, 11-foot barn-door kite using a full-sized parachute. Such endeavor requires more than ordinary equipment, and the big kite is flown from a power-winch made from old washing machine parts and mounted on an elaborate trailer equipped with a directional-control mechanism and a cowcatcher. Since there are no cows where Tony operates his gear, it could be concluded that that is a touch stemming from an earlier life as a railroader, which Tony wasn't. He says it pleases the children.

In the mid 1950s on the seashore in Westport, Connecticut, on Fourth of July eve, a group of our kite fliers sent up their vehicles to 200 feet. At the hand position of the line they tied sparklers, which were quickly ignited. As they burned, the fliers released their kite lines so that the kites rose another 200 feet, pulling the dazzling sparklers with them over the water. The effect was brilliant and as patriotic, if not as commercial, as the fireworks display that went on next night.

Another kite illuminator is the night light in the sky. This is a simple matter of attaching a lighted searchlight (small) to the lead line 100 feet below the kite, letting the kite soar. The lit searchlight will jig its way in the night sky like some bright star. The next day there will be numerous reports of UFOs.

Hummers or buzzers are challenging as well as historic bits of kite fun. Hummers (the Chinese used flutes as well), attached by a tightly drawn line to the cross-sticks in the kites, hum and whistle and buzz according to the amount of turbulence in the air. An invading army was scared off by the sounds of thousands of screeching hummers sent up by a besieged Chinese city, according to legend.

Hummers on kites were really the first of the early storm warning instruments, long before the Weather Bureau existed. In China, the farmers set hummers in kites that were left flying all night. The intensity of the wind was indicated by the humming sound of the kite. However, if the wind was gentle, it would lull the farmer to sleep. A change in the pitch of the hummers would serve as a storm warning, and the kite-farmer was wakened and would charge into the field to protect his crops or reap them throughout the night.

Here's how to make a two-stick hummer: Add an extra stick between the spokes about two inches from the ends. Fasten the covering around this stick so that the edge string is exposed above it. Cut a strip of the cover material about four inches

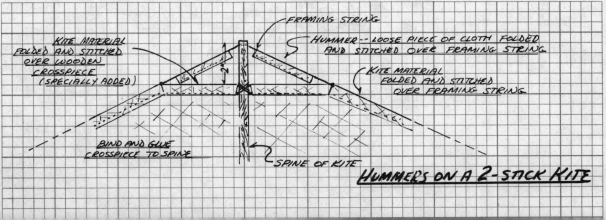

wide and a little shorter than the length of the exposed string. The hummer is then set into the top of the kite and the tail fastened to the string tied to the lower spokes of the kite.

At one time the greatest extracurricular activity among kite fliers was the sending of "messages" or "travelers" up kite lines. These are usually made of paper, with a slot to permit their being placed on the line. The wind shoves the message up the line very fast, where it stops abruptly at the bridle attachment. Several such papers traveling at spaced intervals up the line make a pretty sight, but if too many gather at the bridle the kite is likely to become overloaded and settle down in a tree—usually the kite-eating type.

Anyone stimulated by Rube Goldberg contraptions should get a kick out of building the mousetrap messenger depicted in the accompanying illustration. Goldberg (though not the drawings) would explain the operation something like this: Contact with the cork stop (A) causes a plastic straw or ⅛-inch dowel (B) to tip the mousetrap (C) on which a sail (D) has been mounted. The sail snaps down, but is prevented from clamping down on the flying line (E) by the opposing pull of a rubber band (F). The contraption now slides back down the kite line; a simple resetting of the trap will raise the sail and the wind will send it skyward again.

The trick in putting together the mousetrap messenger involves finding a rubber band with the correct tension for balancing the mousetrap's pull when the trap is half sprung. Use a *light, small* mousetrap, both because the thing won't go up in the air if it's too heavy, and because a light mousetrap has a highly tensioned spring.

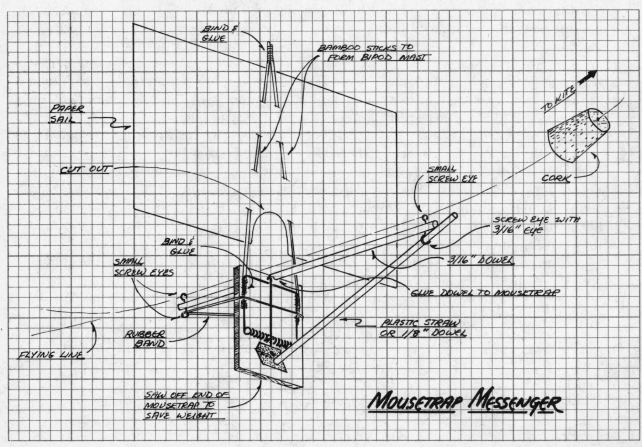

The late and revered E. A. (Mac) McCandlish, one of the world's greatest exponents of the kite-flying hobby, evolved a simple device to send tiny plastic parachute jumpers up a monofilament line and kick them off just about the time they thought they had reached some form of a haven aboard the kite. Mac bought the little jumpers for a dime each in large quantities. He simply inserted a bent common pin through the top of the little plastic parachute canopy, hooked the assembly on the kite line, and they took off. Flying Scott sleds, which have an extremely high flight angle, the objects reached elevations of a thousand feet or more when a snap on the line tossed them up and away. Quite often the things were caught in a thermal and just went on up and out of sight. It is imagined, with some justification, that there are several hundred of these little skydivers lying around the wheat fields of Kansas and oil fields of Oklahoma, with a possible sprinkling of them in Canada. Some may have been found and mistaken for the mummies of early-day flying-saucer pilots. Yes, they are green.

More serious-minded Will Battles, a chemist turned inventor, designed and built what he calls an Astrozoomer, which is a line traveler that goes up the kite line and then back down again as long as the kite remains aloft and the device hangs together. A fairly large plastic delta wing, it is equipped with a hinge device which allows it to form a vertical sail on the ride up and flip back into a sleek delta aircraft when it strikes a cork stop near the kite. Power is supplied by rubber bands. Will added a little wire hook release to the device which permits the dropping of light objects from the Zoomer as it makes its first contact with the stopping device.

Jack Aymar, an avid flier of Eddy kites in Florida, contrived such a zoomer years ago but never patented or marketed it. The zoomers come down very fast, an estimated 50 or 60 miles per hour, depending on the elevation and angle of the kite. They may be stopped at the anchorage for adjustment or loading if one doesn't mind losing a finger or two. A catcher's mitt is suggested.

Many years ago when kites were being taken seriously by those intent upon inventing the airplane, a courageous soul affixed a chair to a pulley on a kite line and opened an umbrella to pull him up to the kite, or partway, anyhow. Kite history, which is pretty scanty, reveals this brilliant innovation but fails to note what happened to the innovator. It is safe to assume that he probably fell, but on his head, and wasn't injured in the slightest.

Dropniks are always having suggestions made to them of dropping cats and other small creatures, using parachutes of course; but most dropniks are kindly fellows who wouldn't dream of such a thing. They are so tenderhearted that they even feel bad when a beloved little dummy character misfires deployment and falls to a certain "death" on the cruel and gravel-surfaced earth. Many live creatures have been lofted on kites, however, but usually with protective devices that prevent falling off. Such experiments do no good, undoubtedly terrify the creature and, happily, no known cases have been brought to our attention of late.

One of the most ingenious rigs in which a traveler is used was created by George E. Henshaw, who made the first bird's-eye-view photo of New York City by a camera lofted 500 feet. His photo took in an east-northeast view of the city and focused on Washington Square. Here is the way it was done in the year 1895.

A small box camera was attached to a traveler which was set up to trip the shutter release when contact was made at the kite head at 500 feet. The camera returned to the flier on the ground, who then reset it, sent it up repeatedly and thus made a series of pictures which compare with pictures made with more modern equipment or via airplane.

Unbelievably, the photos were made on glass negatives. The camera was carried up on a train of kites made by a fabulous kiter whose name rings like a man falling down a flight of metal stairs—Gilbert Totten Woglom.

All kite fliers have a longing to learn what it's like up there on a kite, looking down at the earth. They could easily hop in an airplane and get the same results, but that would defeat the esthetics, so some, who are definitely not dropniks, go in for kite photography whereby the camera is lifted by the kite and triggered by a number of ingenious devices including burning fuses. But it takes a graduate dropnik to invent the devices that really work.

One dropnik tied a long line to the camera trigger, assuming he could just pull on it when the kite got aloft and snap at least one picture. It would have worked fine except that he forgot that the same wind that lofted his kite and heavy camera acted also upon the trailing line. If he could have jumped 60 feet and caught the line with any degree of certainty, he would probably have gotten a fine picture.

Advances have been rapid in this particular endeavor. Small timers, some electrically actuated from battery power, will do the job, but a lot of experimenting has taken place.

Robert Ingraham describes an incident he had which involved a large winged box kite with a small box camera mounted on a sloping platform at the bottom of the forward triangular cell. The angle was to ensure the inclusion of the kite flier on the ground manipulating the kite in the anticipated photo. The triggering device had all the aspects of another Rube Goldberg invention except that it wasn't quite as sensible. A rubber band was attached to the camera trigger which, when released, snapped upward. The release mechanism was two weights hung by a thread from the anchorage of the rubber band, and it ran alongside a block of wood covered with fine sandpaper. In theory the swinging weights would fall when the thread became worn through by the sandpaper. The swinging would be created by gently rocking the kite. Timing of the action was about as certain as the date set for the millennium. What happened was not exactly as planned.

No one had ever told Ingraham that kites have a center of gravity, which if drastically altered in flight, causes several aerodynamic mutations with devastating results. While the kite went up on a running launch and maintained correct angle quite well in spite of its added weight in the nose, the first slacking of line terminated the experiment with awful suddenness. The big box kite, all eight feet of it, stood on its nose and went screaming straight for the ground. What happened to the kite and the camera is referred to by insurance people as a "total," but, would you believe it, a picture was taken. Despite the damage that followed, the weights apparently fell off just prior to the crash and the up-angled camera got a nice view of a portion of Highway 90 running from Silver City, New Mexico, to Lordsburg, by way of Mars. What is more, a car is shown clearly climbing up that highway overcoming a 90-degree slope—if you can call 90 degrees a slope.

According to Ingraham, "dropniks should never monkey around with photography, having mentalities unable to cope with such intricacies, but as scientists in other fields they perform a notable service to humanity. One endeavor they engage in is disposing of such bits of pollution as beer cans, which are lofted on their kites and dropped into dumps. Any kite flier who drives one mile on a highway to his favorite flying area can stop and pick up a large number of beer cans. Taped on the flying line at intervals of three or four feet near the kite, with a single strap of draftsman's tape, the light aluminum cans can be dropped in sequence by a hard snap on the line, which rips through the restraining straps with a strong ripple. The cans fall away like a stick of bombs and make a breathtaking spectacle as they fall slowly down, sparkling in the sunlight. The scientific part is the timing the dropniks are forever doing with the hope of disproving the falling weight theory Galileo came up with several hundred years ago, which has never been challenged."

Weights of varying amounts do not fall at the same speed. A Coke bottle makes it to the ground about twice as fast as an aluminum beer can. It takes about 15 seconds for the can to reach the ground, whereas a Coke bottle takes about 5, when the elevation is about 2,000 feet. The trouble with most dropniks is that they never know how high a kite is. However, they feel that Galileo was confused, as anyone must be who would walk out on the balcony of the Leaning Tower of Pisa. Suppose it finally fell over.

Nevertheless most dropniks feel that the ancient Italian scientist was a blood brother and provides one of the best excuses they can think of for conducting their endless experiments. As far as we know, no psychoanalysis has ever been made of a true dropnik, but it might prove interesting. The most avid of the cult are usually little guys who have spent a lifetime looking up at almost everything. Even the post-office boxes assigned to them are always six inches above their heads, calling for short energetic jumps to see if they have any mail. Short dropniks admire heights of any sort and have uncontrolled desires to drop things from them. Throwing rocks from skyscrapers or the Astrodome bleachers is frowned upon by authorities, but kites are perfect platforms and the areas below them are usually uninhabited unless by sheep, cows, gophers and the like.

Since the avidity of dropniks is relative to their height, a six-foot four-inch member of the society wouldn't be considered more than lukewarm to the idea, but John Gibson, an eighteen-year-old kite flier, invented the vacuum release, which was a big step forward as a means to drop things when you wanted them to drop and not before. John, who is a serious student bent on a mining engineer's career, is the technical assistant to David Omick, who invents the things to drop. Beginning with a small rubber vacuum cup which he stole from his younger brother's dart set, John found that by placing the cup on a piece of Formica, it held firmly for about five minutes with a certain amount of weight tugging on it. That's where the science comes in. There is no such thing as an absolutely smooth surface. If there were, a lot of problems encountered in this world of technology would quickly be solved. Formica, despite its polished surface, which feels slick to the hand, has tiny abrasions through which atmospheric pressure finds its way to destroy a vacuum. The biggest advantage of this material is its lightness, and that's why John chose it for his invention of a drop release.

One of the problems of launching a payload to be dropped from a kite is that of the violence, which is difficult to avoid, at the start. It is therefore very important that the load isn't tripped by such movement as is likely to happen with crude devices such as pipe cleaners wound a turn or two to be shaken loose. The vacuum cup is ideal, therefore, and John went on to using the large ones found at stores where they sell car luggage racks. And big cups are necessary when it comes to handling loads like One-Jump Waldo. But that's another story.

Dropniks who prefer to send things up flying lines to fall when they reach the kite include Jack Van Gilder of Seattle, who stumbled upon a clever release mechanism while indulging in an American pastime of bending perfectly good paper clips out of shape. If you've ever wondered what happens to all the tons of paper clips manufactured every year, this is evidence of where some, at least, enter oblivion.

Jack attaches little paper parachutes or whatever to an assembly fashioned from the clips with a pair of needle-nose pliers. As long as the parachute tugs the assembly along the line, it remains locked. When the stop is reached, a disengagement occurs and the object flutters away. Sometimes the clip assembly will come jingling back down the line to be used over again, depending on the force of the wind, but if it doesn't it is easy to attach still another and another until the lift capacity of the kite is overcome by the weight of accumulated metal. But that's a lot of paper clips.

Much has been said about the "best laid plans of mice and men" but nothing about those of kite fliers who contrive to drop things from their kites. They too often go awry and for a hundred reasons. Premature deployment of parachutes, tangled static lines, timers that fail, fuses that go out, unexpected power dives of kites, and faulty engineering all contrive to frustrate. Sometimes overloaded kites break their tethers and go whirling away to crash and make a mess of tangled wire, cloth, screw eyes and wide-eyed little dummy men.

One dropnik tells of the breakaway of a huge, two-celled triangular box kite laden with two dummy parachute jumpers and a heavy timer. The craft landed almost intact, having glided in smoothly with the added weight at its nose. But it began to roll in the high wind, and the poor kite flier chased it for about a half-mile trying vainly to capture it before the damage got worse. It was futile, and he says it required two hours of work with cutting pliers to get the thing apart and salvage the deployed parachutes, jumpers and release equipment.

A successor kite, with a heavy timer fastened to just the correct place on the keel, went into violent power dives when the timer slipped its mooring and slid down the keel to the rear cell section. With the definite shift of the center of gravity, the kite became "redlined," or overpowered, and a terrible destruction was in the immediate offing. There is only one way to bring a kite out of such power dives, which in reality are half-dive and half-climb as the craft is tacking flatly against the wind. Each wild circle brings the kite closer to earth, as the loss of elevation in each dive is fractionally compensated for by each climb out.

Such accidents are all part of the game of dropniking and sometimes create thrilling and unforgettable episodes in heretofore unwritten kite history.

As told by the dropnik, relating to this particular incident, the kite line was tied to the door handle of a truck and the pressure was so great on the kite the line was tautened to a point where it was impossible to get it untied in time to save the craft and payload. The only way an overpowered kite can be saved is to give it slack line immediately and "float it out" and land it somewhat gently. With this an impossibility, the flier could do little but stand and watch the big craft scream its way down to an inevitable crash.

In this case the kite went out of sight beyond an old airplane hangar, and the flier never saw the impact with earth. But experience had taught him that it was pretty terrible. But in all the gyrations and the resultant centrifugal force, the model parachute jumper was thrown high and wide, his parachute deployed and a safe landing effected. That portion was a thrill, he says.

When you walk out to a wreck like that, quite slowly, of course, as there's no need to hurry, there's a fascination in the anticipation of what you'll find. The psyche of man includes a strange preoccupation with violent destruction. But this kite flier was puzzled by the continued tautness of the flying line as he walked along; just as taut as it had been prior to the crash. The reason was quickly discovered. Striking the earth head on, the three-eighths-inch wood spar longerons of the kite had been driven more than six inches into the ground. The forward bridle connection had been buried with the end of the keel spar and the entire wreck was pulling as hard on the line as prior to the crash. When the 250-pound-test nylon flying line was cut and released, it flew back more than 20 feet, attesting to the tension created and resultant stretch. The timer was a total loss, as well as everything the kite was made of, with the exception of the fabric. And that was torn.

Another dropnik, with an obsession to learn how much weight a small parachute could successfully lower to earth, fastened a small pilot chute to a five-gallon can and rigged a crude deployment mechanism. The assembly was tied to the forward cell section of a tetrahedral winged box kite with about 10 feet of line, at the end of which a pipe cleaner was used to affix the can and parachute assembly. Pipe cleaners are highly useful in dropniking, as they can be made to untwist easily by jerking on the kite, yet hold firmly under less violent conditions. They are also useful if the kite flier smokes a pipe. Whatever, in this case, the usual jerking on the flying line failed to disengage the pipe cleaner's grasp, and the flier resorted to violent vertical rocking of the big kite in order to get the can in motion, thereby increasing the activity. He finally got the can swinging in big arcs which would have eventually flexed the wire pipe cleaner to the breaking point, but he was in a hurry and overdid it. The can made a final great swoop forward, upward, backward and right down through the front cell assembly. Had the breakup of the *Hesperus* on the rocks been recorded, the sound would have been similar, this dropnik said. And, believe it or not, that parachute popped out and lowered the entire wreck to the ground quite gently.

"Lt. McLoughlin" is a 15-inch-high parachute jumper with a record of successful jumps longer than your arm if inscribed in six-point type. Made of blue denim and stuffed with bits of foam rubber, Mac has a face painted with textile paint, a flying suit, crash helmet made from a cutaway rubber ball, plastic boots filled with lead shot and carries a complete parachute pack right down to hesitator straps and ripcord pin. He is the creation of Bob Ingraham, who has contrived a long line of such jumpers, beginning with a crude character named "Fearless Fosdick."

McLoughlin, named after a longtime friend of his boss, who is the editor of *Kite Tales* magazine, ranks right along with "Lucie," the family cat, as a family member, and aside from having to sleep in the garage, is given every consideration granted that ancient feline. All kite-flying expeditions made by the editor include Mac, who is usually carried in a suitcase along with other paraphernalia, but now and then allowed to sit in the car like a French royalist going to the guillotine in a tumbril.

Ingraham says he suspects that Mac doesn't like sky diving and would prefer

So fearsome and imaginative are the dropniks created by dedicated kite experimenters that it would take a new book just to list them. Nevertheless, Bob Ingraham's "Fearless Fosdick" embodies almost all the skills and imagination needed to take off on a career of dropniks.

From time to time, in his wonderful quarterly **Kite Tales**, Ingraham recounts some of the more feverish adventures of his hero, Fosdick. It's better than the perils of Pauline. (*Photos courtesy Bob Ingraham*)

Fearless Fosdick was the first model parachute jumper to be dropped from kites by Bob Ingraham. Fosdick, now retired, was made of denim and stuffed with old nylons.

Fearless Fosdick sometimes "hung on the line"— a malfunction that occurred when the ripcord line failed to release from the parachute pack.

An alarm clock timer dropnik device, invented by the late Ed McCandlish, a founder of the American Kitefliers Association. The unwinding alarm key would wind up a short nylon line until a pin was pulled, thus releasing the payload.

having remained a sort of an earthbound Pinocchio rather than a parachute jumper earthward bound. He becomes quite sullen and uncooperative before jumps and is suspected of having hung on the line tightly, refusing to let loose after the drop mechanism had functioned properly. Mac's life has been a series of horrors consisting of sickening drops from a thousand feet or more during which there is no assurance of anything successful in the deployment of the parachute. In fact, there have been many cases where malfunctions have occurred and the poor little guy plunged the whole way with the parachute still tucked safely in the pack.

Intensely interested in parachutes and their proper function, Ingraham says it is nothing short of amazing how the most cautious rigger can make errors that result in fatalities. In real parachute packing, the rigger uses lead shot bags to hold down the pleated folds of the canopy, counting each one inserted the same as a surgeon counts sponges. A recount, upon removing the bags, is vital to ensure that none is left in the pack to cause almost certain malfunction. But there are cases where counting has been faulty and the results tragic. This same thing can and does happen with models

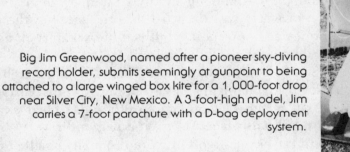

Ed McCandlish used this shapely inflatable dummy to startle passersby by suspending it from a large kite. It was released by an alarm clock timer and fell slowly because of its light weight. No harm came to the dummy but lots of people thought they had seen someone fall to a terrible death.

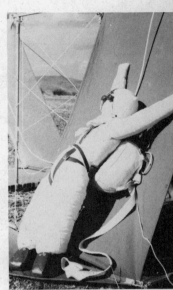

Big Jim Greenwood, named after a pioneer sky-diving record holder, submits seemingly at gunpoint to being attached to a large winged box kite for a 1,000-foot drop near Silver City, New Mexico. A 3-foot-high model, Jim carries a 7-foot parachute with a D-bag deployment system.

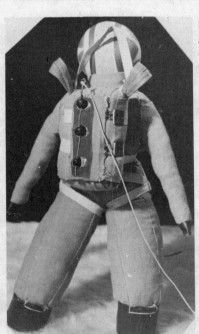

Details of the parachute pack and opening mechanism used on "Lt. McLoughlin," favorite model jumper made by Bob Ingraham, avid dropnik as well as internationally known kite flier and builder. Strap at the back of the crash helmet, which is a modified rubber ball, is attached to a release mechanism. The static line and ripcord pin pull out when the jumper falls away, releasing the parachute. "Mac" has made over a thousand jumps, some of them long-delayed types when special packing methods are used.

What appears to be a "standing landing," which is the type most sought by sky divers, is actually a "studio" shot of "Lt. Elwood Spottswood," one of Ingraham's crew of fearless parachutists. "Spottsy" once traveled two miles before coming to earth on a golf course near startled players.

too. Clothespins, used in place of shot bags by dropniks, are sometimes left inside the folds of nylon with equally devastating results. On one occasion a large safety pin, used to hold the folds together during packing, was left in, and the results were awful. One of the most common errors is forgetting to secure the static line during the excitement of launching, setting the timer and other procedures.

It's a little sad when you realize what you haven't done, and you sit out there under the kite knowing full well that your jumper is doomed. But it's just plain fiendish when you deliberately unhook the shoulder straps prior to launch, as was often done to "Fearless Fosdick." One can only imagine the horror Fosdick briefly endured when he saw his parachute deploy but float off horizontally while he continued down vertically.

Some of the experiments made by dropniks are silly but provide extremely funny incidents. One was the lofting of a gallon plastic jug full of water under a parafoil. The purpose was to study the impact resistance of the material the jug was made of, although no manufacturer had requested such experimentation. At a height of about 20 feet, the jug simply split apart, obviously being defective, and the entire gallon of water was dumped into the faces of the experimenters. As people have a tendency to open their mouths wide when looking sharply upward, a goodly share went down gullets of the dropniks.

Some dropniks have "drop bags" which attach to the timer. The end fastened to the drop mechanism falls away and dumps various items, including flour, which makes a beautiful cloud in an otherwise clear sky. On one occasion a big load of desert soil was placed in such a bag and a very dirty but impressive cloud created high in the sky. Forgotten were the many small stones included, and as the conspiring dropniks looked upward, marveling at their unique creation, said stones came whizzing down at bullet speed, one of them clipping a sensitive bald spot.

The variety of "drops" by dropniks is endless, and some create beautiful sights such as the release of a 150-foot roll of bright-colored plastic surveyor's tape. The unrolling across the sky makes a fantastic scene, and its trailing from a kite as a superlong tail, twisting and turning in the wind, is an unforgettable sight. If two rolls are added together, the 300-foot streamer is even more spectacular. Weighted crepepaper streamers, the same as used by smoke jumpers to determine wind draft effect, fall as streaming droplets of colored rain.

The principal challenge to the dropnik is that of suitably releasing whatever is to be dropped at the proper time. The number of contrivances invented and innovated—from alarm clocks to burning fuses—is legion, but most are crude and subject to malfunction and best left to the more dedicated dropniks.

A useful tool to have around when you are flying gimmicks is the standard old-fashioned pipe cleaner. This fuzz-covered wiring can be turned and coiled and bent to fit many situations without acting as an abrasive that may cut the kite line. To keep from overloading, tie a pipe cleaner ten or fifteen feet below the kite. This will stop the messengers from piling up on the bridle line.

Warning: Do not load too many messengers on the line. A surfeit of travelers will change the angle of the bridle line. This may be disastrous.

Be sure that the center hole is not too large, otherwise messengers will fly right through and up into the bridle line and change the angle of ascent and descent.

Bob Ingraham ties a light thread line to a dead light bulb which he jerks loose at

300 feet. It makes a great bomb. A friend of his tried it and bombed his own car. Never again.

Note: The drop lines, except in fishing, shouldn't be more than a couple of feet long. Otherwise the line starts to swing and a pendulum effect is created that is very difficult to stop and may snarl your lead line.

A great accessory of kite flying for the oldster who doesn't want to run is the plain fishing rod and reel. I introduced the rod and reel technique to startled kite fliers in Central Park in New York City some thirty years ago. It has been criticized as a crutch to the sport, the contention being that the rod and reel do all the work that the flier should be doing. Nonsense. There is as much skill lifting a kite by rod and reel as there is in getting it up by running into the wind. More so, as a matter of fact. With rod and reel you can manipulate the kite so that it catches upgoing currents no matter how slight and retrieve the line more rapidly. Furthermore, you can cast the kite with a rod and reel. A bit of practice and you will find greater joy in using this technique, which will give you more flying dates because with rod and reel it will be possible to fly in no-wind days.

Welcomed by the dropnik fraternity is the little Graupner timer, a German-made jewellike mechanism which was designed as a dethermalizer for model airplanes and nothing else. While the Graupner is incapable of holding up other than the lightest of weights, its tiny release lever, when actuated by rubber bands, can be utilized as the triggering mechanism to release heavier loads. One adaptation is the

It takes considerable ingenuity to rig drop release mechanisms that work. This positive action wooden plug, devised by Ed McCandlish, contains two dowels held together with a rubber band. A hard pull separates the dowels, used as a part of the kite's flying line, momentarily, and the object to be dropped falls away.

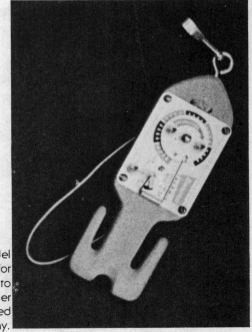

The Graupner mechanism, built as a dethermalizer for model airplanes, is used by dropniks to trigger stronger mechanisms for dropping heavy objects which cannot be fastened directly to the timer. It is actually a precision-built spring-wound timer similar to those used as a kitchen appliance. It is manufactured in Germany.

Dropniks need special kites to carry some of the loads they send aloft. Objects range from light aluminum beer cans to five-gallon containers. One dropnik even dropped a complete kitchen chair. It looked funnier hanging under the kite than when falling, but not much. This early-day kite, with a 14-foot wingspan, was developed by Bob Ingraham at age 16 just to carry junk up into the sky.

mounting of the mechanism on a wood block and adding a small hinge. The weight of the object to be dropped rests upon the hinge, not the arm, and the movement of the arm releases the rubber bands holding the hinge section upright. The Graupner timer can be duplicated on a larger scale by modifying a small oven timer—if one can sneak it out of the house and into the workshop.

Parafoils, especially the larger ones, are the best kites from which to drop objects, as they are great heavy-load carriers, surer on launch and climb quickly to the desired height. However, large box kites have served such purpose admirably for many years. The parafoil has the advantage of remaining undamaged in crashes, which are more likely to occur when loads are involved with its flight.

One-Jump Waldo is the creation of Bob Ingraham and his associate dropniks who have unlimited uninhabited spaces in which to conduct their experiments. Waldo is a man-sized foam-rubber dummy stiffened with a plywood backbone who carries a 16-foot parachute donated to the cause by Dave Williams, who flies full-sized parachutes as kites. Waldo has a beautifully designed parachute pack and, aside from having abnormally wide hips, is quite a manly figure but not exactly a handsome one. In fact he is so ugly that the only expression a little three-year-old girl could think of upon first getting a glimpse of him was "yuk!"

Waldo, parachute and all, weighs 11 pounds and exits from a 42-square-foot Jalbert parafoil when making exhibition jumps. His nickname is the result of his first jump when he chose to land on top of the only building in a 60,000-acre area, and it was assumed he could never be retrieved. But he was and has gone on to a fame of sorts.

Release of the big jumper is accomplished by one of John Gibson's vacuum cup assemblies, with the cup attached to a short section of aluminum tubing to prevent twisting in the wind. The cup is fastened to an aluminum plate mounted on Waldo's shoulders and bleed-off time is about five minutes under normal conditions. Once aloft no one would suspect that the jumper was other than a daring human.

It has been said that people watch race drivers and sky divers with a faint hope that they will be dashed to death and provide a morbid thrill. But this isn't so. Full deployment of a parachute when it can be seen usually brings cheers and expressions of relief from watching crowds. Race drivers crossing the finish line safely bring forth great ovations from the stands, while the twisting, turning and burning of a less fortunate driver's car stuns a crowd into silence and dismay. There may be some who get an abnormal kick out of tragedy, but they are victims of mental quirks unexplainable.

One-Jump Waldo, asked to make an exhibition jump at an air show early in his career, had the misfortune of having a hesitator strap tear away at the start of parachute deployment. At 500 feet elevation the unopened chute rolled down to lodge between his feet, and he plunged to earth head down to land with a terrible-sounding and far too realistic crunch in the dust before 2,000 spectators. The groan from the crowd during the seconds of the fall was in unison and real. The silence that followed when Waldo lay near the hardstand, his head against his chest, testifies to the reality. No one in the crowd had any illusions that the jumper was real.

For those of you who are eager to get started on the sport of dropping items on yourselves or curious bystanders, the dropper shown in the accompanying diagrams can be constructed in a few minutes from a scrap of wood, a wire coat hanger and a rubber band. The ideal thickness of the wood is ¼ inch to ½ inch, but a scrap of shelving will do if you can't find anything thinner. As for the wire, use the thinnest

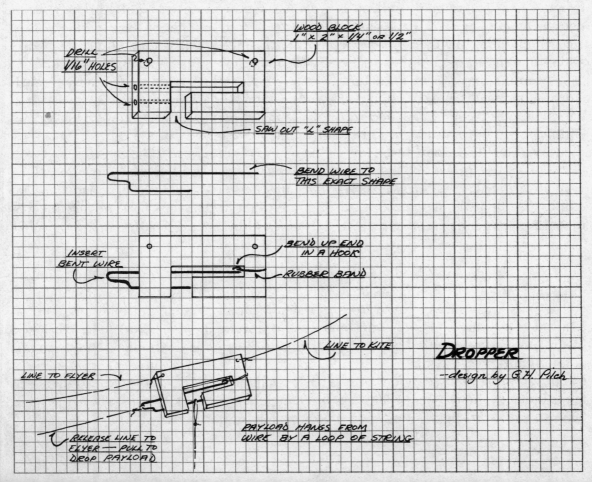

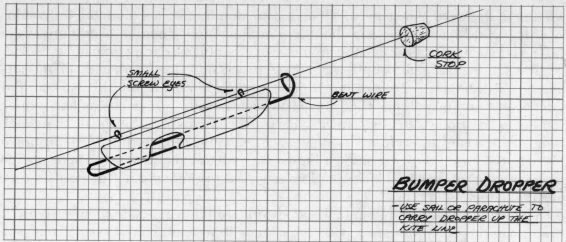

SMALL
SCREW EYES

BENT WIRE

CORK
STOP

BUMPER DROPPER
-USE SAIL OR PARACHUTE TO
CARRY DROPPER UP THE
KITE LINE

coat hanger you can find. The ingenious Mr. G. H. Pilch, creator of this dropper as well as the kite on pages 119–20, recommends using a bicycle spoke. To make the dropper, simply saw and drill the wood as shown on the plan, bend the wire, attach with a rubber band, and you're ready to drop things.

This is a stationary dropper—that is, it doesn't travel up and down the kite line like a messenger—and it requires a special release line to operate it. Be careful not to get the flying line and release line snarled when you're letting out the kite. If you have a helper, it's a good idea to have him stand a few paces away, paying out the release line as you pay out the kite line. To operate the dropper, just tug on the release line.

If you have built a Pilch dropper, or even examined the plans, the bumper dropper (as diagrammed) will pose no construction problems. This dropper, however, is a messenger: it carries its payload up the kite line. So be sure to "fly" it on a smooth kite line like nylon monofilament. String (or monofilament with knots) won't slide smoothly through the screw eyes as the messenger travels up toward the kite.

The release mechanism is slightly different from the one on the Pilch dropper. It stops its payload when the bumper smacks into a stop—here shown as a cork—that has thoughtfully been attached to the line ahead of time. So it's important for the sliding metal wire to move freely within the wooden body of the device. Balsa, by the way, is an ideal wood, since it is light and travels easily up a kite line.

The motive power for the messenger can be a paper sail or a toy parachute. One variant of the dropper has the parachute attached to the release mechanism. The chute tugs the little device skyward—then with the triggering of the release mechanism, the chute falls earthward and the dropper slides back down the line.

The self-adjusting bridle is the holy grail of kite fliers, everlastingly sought, never gained—even though the heart is pure, as is always the case with kite fliers.

It was unattainable until recently when Benn Blinn, white-haired, gentle-hearted Columbus, Ohio, millionaire, entrepreneur and gadgeteer, shrieked "Eureka!" and reinvented the self-adjusting bridle and revolutionized kite flying. It is impossible to sail a kite as you sail a boat. Unlike a boat, a kite cannot be made to luff or sail into the wind, nor can reefs be set in its sails. Some of the skillful fliers can make it dance and do other tricks, but basically, the average kite goes where the wind takes it, for the bridle position cannot be adjusted from the ground.

Not all dropniks drop everything. They use their kites to suspend various objects high in the air. One of the most popular items is the Stars and Stripes flown from the flying line, not from the kite itself. That would cause too much drag. This flag was flown from a large delta-wing kite by Dick Robertson of Austin, Texas.

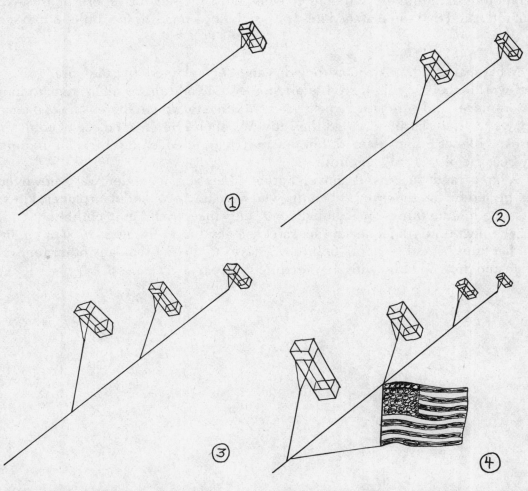

Raising Old Glory. A kite flier may display his virtuosity as well as patriotism by "raising Old Glory to the sky" on the Fourth of July. Use as a minimum a 10-pound test line and a family of similar kites. The first kite should go up on at least 300 feet of twine. Once up, turn the line of this kite over to your co-pilot while you go down the field to fly a second kite up to an altitude of 150 feet (half a ball of twine). With both kites in the air, bring the lines together and tie them to each other. Run the two kites out another 200 feet. Fly the third kite on the second half of the ball of twine and tie it to the main line. Repeat with the fourth kite, which now becomes the main line. Having secured the flag to a very light stick, tie the upper end to the main line below the point where the third kite is tied and run a cord 10 or 15 feet long from the bottom of the kite to the main line. Let the main line out another 100 feet and whip Old Glory into the sky.

Blinn's contrivance is a simple one, just as simple as the wheel once it was invented. Writes Blinn: "The automatic bridle forms a triangle at the lower point of attachment where the kite attacks the wind most efficiently. The trouble is that sometimes the attack is greater than the kite can take. Therefore, it is best to attach an elastic material of some kind at this juncture of the kite body and bridle. This stretch material in the bridle will allow the kite to automatically adjust its attitude of attack as though the point of attachment had been moved up to the bridle." When the wind dies down, according to Benn, the bridle, of course, returns to its original position. Also, the automatic bridle takes care of a lot of shock, which is about the only reason the line breaks in critical wind turbulence.

Before we leave Benn Blinn and his magic bridle, it must be noted that he is one of the greatest of the latter-day fliers. It was he and the late Walter Scott who undertook to fly kites across the Atlantic some years ago. Though they failed in the noble attempt to "communikite" with our cousins across the sea, the reports on this experiment indicated that some of the kites were sighted as much as fifty miles out to sea.

What makes dropniks do as they do can't be explained, but they don't care. In a cruel world where children are literally forced into adulthood, there remain in most of us impulses and curiosities considered childlike for which there is no explanation. Why we have so sharply divided the activities of children from those of adults in all senses is likewise unexplained, but we are forced to cover and hide the impulse to play because play is only for children.

A great and successful movement of liberation is under way, however, as exemplified by the thousands of adults who have taken to model airplanes, kites and a host of other fun things once thought to be only the playthings of children.

The next time someone says he can't see any fun in flying a kite you might tell him that kites have done more to lift man's eyes to the sky than any other innovation of man and provided him with an unending source of joy.

8 FISHING WITH KITES

"The kite is such a wonderful fishing machine," says Captain Tommy Gifford, the dean of U.S. charter-boat captains. "The kite will take more fish than any other method of presenting bait." And Captain Gifford should know—he has caught tuna, swordfish, marlin and other prize fish by using a kite to carry baited fishing lines to water surfaces hundreds of feet away from the noise and wake of the boat.

Gifford also has taught the sport of kite fishing to numerous seasoned anglers who thought they knew all the tricks for taking trophy fish from the deep seas along the coasts of the United States. But kite fishing is an ancient art, almost as old as kite flying itself. The idea may have originated thousands of years ago when the kite of a Melanesian native accidentally dipped a little too close to the surface of the sea and a hungry denizen of the deep made a grab for the man-made bird. By attaching a lure and hook to the kite line, and letting it drop to the water surface again, the ancient kite flier probably got the fish. He then announced to his friends that he had discovered a new way to mix business and pleasure.

At any rate, the idea seems to have caught on quickly and spread around the world because there is evidence that peoples of some early cultures were hauling in fish on kite lines before the rest of the world was even aware that a few palm fronds tied to a framework of sticks could ride the air currents. Some form of kite fishing is still being used in the Southwest Pacific. Historian Wayne J. Baldwin records that in Micronesia a ball or ring of spider web is used as a lure to catch the mighty garfish. In some parts of Asia a running noose is attached to a kite to snare the fish. A form of kite fishing, better known as skip-fishing, was popular in the earlier days of American history. But that sport gradually faded as casting and spinning reels, spoons, outriggers and other precursors of modern fishing gear began to dominate the scene. However, with better kites and improved kite-flying techniques, the old sport has been revived and married to the newer types of fishing tackle. And kite fishing is today more popular than ever before.

My own initiation to kite fishing dates back to the 1950's while practicing a bit of old-fashioned skip-fishing from the beach at Truro, Massachusetts, on Cape Cod. My kite was about 200 yards offshore, beyond the curling combers of the sea, and my baited and weighted lure on a 20-foot drop line was skipping along the surface of the water.

Suddenly, the kite dropped about 50 feet and I felt a terrific pull on the line. My nearly automatic response was to reel out in order to keep the kite in the air. As the kite sailed upward again, a big striped bass was lifted out of the water, hooked on the lure. At times the fish was 10 feet out of the water as the kite pulled skyward and I pulled the line toward the beach. One of the many passersby who stopped to watch the ensuing battle screamed, "Look! He's hooked a flying fish!"

After a half-hour struggle, I managed to haul the striper in close enough to gaff it. And to my immense satisfaction, the fish weighed in at 20 pounds. Since that debut, and with some practice at modifying my own drop-line technique, I have hooked seven- to ten-pound bluefish with almost monotonous regularity while kite fishing in Long Island Sound or in the Atlantic off Montauk Point.

An experienced kite fisherman can fly his bait to almost any point in the water that he chooses. And he can fish up to a quarter mile from shore or troll among rocks or in a pounding surf where no boatman would dare travel. And no special tackle is needed; the same rod, reel, line, swivels and artificial lures or live bait used for conventional fishing are used. However, the choice of kite is important. Since the kite is to be used in a watery environment, the kite materials should be impervious to water. A paper kite or a kite made with light wooden strips obviously would not withstand the rigors of kite fishing or more than one accidental soaking in the water. The best kites are those made of good sheet plastic, such as Mylar, although a fabric-covered kite with lightweight metal or substantial wooden framing would be satisfactory. And the Rogallo-type plastic flexible kites are excellent for kite fishing.

A good rule of thumb in choosing a kite is to figure on about one square foot of kite surface for each pound of fish you hope to catch. An inexpensive toy-store kite generally can handle a fish weighing up to two or three pounds. If you are going after fish that weigh up to ten pounds, you will need at least a good square yard of kite surface.

A heavier line is needed, of course, for bigger fish. And if you are going after a really big catch, you will need a rod and reel big and heavy enough to handle the fish, just as in conventional fishing. For starters, however, load an ordinary fishing reel with 20- to 40-pound-test monofilament or nylon line. The fishing line will also be your kite line. Some kite fishermen operate quite effectively with a big spool of heavy kite cord. But you will find that it is easier to launch and control your kite with a good strong fishing line on ordinary bait-casting tackle.

Drop-line kite fishing is less complicated than the other basic method of employing an outrigger or trolley system to carry a separate fishing line in tandem with a kite line. With the drop line, the lure or bait and a suitable weight are attached to one end of a leader, and the other end of the leader is fastened to the kite line. The leader may range in length from several inches to many feet, depending upon the distance between the kite line and the surface of the waters being fished. The trolley system, described in greater detail later in this chapter, requires the proper positioning of two separate lines held together by clothespins or similar devices so that the fishing line drops away from the kite line when a fish strikes.

The beginner also should make sure he has an adequate supply of quarter-ounce and half-ounce weights in his tackle box. The amount of weight needed is something of a trial-and-error matter at first, but it can be a critical factor in maintaining effective control. A weight overload will tend to drag the bait too deeply in the water, but a lack of weight on the line can result in a lure swinging in the air beyond the reach of even a flying fish. If your first guesstimate of the situation is wrong, you can add or subtract lead in quarter- or half-ounce weights.

The next step is to check the wind direction. Because of temperature variations between land and water, there almost always will be a breeze around the shore of a large body of water. A direct offshore breeze is ideal, but any offshore breeze is suitable for launching the kite. If the wind is parallel to the shore, try to find a pier or jetty to take the best advantage of the wind direction. An island with a lot of beach area gives you the most options; a lake or reservoir with trees close to the shoreline cuts the options considerably, and you may have to walk or drive around the edges of the lake until you find a satisfactory site.

Once you have found a good location, tie the end of the fishing line securely to the bridle of the kite. Then send the kite out about 200 to 250 feet, lock the reel, and pull in the line from the tip of the rod until you have enough slack to fasten the leader, or drop line, which carries the weight and lure, to the kite line.

The leader should be 20 to 30 feet long, long enough to troll or skip the lure through the water. And adjustment of the small lead weights will help achieve the proper distance of the lure to the water surface. There are two other techniques that help the kite fisherman control the position of the drop line. He can raise or lower the tip of the fishing rod to lift or drop the lure. And he can reel out kite line quickly to lower the lure; reeling in rapidly has the opposite effect of lifting the lure.

With these factors considered, the art of drop-line kite fishing becomes a matter of remote control trolling. To troll out, you release kite line slowly. To troll toward shore, you reel in slowly.

A strike is easy to detect—about the same, in fact, as in conventional fishing with the same kind of tackle. And once the fish is hooked, it is landed simply by reeling in the line. Generally, with pressure from two sides—the kite pulling from one direction and the fisherman pulling from the other—the hook becomes embedded more firmly than when the pressure is only from the pull of the angler. A larger kite gives some obvious advantage, especially if the fish is bigger than expected or puts up more of a fight than anticipated. A fighting fish also lends added excitement to the sport, but the kite fisherman should be alert to wild maneuvers such as the fish making a sudden lunge at right angles to the kite line. The kite will dip sharply and you may have only a few seconds to demonstrate that people can think faster than fish. You may lose not only the fish and lure, but the kite.

However, once you have learned how to select the proper kite fishing rig and how to use it effectively, chances are you will catch more fish in any body of water than would be possible without the use of a kite for a sky hook. If properly maneuvered, the lure can be presented to the fish in a more natural manner; the bait is dropped or skipped at the surface with a minimum show of line. The bait appears far from the man-made vibrations of boats churning through the water or heavy feet clomping on a rocky shore. And the kite fisherman can spot the bait in the area where he sees bass, for example, popping the water surface from below. It is not unusual for an experienced kite fisherman to drop a lure within a yard of a fish seen surfacing 250 feet away.

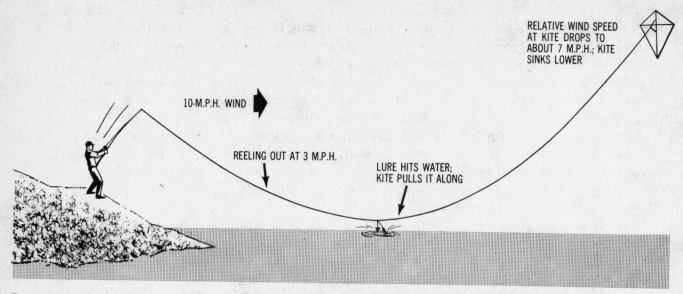

The windage chart put together for **Popular Science** magazine by expert George Daniels and the author is a graphic illustration of the drop-line method and its simplicity of operation.

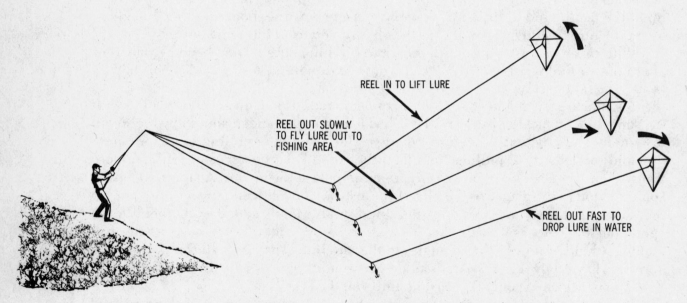

A second chart shows the action necessary to fly lures or bait to the areas where the fish are located. Using the wind, the line will go much farther than a cast. Although Daniels' chart shows a rod and reel in use, they are not necessary—just a hand-over-hand reel will do.

A second method of kite fishing, used primarily by boat fishermen, uses a trolley system of two or three lines connected with clothespins, pulleys, spring-loaded trips or triggers, and other devices. The basic system uses two lines, one for the kite and the second for the fishing line. The fishing line is rigged through a clothespin on the kite line. When a fish strikes, the fishing line pulls free of the kite, which remains in the air. The angler then plays the fishing line in the same manner as in conventional bait casting or trolling. The main advantages of the trolley method are that, as in drop-line fishing from the shore, the kite carries the fishing lure much farther out than it could be cast. Again, assuming that fish avoid boat noises and other "bad vibes" associated with the presence of humans, the lure is presented in a more peaceful setting. The lure also can be presented with a more enticing motion and can be held more easily near the surface of the water. The big disadvantage to trolley-line kite fishing is that the fisherman simply does not have control of his line at the most critical instant of the sport—when the fish makes its strike. A period of 10 to 15 seconds can elapse from the time the fish hits the bait until the fisherman adjusts the tension on the line. During this period, the fishing line has become disengaged from the clothespin or other triggering device, a good many yards of slack line have drifted down to the water, and the fish may have had a chance to finish off the bait and leave the area before the fisherman has had a chance to set the hook. If the tension is not set

Skip fishing or kite fishing is exactly what it sounds like. You fish with a kite leading the bait, hook and lead weights through the water—from the land. Recently, there has developed a new form of kite fishing from boats. (*David Stemple*)

properly at the crucial instant of the strike, the fisherman may lose the lure or snap the line. And, too often, the angler merely reels in an empty hook beneath an immutable kite still sailing above the boat.

However, Captain Gifford and many other anglers of the deep seas swear by the technique. And they have managed to keep a significant proportion of the taxidermy industry busy with carcasses of marlin, swordfish and other piscatorial winners snared with trolley kite fishing rigs.

Except for the argument that kite fishing from boats is worthwhile because the boats may disturb nearby fish, there are some anglers who are persuasive in their philosophy that kite fishing and boat fishing are somewhat redundant: if you have a quiet boat, you don't need a kite to reach the far-out fish. But there are enough sport fishermen who get seasick, even at the sight of a boat, to warrant serious consideration of the advantages of drop-line kite fishing. One angler noted for his prowess at deep-sea fishing without getting his feet wet is Al Kretschmar of Miami, Florida. Kretschmar probably holds the world's long-distance record for fishing by kite with a cast of over a half-mile. He uses a kite made of bamboo framework covered with nylon. Kretschmar's fishing kite, which has helped snare many barracudas, is equipped with plastic floats so it can be retrieved easily if a wild barracuda suddenly zaps to the side and pulls the kite into the drink.

Kite innovator Dom Jalbert has devised a trolley system with a spring-loaded trigger device on the kite. The fishing lure is carried up the kite line trolley on a wind-filled parachute. When the chute reaches the end of the line, the trigger releases the baited fishing line.

But back to Captain Gifford. He is credited with having caught more fish with kites than anybody else who has tried the sport. Gifford's kite usually is fashioned like an Eddy kite with a framework of fiber glass and a covering of silk. The kite line is reeled from a big wooden spool that he feeds out behind the boat, which may or may not be moving when the kite is launched; Gifford prefers to anchor the boat while kite fishing and reportedly can get his tailless kites into the air when there is almost no breeze at all.

For catching sailfish, a popular item among deep-sea kite fishermen, live bait is used. And the bait generally is pinfish. The bait is suspended so that about half of the pinfish is in the water, the half with the hook affixed above the water. The bait wriggles and offers some motion as the kite moves or the boat rocks gently in the waves. Actually the pinfish (or sardine, mullet, or whatever) is free to swim in the position it is held by the kite. The important consideration is that the live bait should give the appearance of a natural forage fish from the perspective of the fish you are trying to catch; the game fish will be looking up and should not be able to spot the hook and leader suspended on the top side of the water surface by the kite.

Gifford has worked the Atlantic from Nova Scotia to the Caribbean with his trolley kite-fishing method and was the first to catch many species such as white marlin and tuna in coastal waters of the United States with a kite.

On the California coast, deep-sea kite fishing had a much earlier beginning. It began in earnest around 1912 in an area called the Doldrums, off Santa Catalina Island, where a colony of bluefin tuna had eluded expert anglers for years. The tuna liked the Doldrums because it also was home to a school of flying fish, and the tuna ignored any bait that did not pop out of the water occasionally. The only time an angler got a strike in that location was when he pulled hard on the line so that his bait skipped.

The freaky behavior of the tuna inspired a California charter-boat captain named George Farnsworth to try the old trick of skip-fishing with a kite.

The imaginative Farnsworth is also the inventor of an original fishing kite, which he named the Tunaplane. In his youth, he had flown every type of kite—the Eddy, box and even the barndoor, according to kite historian Wayne J. Baldwin. Farnsworth used the first fishing kite around 1908 or 1909, although Baldwin reports that at that time *The London Daily Mail* described a new method of fishing whereby a second line—a baited fishing line, that is—could be attached to the newly invented box kite, which would carry it to the fish.

At that time, even as it is today, the Tuna Club of Avalon, on Santa Catalina Island, was a renowned fishing shrine. Captain Farnsworth would report all his tuna trophies to this club, which had been founded in 1898. For a long time, he kept his kite fishing secret even from fellow members of the club, who were perplexed and frustrated seeing him come in day after day with such prize catches. There were many fine fishing experts in that club, including Zane Grey, who was an authority on the subject.

Every time Farnsworth returned from the fishing grounds, a huge crowd met him at the dock. One day he inadvertently revealed his secret—coming into the harbor trailing a kite 100 feet in the sky with an American flag attached to the line. The kite aloft was the old-fashioned barn-door kite, described thus: it was constructed of unbleached muslin or similar cloth material sewn around the edge, had a three-leg bridle, with the bottom leg adjustable, and a series of cloth tail-sections. The stronger the wind, the more tail was needed. The material was waterproofed. The sticks were spruce, ½ inch by ¼ inch in size. The cloth tail section was 6 feet by 4 inches wide. The lengths were fastened together by safety pins, with one section of tail for light winds and four sections for strong winds of up to 25 knots. The three-leg bridle was adjusted according to the wind speed. The longer the lower leg, the flatter the kite flew. In light wind the kite was flown as close to the water as possible, and in high wind it was lofted as high as 300 feet.

With a bit of practice, Farnsworth made the bait jump and skip like a flying fish. The tuna went for the kite-skipped bait, and before long Captain Farnsworth was booking anglers by the score for kite-fishing trips to the Doldrums.

By the following year the bluefin tuna population off Santa Catalina had been stabilized by kite fishermen who copied the Farnsworth technique. And Captain Farnsworth went in search of other piscatorial thrills with a passenger named Bill Boschen, who used a kite to cast bait to the first broadbill swordfish ever caught on a rod and reel.

History is a bit hazy regarding the details of the spread of deep-sea kite fishing from the Pacific to the Atlantic Coast. But Captain Tommy Gifford appeared one day with a kite rig on the waters near Montauk, New York, at the tip of Long Island. And charter-boat fishing on the Atlantic Coast has blossomed with kites over the Gulf Stream in increasing numbers since that day.

More recently, a new variation in kite fishing from boats was developed by Edgar Lewis, in the Miami, Florida, area. Lewis uses a tailless square kite, about 30 inches by 30 inches, made of silk covering an X-shaped fiber-glass frame. A special

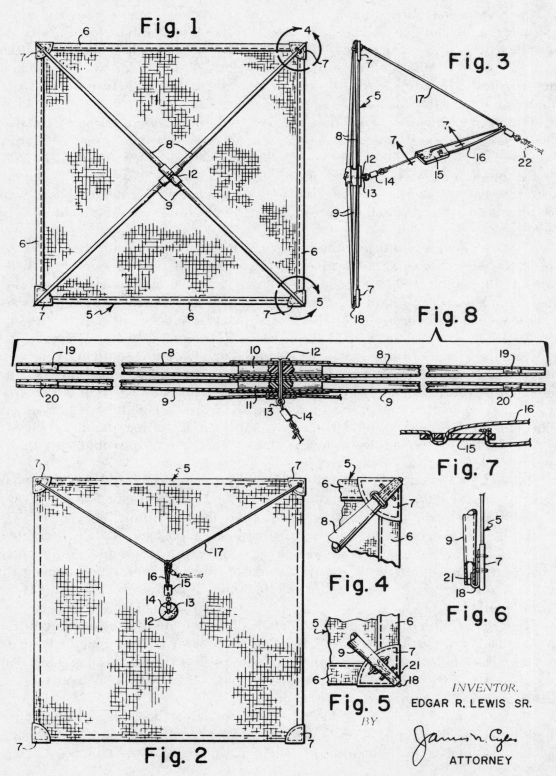

April 18, 1967

E. R. LEWIS, SR

3,314,630

FISHING KITE

Filed Feb. 15, 1966

Fig. 1

Fig. 3

Fig. 8

Fig. 7

Fig. 4

Fig. 6

Fig. 5

Fig. 2

INVENTOR.
EDGAR R. LEWIS SR.

BY

ATTORNEY

1

3,314,630
FISHING KITE
Edgar R. Lewis, Sr., 6690 SW. 98th St.,
Miami, Fla. 33156
Filed Feb. 15, 1966, Ser. No. 527,440
4 Claims. (Cl. 244—153)

This invention relates to a fishing kite whereby to float over the water and support a bait at the surface of the water and with the kite being held above the water by normal air currents.

The kite comprises a square fabric cover that is expanded by triangular rods, having fitment into the corners of the kite and with means connected to two adjacent corners of the kite to constitute a connecting means for a fishing line or the like and with the fishing line being connected to a pivotal point of the rods by adjustable means.

In the drawings:

FIGURE 1 is a top plan view of an assembled kite constructed in accordance with the invention,

FIGURE 2 is a bottom plan view of the kite in assembled form showing a bridle that is connected to a pivotal point of the expandable type rods,

FIGURE 3 is an edge view of the structure illustrated in FIGURE 1,

FIGURE 4 is an enlarged view of one corner of the kite showing the mounting means for the cross or expansion rods,

FIGURE 5 is a view similar to FIGURE 4, but taken upon the opposite side of the kite,

FIGURE 6 is a fragmentary sectional view of one corner of the kite,

FIGURE 7 is a fragmentary sectional view through an adjustable bridle, connected with the kite and taken substantially on line 7—7 of FIGURE 3, and

FIGURE 8 is a sectional view taken through the collapsed rods for supporting the kite in an operative position.

Referring specifically to the drawings, there has been illustrated particularly in FIGURES 1 and 2, a generally square fabric flexible kite 5, formed of any desirable material and having its edges hemmed, as indicated at 6. The kite 5, as illustrated is square in shape and its corners are reinforced by corner tabs 7 that are stitched or otherwise connected to the fabric of the kite.

Adapted to have connection to the opposite corners of the kite, are reinforcing plastic tubes 8 and 9. The tubes 8 and 9 are hollow tubular members, tapering from their central portion to the point where they connect to the corners of the kite. The tubes 8 and 9 are connected together by cylindrical plugs 10 and 11 into the open inner ends of the tubes 8 and 9 and are frictionally held therein and whereby to constitute a pivotal point for the tubes 8 and 9, by a cotter pin 12, that passes through apertures of the plugs 10 and 11 and with the cotter pin having an open cylindrical head 13 and whereby the tubes 8 and 9 are pivotally supported together to swing to and from a collapsed position and to also constitute the spreading means for the kite 5. The head 13 of the cotter pin 12 is connected to a swivel 14 that is connected to an adjustable toggle 15, in a bridle 16.

Each of the adjacent upper corner tabs 7 is connected to a bridle 17, that has connection to the bridle 16 and with each of the opposite corners 7 being provided with hooks 18, that have hooked engagement into the

2

open ends of the tubes 8 and 9 whereby the kite is effectively connected at the ends of the tubes 8 and 9 to spread the kite 5 into a relatively taut position. The tubes 8 and 9 adjacent their outer open ends are provided with plugs 19 and 20 and whereby the tubes 8 and 9, with the plugs 10 and 11 are sealed against the entry of air or water. The ends of the tubes 8 and 9 are connected to the tabs 7 by wire loops 21 and so that the kite may be collapsed by swinging the tubes 8 and 9 upon the pivot 12, collapsing the kite 5 whereby the kite may be rolled into a relatively small elongated package.

In the use of the device, the kite is spread, as indicated in FIGURES 1 and 2 and the ends of the tubes 8 and 9 are connected to the tabs 7 by the wires 21. The pivotal member 12 fixes the tubes 8 and 9 together and the swivel 14 of the bridle 16 is connected thereto and projects from the central swivel point outwardly for connection to the bridle lines 17. The bridle lines 17 and 16 are then connected to a fishing line 22, upon which the fishing bait is connected, to float upon the surface of the water by the action of the kite, floating thereover.

It will be apparent from the foregoing that the fishing kite of this invention has provided a novel means for fishing from relatively small boats and may be fed outwardly from the boat and floats over the water by the draft of normally prevailing winds. The kite may also be employed to hold a small signal light or a radio antennae and is capable of folding into a slender package by unhooking lower corners and the kite is adjustable as to height by the center bridle. The entire device may be folded into a relatively small package for carrying or storage.

It is to be understood that the invention is not limited to the precise construction shown, but that changes are contemplated as readily fall within the spirit of the invention as shall be determined by the scope of the subjoined claims.

I claim:

1. A fishing kite of the character described including a generally square section of fabric, the fabric upon four sides having a hem, the kite being collapsible and held in an extended floatable condition by a pair of crossed tubular rods, the rods at their central section being pivotally connected together so that the kite may be collapsed, means upon each end of the rods that have hooking engagement with corner tabs for each corner of the kite, the rods being pivotally connected together at their central portion by a cotter pin that passes through apertures and with the cotter pin upon one end being provided with an opened eye and bridle means connected to adjacent corners of the kite for subsequent connection to a fishing line.

2. The structure according to claim 1 wherein the rods are formed of portions of tapered tubular plastic construction, tapering toward outer ends and with the inner ends of the portions constituting the larger ends and with the larger end of each portion being coupled together by a frictional plug, the outer or small ends of the rods being closed by frictionally engaged plugs so that the rods for their major length are hollow and floatable.

3. The structure according to claim 1 wherein the tubular rods are in normal expanding position with respect to the kite to maintain the kite in a fully expanded position and with the rods at their pivotal point being collapsible so that they shift to parallel positions for collapsing the

3

kite, the rods at each end being provided with hooks that are connected to the corner tabs to maintain the rods against displacement from the kite, the bridle being connected to two adjacent tabs and also connected to the eye of the cotter pin and with the connecting means for the bridle having a swivel that is connected to the eye of the cotter pin and also to the bridle and slidably adjustable means for the connection of the bridle to the eye of the cotter pin for controlling the angularity of the bridle.

4

4. The structure according to claim 2 wherein the rods at their outer ends are fixed to the several tabs by hooks that extend through the tabs and that overlie the terminal ends of the rods and means associated with the bridle, comprising a swivel that is connected to a fishing line.

No references cited.

MILTON BUCHLER, *Primary Examiner.*

P. E. SAUBERER, *Assistant Examiner.*

kite rod-and-reel set is mounted on the side of the boat, or the rod can be slipped into a plastic rod-holder mounted on the inside of the boat. The kite reel is equipped with drag to keep the kite line under control; the reel, made of mahogany, is designed so that each complete turn of the reel handle feeds out or pulls in two feet of 60-pound Dacron kite line.

As Lewis explains the device: "With a steady wind of about six knots and up, the kite sets sail with no effort at all. The first clothespin is positioned about 50 feet below the kite, and when that position is reached, the rise of the kite is stopped temporarily.

"Now the fishing line is snapped to the clothespin—but not directly. The angler must be able to control the location of his bait; therefore, his line must run freely.

"Attach a small plastic ring, or a swivel, or an ordinary paper clip, to the fishing line just above the swivel that joins the line to the leader. Let's say a paper clip is used. Snap the paper clip into the clothespin.

"Next, the kite line is again let out from its reel—and the fishing line must be played out at the same rate. When the second clothespin comes up, attach the second fishing rig, if wanted, in the same fashion. Then let the kite fly until it reaches the desired distance from the boat. Lock the kite reel to prevent more line from slipping off. Release or take up fishing line as required to keep the bait flipping at the surface.

"When a fish takes the bait, the fishing line snaps from the pin. Obviously, there is a lot of slack—which works to the angler's advantage. By the time he cranks to tight-line status, the fish usually has the bait and can be struck immediately.

"The kite remains aloft, out of the way, while the fish is fought, landed, or lost. Then, of course, the kite must be cranked boatward so the pins come in reach to accept new rigs.

"With live bait on the line, the angler has his choice of drifting or anchoring. Drifting generally is best, especially if sailfish are of primary concern.

"Since the kite flies down-wind, ahead of the boat, drift fishermen can easily fish deep baits on the other side at the same time—thus attacking fish from all directions."

The Lewis kite fishing gear also serves as an outrigger for trolling with lures or trolling bait. Captain Lewis advises that when baiting the line with live bait, the angler should secure the hook in the flesh of the bait just back of the head and forward of the dorsal fin, being sure that the backbone is not injured. This allows the kite fisherman to play the bait near the surface of the water with the leader completely above the water. In trolling, the bait will rise to the surface as with any outrigger bait.

One precaution: the kite line tends to wear just above each swivel after repeated use. So the angler must inspect the line near the swivels frequently.

Lewis also recommends that the angler tie 8-inch strips of ribbon of any color at the swivel where the leader wire is secured to the fishing line. These markers will help you to tell where the bait is located, and the ribbons are particularly helpful in locating the bait when bright sunlight makes it difficult to follow the bait on the water.

Captain Lewis uses three different kites, depending upon the strength of the wind. The largest is what he calls a light air kite, for use in breezes of about 6 miles per hour. For a moderate breeze of about 12 miles per hour, he uses a medium breeze kite. And the third is put to use in heavy winds. Although designed primarily for flying from a boat, the Lewis kite also performs well on land.

Lewis and other kite fishermen who work from boats have found that the cockpit or cabin of a boat or any large superstructure can produce enough mild turbulence to make kite launching difficult. As a result, the angler should try to find a spot that provides clearance from wind interference; one solution to the problem is to stand on the gunwale of the boat while raising the kite.

After a kite has been used for a while in sea waters, says Lewis, salt brine will accumulate in the fabric of the kite cover, if a covering of silk or similar material is used. The salt brine will interfere with the porosity of the kite surface so that the kite will fly erratically, if at all. The cure for this problem is to stretch the covering taut and spray it occasionally with fresh water, then let it dry. Never stow away a kite when it is damp.

And if your kite should fall into the water, Captain Lewis adds, never attempt to pull the kite toward you. Instead, move the boat to the kite to retrieve it. As you will discover the first time your kite gets dunked, the water has an effect similar to air lift on a kite, and tugging on the line will tend to drag the kite below the surface of the water.

Another lesson learned by Captain Lewis that he is quite willing to pass along to kite fishermen is that of the choice of kite colors. His first kites were covered with red silk, but he discovered that other boatmen who were not familiar with kite fishing mistook the kite for a distress signal. He was "rescued" so many times that he finally switched to kites covered with black fabric.

Captain Lewis has set many records of catches with kites in waters of the Florida area. On one trip with his charter boat, the *Re-Run*, seven kingfish weighing from 30 to 60 pounds were taken within two hours. And catches of five to six sailfish per trip are not unusual. Outdoor writer Vic Dunaway reported that on one kite-fishing trip with Lewis, the catch over a four-hour period included three sailfish, a barracuda, and a blackfin tuna. "It was a good trip," Dunaway commented, "but compared with other kiting excursions we have taken off Miami and the Upper Keys . . . certainly not phenomenal."

Another outdoor writer, Nelson Benedict, reported on a kite-fishing trip to Alligator Reef, off the Florida Coast, with Gar Wood, Jr. They were aboard the charter boat *Checca*, piloted by another enthusiast of the Lewis method, Captain Jim Albright.

Benedict wrote: "Capt. Albright had two baits working on the kite line. They produced eight sailfish strikes and five releases in four hours of actual fishing time. The billfish tally might have been much higher had not the live mullet proved equally attractive to a swarm of very hungry kingfish."

The *Miami Herald,* in its report of the 1968 Met fishing tournament, listed five sailfish and a 115-pound white marlin taken by baits suspended from kites on one boat captained by Randy Lacey and an 82-pound sailfish caught by a kite fisherman in a competing boat. In the same tournament week, a kite sailed from Captain Don Gurgiolo's boat was responsible for a new amberjack record of 82 pounds in the Light Tackle General Division.

Among the many other remarkable stories that can be told about kite-fishing experiences in Florida waters is the report of a cruise by Captain Lenny Bierman, who took a pair of visitors out of the Venetian Causeway merely to show them how to

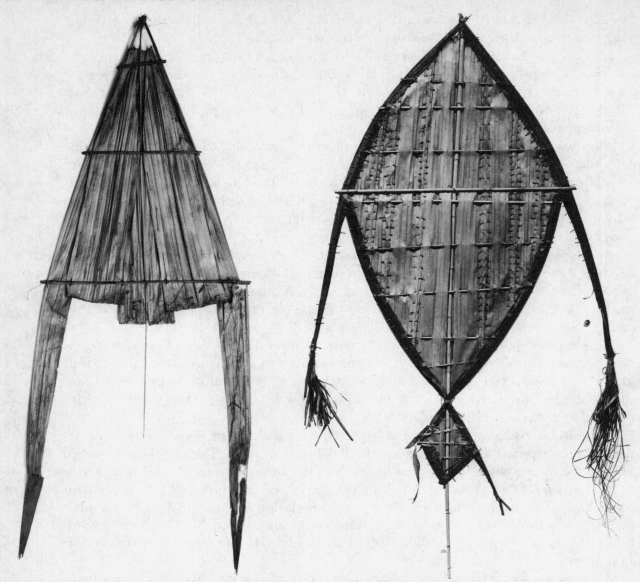

Two examples of primitive kites adapted by Polynesian natives for use in fishing. (*British Museum*)

set up a kite-fishing rig on a boat. While giving his free demonstration from the deck of a 29-foot craft, the pilot and his passengers were almost literally besieged by game fish going for the kite-suspended bait. After catching two amberjacks weighing 93 and 103 pounds plus eight sailfish, the visitors were convinced that kite fishing was, in the words of Captain Lewis, "the greatest invention since the spinning reel."

In fact, fishing with the aid of a kite is so rewarding that one expert recommends: "If you don't get any action in 10 minutes, you are wasting your time in that area and you should move to another spot."

How do you pick the "right spot" for kite fishing? One good trick, both for kite fishing from a boat and for drop-line fishing in the surf, is to "follow the birds." Game fish usually prowl in areas populated by the smaller bait fish, and birds that can hover above the water and watch for schools of such fish compete for the piscatorial morsels. Thus, a flock of birds hovering over a particular area and diving into the water is a good old Indian sign that a school of fish is there. And that is the area where the kite fisherman should spot his bait. Fishing in bays is always better when the tide is moving, either in or out. The tide flows are accompanied by an increased amount of activity by the fish; conversely, the action diminishes when the tide is slack.

The kite fisherman also should understand something of the psychology of the game fish. For example, the reason fishing usually is better at dawn and at dusk is that game fish or bait fish found near the shore tend to seek protective cover when light from the sky is bright enough to illuminate the water all the way to the bottom. But given a bit of darkness and increased shadows along the shore, the same fish will leave the secure holes and rocky fortresses on the bottoms and go on the prowl for food.

Of course, if you are familiar with the holes and rocks of a particular fishing area and can spot your bait in the places where the fish are likely to be hiding, you frequently can tempt them into making a quick grab for the lure even in bright light.

On the question of whether to use an artificial lure or live bait, a group of scientists at the Miami Institute of Marine Science have come up with a good argument for going the live bait route. In experiments on fish behavior, they have found that live bait fish send out a sort of distress signal in the form of low-frequency sound waves. The bigger game fish pick up the distress signals and home in on the hapless prey held on your fishing line. It is the angler's version of the predator game call used by hunters to lure wild animals by producing the sounds of an injured rabbit or whatever. Game fish have been known to zoom out of a 60-foot hole to hit a live bait fish emitting the low-frequency death rattle, and in deep-sea kite fishing a properly hooked bait fish can attract a stampede of amberjacks. The bait fish will be able to wriggle about in the water and produce the distress signal that game fish find so attractive.

An experienced kite fisherman not only can drop his bait within a few feet of where he has observed a particular game fish popping the surface, he also can in many instances keep the bait out of the mouth of an unwanted predator. The trick is simply to lift the bait out of the water until the predator has passed by—a feat that obviously is easier to handle in the ocean, where the angler can identify the species by their size and other characteristics. However, a Florida kite fisherman claims to be able to maneuver the bait so precisely that he can present it to a particular amberjack in a group and prevent the others from hitting it. There is no other way, with the possible exception of using a harpoon or spear gun, for an angler to manipulate a bait into the mouth of the one fish that he wants to catch. But it's almost a guaranteed dividend of kite fishing, after some practice.

Because a kite affords ultimate control of the bait, the kite fisherman also is able to avoid the patches of weeds that frequently foul up the tackle. Even in the Gulf Stream, Captain Lewis has observed, there are periods when trolling is "all but impossible" because of the islands of floating seaweed. "But I just put up a kite," Lewis continued, "and manipulate my bait up and down between the islands of weeds."

Another frequently overlooked advantage of kite fishing is the great economy of the sport after the initial investment in the kite and presuming the angler takes proper care of the kite used for fishing. But beyond that investment there is practically no further expense involved in going after big fish. In many lake and ocean areas, the fisherman with a kite can do about as well from a good shore position as he can with a boat; in certain instances, such as fishing in rocks or reefs, he can score better with a kite than would be possible by casting from a boat with conventional tackle. So the kite has sometimes been called the poor fisherman's boat.

Even when used from a boat rather than from shore, a fishing kite offers great economies. Most boaters report that they get more fish per gallon of engine fuel, sometimes as much as a fivefold increase, after learning how to handle a kite-suspended lure. They just turn off the engine and launch the kite.

Now, back in the old days, before kite fishing became popular, a deep-sea fisherman may have spent five to ten years trying to catch a sailfish to have mounted on the wall of his office or den. Naturally, anybody who has devoted ten years of Florida vacations to the goal of catching a single sailfish would be mighty proud of his endeavors. So the atmosphere in the country club back home can become suddenly quite chilly when a young upstart announces at the bar that he has just returned from his *first* charter-boat trip with *two* or *three* sailfish—caught with a kite!

A somewhat different kind of hazard was encountered by our own Bob Ingraham while fishing with a drop line from a kite over a New Mexico lake. Ingraham had just hooked a fine fish when a sudden wind gust caught the kite and yanked the fish some 50 feet into the sky. A pair of golden eagles soaring over the lake at that moment flashed toward the gleaming fish like a team of fighter pilots. By the time Ingraham reeled the fish in there was little more than a skeleton attached to the hook.

9 KITE RIDING AND GLIDING

Just about everybody who has ever sent a kite aloft has speculated on the possibilities of the kite flying him rather than the other way around. The feat is not, after all, very difficult or complicated. All you need is a wind that is strong enough, and a kite that is big enough and steady enough.

So it is not really very surprising that records of man-lifting kites go back almost as far as records of any kites at all. Predictably, the peoples of the Orient appear to have been the first to construct man-lifters. The accounts are quite serious: kites are used to fly people in and out of besieged cities, or to send spies aloft to get a good view of what the enemy is doing. There is no record of anybody riding a kite for fun. Occasionally, the practice is put to some bizarre uses. Marco Polo recounts how man-lifters were used as a sort of fortune-telling device by Chinese sailors. Before setting forth on a voyage, he relates, captains would scan the waterfront for someone drunk enough or stupid enough to go up in a kite. Once found, the victim was tied to the framework of the kite and launched into the air. If he flew, it was an omen that the voyage would go well. If he didn't fly . . .

Japan, too, used man-lifters many centuries ago. One tale relates how a twelfth-century hero, Minamotono Tametomo, sent his son by kite from the islet of Oshima to the town of Kamakura on the Japanese mainland. Since the distance in question is about forty miles, we may conclude either that the twelfth-century Japanese used extraordinarily long kite lines or that the tale is somewhat exaggerated. Another famous Japanese story tells how a master thief—his name variously given as Ishikawa Goyemon or Kakinoki Kinsuke—used a kite to loft himself to the top of Nagoya Castle in a vain attempt to steal the gold dolphins that adorned the roof. Unfortunately for him, he succeeded only in breaking off a fin and getting himself boiled in oil when he later got caught.

Lifting people by means of kites remained strictly an Oriental accomplishment until the eccentric English schoolmaster George Pocock decided to try it as a follow-up to his attempt to put the horse out of business by developing a system of towing carriages over the highways with kite power. Although the event attracted little attention at the time, Pocock's posthumously published book, *A Treatise of the*

Early experiments with kite riding—in this case for military use in Buenos Aires, Argentina—often involved an observation car or seat being lofted by a kite flotilla. (*New York Public Library*)

Aeropleuristic Art, describes a series of tests conducted about 1825 in which passengers rode into the air in an armchair attached to a kite line. And the first of the kite riders was probably the inventor's daughter, Martha Pocock. The account describes her ascent to a height of one hundred yards and, "On descending, she expressed herself much pleased at easy motion of the kite." Pocock's son also rode in the armchair "to the brow of a cliff, two hundred feet in perpendicular height." The kite itself was made with a covering of canvas and was thirty feet high.

A basic requirement of a man-lifter is that it be steady as well as big. And the flat kite of the nineteenth century was not notably steady. For this reason, the people who were lifted into the air by kites typically did not cling to the line itself, but were seated in a chair that hung down from the kite. Some improvement came with Cap-

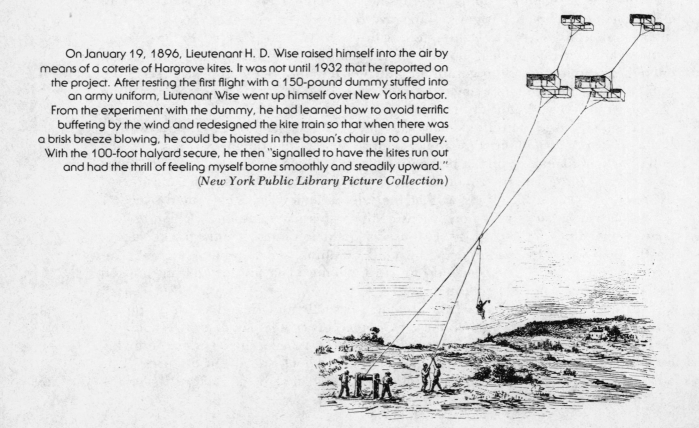

On January 19, 1896, Lieutenant H. D. Wise raised himself into the air by means of a coterie of Hargrave kites. It was not until 1932 that he reported on the project. After testing the first flight with a 150-pound dummy stuffed into an army uniform, Liutenant Wise went up himself over New York harbor. From the experiment with the dummy, he had learned how to avoid terrific buffeting by the wind and redesigned the kite train so that when there was a brisk breeze blowing, he could be hoisted in the bosun's chair up to a pulley. With the 100-foot halyard secure, he then "signalled to have the kites run out and had the thrill of feeling myself borne smoothly and steadily upward." (*New York Public Library Picture Collection*)

tain B. F. S. Baden-Powell's "Levitor" design, of 1894 and afterward, in which a train of medium-sized kites proved to be as powerful as, and steadier than, a single giant man-lifter of the Pocock variety.

Orthodox kiters contend that a true kite must be tethered. Orthodoxy, however, has never been allowed to stand in the way of those who felt there should be more to kite riding than dangling in a chair or going nowhere several hundred feet up on a relatively stationary kite frame. The next logical step, therefore, was towing a man-lifter. After all, all sorts of traction have been used to launch kites, including small boys running, horses, motorboats, steamships, and in our own day, helicopters.

The first person to use traction to launch a man-lifter was a French inventor named LeBris. In 1857 he designed a vaguely bird-shaped glider that was launched from a horse-drawn carriage with LeBris lying flat inside the bird's body. The bird rose, but when the horse bolted, the line snapped, the end wrapped around the coachman, and the poor man was hauled kicking and struggling into the air. LeBris' glider thus became the first kite to combine all three possible methods of flying: the primitive dangle, the advanced traction, and the ultra-advanced free flight.

Among the most spectacular of the towed man-lifters were those designed by Alexander Graham Bell, inventor of the telephone. His largest model was launched by towing it behind a steamship. It was an immense box kite, or cellular kite, made of a honeycomb of 3,393 silk cells. Bell named the 208-pound kite the *Cygnet* and it was launched over Baddek Bay in Nova Scotia in December, 1907; a steamship towed the huge kite into the wind and it rose to a height of nearly 170 feet. It floated gracefully

In 1908, Alexander Graham Bell developed the circular multicellular kite, which he sent up from Cape Breton Island in Nova Scotia. In 1903, he had written that "a properly constructed flying machine should be capable of being flown as a kite and, conversely, a properly constructed kite should be capable of use as a flying machine when driven by its own propellers." (*National Geographic Society*)

for some seven minutes with a pioneer kite rider, U.S. Army Lieutenant Thomas E. Selfridge, lying on his stomach in the center of the kite. Unfortunately, the crewmen were so startled by the sight of a man flying in a kite above them that they forgot to cut the kite's towline when it descended gently onto the water. The kite was dragged through the water and destroyed, but Lieutenant Selfridge survived with only a cold dunking.

Ironically, the same Lieutenant Selfridge later became the first fatality in the history of powered aviation. He was killed at Fort Myer, Virginia, while making a test flight of a plane built by the Wright brothers.

Dr. Bell had previously flown a huge multicelled kite, the Frost King, with a 165-pound man aboard. The Frost King was launched in 1905, also in Nova Scotia, and lifted some 62 pounds of rope and ladder in addition to the unnamed kite rider. The kite contained 1,300 cells made of silk and arranged in 12 layers. Details about how the Frost King was launched are scanty, but Bell was known to use horses to tow kites when the wind was slack.

Like the Wright brothers, Bell intended his experiments with kites to provide information that could be used for building airplanes. Bell believed that his honeycombed man-lifters could be outfitted with a gas engine that would provide forward propulsion while simultaneously blowing air toward the cellular kite to give it the necessary lift. Bell finally did produce a flyable airplane in 1908, although it was designed as a biplane rather than as a gas-engine-powered tetrahedral kite. Bell's airplanes, the first to fly over Canada, also had such features as a tricycle landing gear and wingtip and hinged-surface ailerons, innovations in airplane design.

In fact, Bell's airplane experiments received more attention than the Wright brothers' work in the first decade of the twentieth century, and many people believed that Alexander Graham Bell rather than the Wright brothers invented the airplane. It was through experiments by Bell and the Wrights, using human kite riders, that the big breakthroughs in powered flight were made.

The bulk of kite-riding enthusiasts add a third type of kite riding to the stationary dangle and the towed ride: the free glide, or hang gliding. This viewpoint is hotly contested by those purists who maintain that a kite, by definition, is a tethered structure. And it is certainly true that many gliders and soaring devices owe little or nothing to kites—the long-winged sailplane, for example, isn't a kite by anybody's definition. Yet, over and over, the inspiration for manned flight has come from two sources: birds and kites; and both the earliest and most recent versions of gliding flight were attained by variations of kites. In 1804, the pioneer inventor Sir George Cayley built the first glider by mounting an arch-top kite flat on a stick fuselage; the kite served as the glider's wings. In 1849 Cayley succeeded in flying a 10-year-old boy in a larger model that he launched by rolling it down a hill. Several years later, Cayley launched his coachman to make a similar flight. Despite the successful flight, the coachman picked himself up, dusted himself off, and resigned his service with the declaration that henceforth he would travel only by horse.

Another pioneer aeronaut who deserves mention, although he was not, strictly speaking, a kite rider, is the German engineer Otto Lilienthal, who designed and flew on a variety of gliders. Lilienthal, who was born in 1848, began his experiments around 1891; he would grasp the frame of his device about his shoulders and run down a steep hill. When enough lift developed to carry the glider into the air,

Lilienthal would retract his legs and soar like a bird. He made hundreds of such flights, none extending over a distance of more than 1,000 feet, until one summer day in 1896 when his craft stalled at an altitude of about 50 feet and he plunged to his death.

Lilienthal's gliders owed more to birds than kites in their design; one even had flapping wingtips.

However, he is still honored by modern kite riders as the true father of glider flight, and his birthday is observed each spring by hundreds of American kite riders who gather for contests and other festivities. Winners are awarded an "Otto." Although dead these many years, Lilienthal held the Self-Soaring Associate Card #1.

Every schoolboy and girl learns that Wilbur and Orville Wright are credited with the invention in 1903 of the airplane. What most schoolchildren fail to learn is that the Wright brothers were also adept in the sport of kite riding, in both tethered and free flight. And the site of their several years of experiments in riding on a glider modification of a Hargrave box kite was the same beach at Kitty Hawk, North Carolina, where they later made the first powered flight. Kitty Hawk was a natural setting for kite riding because of the wide expanse of treeless terrain and the almost continuous oceanfront winds. In 1902, the Wright brothers were granted a U.S. patent for "certain improvements" to permit better control of a kite by the person riding it.

After the Wright brothers, manned flight became the domain of mechanical devices. In the era of the jet plane, the practice of flying from a flimsy kite seemed like a late-nineteenth- and early-twentieth-century eccentricity. But beginning in the 1950s and 1960s, kite riding returned again as the sport of those who wanted to feel the sensation of flying with their own bodies, not through the intermediary of a machine. Modern kite riding is of two main kinds: towed flight, usually behind a motorboat with a launch from water skis, and hang gliding, free flight with a launch by running downhill into the wind until the kiter becomes airborne. There are, of course, mixes of the two, involving kite riders who become airborne while the kite is under control via a kite line, until they reach a point in their flight at which they release the line and make a free-fall glide to earth. Finally, there are many daring young men and women who have jumped out of airplanes, plunged from high-flying balloons, and leaped from 12,000-foot mountain peaks to glide earthward on kite wings at speeds of more than 50 miles per hour. One expert performer of this art, Gary Warren, describes the sensation of kite soaring as "the closest thing there is to flying like a bird."

There appears to be a regional bias in the forms of kite riding. In the Northeast and California, where sea cliffs, dunes and inland hills provide good downhill launching spots, the amateur sport of hang gliding prevails. In Florida, where there are no hills, but the offshore water is calm, water-ski kiting is the preferred method, and the sport is dominated by exhibition-giving professionals. Each variant of kite riding has its partisans, but they are coming together, particularly since the adoption of the flexible Rogallo wing kite by the water skiers has made possible extended gliding flights of a kind that was impossible with the flatter, stiff, Eddy-style kite that was formerly favored.

Water-ski kiting is somewhat older than hang gliding, and the early water skiers faced—and were often drowned by—a number of problems. Among them was the propensity for towlines to get tangled in the boat propellers. Or the nylon that the tow lines were made of would melt if it came in contact with a hot boat motor. Today, boats used for water-ski kite riding are equipped with special removable aluminum towline posts that eliminate those hazards. And two people are assigned to each boat, one to drive the boat and one to handle the towline; the old way of using one man in the boat to both drive and handle the towline resulted in many unfortunate mishaps for many early water-ski kite riders.

A second problem was even more basic—that of holding on. As the veteran water-ski kiter Jack Wylie reported to the American Kitefliers Association, in the days before a special harness seat was designed for kite-riding competition "we had to use all our strength simply to stay on the kite, thereby making any degree of control impossible for any but the strongest athletes."

Wylie stated that before the Rogallo kite, to lift a water skier the kite needed to be 17 feet in length and 16 feet across the wing bar, using aluminum tubing for the frame and plastic or nylon covering. However, Wylie commented that while such a kite would lift his 196-pound weight in a relative air-speed of 30 miles per hour, "trying to bank it or hold it in a crosswind was like trying to hold a sailboat upright in a crosswind by holding a single rope attached to a 16 foot mast." The American Kitefliers Association questioned the emphasis on muscle power in kite-riding competition and stated editorially in its publication, *Kite Tales*, "We would think that water ski kiting should be anyone's sport who is reasonably athletic, not just for those extra big and strong individuals. It is about as silly to require kites that take giants to fly as it would be to increase the size of the discus so that only the Jolly Green Giant could throw it. . . .

"Is it muscle the sport is after, or is it coordination and skill? In view of the somewhat hazardous aspects of the sport, we think the ski kiters might better take up weight lifting and forget the urge to get up into the wild blue yonder."

Fortunately, water-ski kiting has come a long way since those early days. Max Coombs of Miami, Florida, is among the versatile water-ski kite riders who have branched out into performances on the ABC-TV network's *Wide World of Sports*, plus hundreds of other spectacular appearances throughout North America. Coombs, who also claims to be the first kite rider to make a flight on a kite towed by a helicopter, has designed his own kite for such work. It is a 38-pound Coombs Delta Wing Kite that folds into a package that can be transported on a car's ski rack.

A Coombs kite with a man aboard can be launched by three men towing it into the wind, as well as by towing with a car or a large motorcycle. However, like the other experts, Coombs does not recommend that beginners make their first flights over dry land; he suggests that novices practice over water using a boat with a minimum of 50 to 100 horsepower.

Coombs made his first kite ride with a helicopter tow on September 23, 1970, from North Miami, Florida. After being towed aloft by the copter to an altitude of 200 feet, he tripped a release mechanism and glided to a perfect landing on Biscayne Bay. He repeated the helicopter tow lift the same day and ascended to 450 feet before disengaging and gliding down to the waters of Biscayne Bay. On two subsequent kite rides using a helicopter tow, Coombs flew in street clothes and glided to safe landings on the ground in front of television cameras.

I have witnessed Coombs descend from a height of 200 feet and land neatly on the lawn of his Florida home. The lawn is 20 by 30 feet. On his way down after cutting his line, he maneuvered between rooftops and telephone lines with the grace of a ballet dancer.

In other mind-boggling performances, Coombs has launched himself by leaping off bridges and by sailing gracefully through the skies at the controls of his kite while a bikini-clad aerialist swings on a trapeze suspended ten feet below the kite frame.

In the kite-riding field, Max Coombs is at the top of the "Who's Who" list. At his school in Miami, Coombs builds his own kites and sells them to customers who have passed the full course of instruction. The girl on the trapeze obviously trusts Max. (*Max Coombs*)

So skilled is Coombs that he can release the flying line, drop his skis into the water and land on the 20-by-10-feet lawn of his home without a flutter. And over the wires as well. The stunt is not recommended for amateurs. (*Max Coombs*)

a b

Coombs in action: (a) from a watery start at the dock, (b) he rises in the water as if water skiing. (c) Now aloft with a bird's eye view of Miami, he's got to look for a landing area, the trickiest part of the ride.
(*Max Coombs*)

c

Coombs and his colleagues take a sunset ride off Miami beach. (*Max Coombs*)

The author meets Max Coombs.
(*Max Coombs photo*)

Probably the most publicized ski-kite rider is Simon Khoury. He is the stunt man in the advertisements that show personalities who walk away from dangerous sports experiences to relax with a drink of Canadian Club whiskey. Khoury likens his experience to "jumping from a cliff with a beach umbrella." He has flown at Cypress Gardens, which he found child's play compared with jumps he made from Jamaican cliffs. He describes one such adventure as follows: "I was leap-frogging islands on a tow when the wind caught my kite and lifted it a hundred feet in the air. The boom camera attached to the kite was a threat to my balance, and I began to swoop toward the island's tower. Within a few yards of the tower, a strong blast forced me up over the tower and not a moment too soon. After that, it was touch and go until I landed safely in the water—on my water skis."

You guessed it. He reported back to the Arawak Hotel and "toasted my happy landing with my favorite whiskey."

In the East, specifically at Mirror Lake in New Jersey, George Blair, over sixty years of age, is the leading exponent and instructor in the ski-kite riding art. He runs the Family Ski School there with his four beautiful daughters as helpers and instructors.

Blair uses five basic kites, three of them flat kites and two delta wings. All are made for him by Ken Tibado of Lake Wales, in Florida, whom Blair considers the father of modern kite riding. Like other great teachers, Blair will not let his pupils solo unless they are both physically and mentally prepared. He has turned down students he thought were not mentally, much less physically, capable of handling this type of flying.

At his kite-flying school outside of Red Bank, New Jersey, George Blair stresses safety first. Over sixty years old, and without a riding mishap, he's a living example of his philosophy.

Spectators at the Southern Sailboat Show in Miami's Marine Stadium were startled to see a sailor step into a harness that was attached to a flying platform—in this case a huge spinnaker or kite sail. Off he flew some fifty feet and then was hauled back aboard the show boat. Impractical, yes, but thrilling. It is only another manifestation of the many new sporting uses that are being made of the kite. *(Miami Metro Department of Publicity and Tourism)*

Blair has flown in many shows, including some in Cypress Gardens. He has flown with Bill Moyes, the Australian rider, as well as Bill Bennett, another Australian, whom he met Down Under when he served as assistant coach to an American water ski team.

In 1964, something new was added to water-ski kiting: tournaments, started in Austin, Texas, with competition concentrated in two major categories—tricks and slalom. A rating system also was established by the American Water Ski Association in Winter Haven, Florida, to classify kiters according to their abilities. In the trick competition, each contestant is allowed two passes over the tournament course while judges in the towboat and in other boats along the course record the tricks performed and score the contestant on his excellence. The rider is attached to the kite by a seatlike harness which in turn is attached to the center of a trapeze bar by a quick-release mechanism. The towboat pulls the kite into the wind while the kite rider ascends to a height of twenty to eighty feet above the water. On each pass, he is allowed a total of twenty seconds to perform all of his acrobatic tricks. The tricks, of course, are done without the skis, which are dropped off when ascension begins.

The slalom competition, patterned after the ski slalom, involves riding a kite over a course marked by six buoys, three on each side of the towboat's wake. The buoys are staggered and each has attached a hose that throws a water spout about thirty feet into the air. The water spouts help the judges to determine whether the contestant has rounded the buoys properly. Each contestant is permitted to make two passes over the slalom course. The towline is set at 130 feet in length at the start of the slalom event, and those who survive the first two passes must compete again with the line shortened to 100 feet. If there are contestants still tied for first place in the slalom event after the first two heats, the towline is shortened again and so on, until there is a sure winner.

Modern kite riding gained its initial popularity as an adjunct to water skiing. And because of occasional concussions, fractures and other injuries sustained by some beginners, many experts recommend that fledgling kite soarers get their initial training over water. Kite soaring is a potentially dangerous sport, and a mishap over water can be less dangerous than a sudden drop over hard land. The most serious, and fatal, accidents have been those in which beginners were practicing on kites being towed by cars and trucks. The major hazard in car-towed kite riding is that the driver cannot easily keep his eyes on the kite rider and the road at the same time, even with the aid of rear-view mirrors. Another danger is that car drivers tend to pour on the horsepower to get the kite into the air and build up too much speed too soon. A third hazard is that drag compensation is difficult to control on some kite launches, and a big kite can produce drag forces under tow that will snap the kite line like a piece of thread. It has been calculated that a big Rogallo kite may require a line with a test strength of nearly 10,000 pounds to be towed safely into a 20-mph wind. At least one fatal accident occurred when a kite line snapped under such circumstances.

For those reasons, experts like Gary Warren recommend that prospective kite riders begin as water skiers, then learn by easy steps the tricks of handling a kite that lifts them from the water surface as they ski. First lifts should be relatively low in altitude, about thirty to fifty feet, so the novice can experience the feel of wind currents and learn how to react to the unseen forces that lift, lower or whip the great kite surface into a sudden stall. In addition to lift and drag forces, the beginner also must reach an understanding with the force of gravity, which eventually wins over all flying objects.

The kite rider must learn all his lessons in solo flights. There are no dual controls on soaring kites or room for an instructor or co-pilot. So the beginner is in somewhat the same situation as John Glenn and Yuri Gagarin were when they blasted off into space as pioneer astronauts; learning to survive in the sky begins in the first second after liftoff. And anybody who hasn't done his homework can be in big trouble.

Moreover, there are no creature comforts for the rider of the big soaring kites. The "cockpit" consists of little more than a body sling and a metal trapeze bar that the rider must cling to for as long as he is aloft; waving to the crowds below could be lethal for the novice kite rider.

Overconfidence is a great danger. If the first ride is a great success at an altitude of thirty feet, the novice may feel it would be just as easy to play Superman and soar up to three thousand feet without further experience. But that could be a serious mistake. Until he has complete command of the kite in all sorts of wind situations, he should work repeatedly at low-altitude flights over water, remembering also that while water is softer than ground, a hard impact on water can break a bone or produce a brain concussion.

Fortunately, water-ski kiting is safer today than in its creeping infancy some twenty years ago. Some exponents, such as Wolandi of Dania, Florida, even claim you can learn water-ski kite riding *without* previous experience in water skiing. Wolandi uses Andi kites which are sold in three sizes, ranging from small for persons up to 140 pounds to a large size that can support most people up to 275 pounds. A medium-size kite, for weights up to 200 pounds, can be towed by a boat equipped with a 50-horsepower outboard motor.

The launching technique of the Andi kites is similar to that used with the Rogallo wing. The rider sits in a crotch harness and holds onto a trapeze while the boat tows the kite to launching speed. For landing, the rider holds his feet up and the man controlling the towline releases the line when the kite rider is about three feet above the water. The kite is equipped with flotation gear to keep it and the passenger from going below the water surface.

Hang gliding, the other main variation of the sport of kite riding, is in many ways a throwback to the kind of gliding done by Otto Lilienthal in the 1890s. One basic difference is that the majority of hang gliders follow the lead of Richard Miller of California, who used a Rogallo-type kite for the airfoil of his pioneering "Bamboo Butterfly" in the mid-1960's rather than the rigid trussed plane surfaces developed by Lilienthal and the Wright brothers and others of that aerodynamic ilk.

One of the major influences in hang kiting—though many times by indirection—has been Domina Jalbert of Boca Raton, Florida. I first met Dom when doing a story for *Life* magazine in the 1950s when he was building unusual parachutes designed from his experience with kites. We have maintained a kite-flying friendship through the years, meeting annually at festivals in Washington and Boston. Dom has not always gotten the recognition he deserves for his pioneering in the kite-cum-parachute gliding world. Much of his work has been as important as that of the other great

The first of the Jalbert riding kites were actually developed as parachutes that could be maneuvered like a kite. (*Jalbert Aerology Lab*)

Domina Jalbert with his parafoil. (*Ben Kocivar*)

pioneer, Francis Rogallo. Hang kiting, rather than parachute jumping, seems to have captured the general public's attention, and there will undoubtedly be more hang kiters than parachute jumpers in this world.

The Rogallo-type kite used for hang gliding differs somewhat from the limp square described earlier in this book (on pages 73–75). For one thing, it is stiffened fore and aft by three pieces of metal: two along the wing edges and one as a central "keel." A fourth tube acts as a spreader. In many respects, the kite resembles a delta wing. Although it is not the most efficient model for a hang glider, it is simple, easy to build, inexpensive, light, easily transported, not too large—the keel averages seventeen feet or so—and a surprisingly good performer. In short, it possesses all the virtues most prized by the youthful amateurs who have promoted this newest variant of kiting.

Instead of simply hanging onto the frame of the kite, the rider suspends his body in a harness attached just ahead of the center of gravity of the kite canopy. A control bar allows the kite to be pointed upward with a forward thrust, while pulling back on the control bar aims the kite toward the ground. Sideways movement of the control bar permits turns by dipping either the left or right tip of the kite wing. To get started, the kite rider runs or jumps from a height and glides about until he lands. And depending upon available wind currents and updrafts, a hang glider can prolong his flight for a surprisingly long time.

Because hang gliding utilizes the Rogallo kite design, it can be operated somewhat like a free flying craft that conforms in a gentle way to the movements of air currents. And control is achieved with a minimum of effort by body movements to shift the center of gravity. When used with skill and caution, the hang glider is a relatively safe contraption, perhaps safer than skiing. Francis Rogallo himself is among the most enthusiastic of all kite riders. He tethers one of his kites to an anchor in the sands of a Carolina beach and lets a wind carry him up into the sky where he may relax quietly above the surf until he is ready to return to earth. And gliding back down to the beach is simple enough because the flexible design of the kite allows for maximum control.

The main hazards of hang gliding are stalls, flying into an obstruction and falling out of the harness. The latter two hazards usually can be controlled by the kite rider simply by employing good sense and caution. A dune area or beach, or desert area, should afford a minimum of obstructions; a kite rider who tries to glide through an urban area or a hardwood forest probably deserves all the lumps he collects. Falling out of a harness is always a possibility, but it is an improbable one.

As for stalls, the kite rider can prevent a major share of such mishaps by understanding the aerodynamics of kites and aircraft in general. A stall occurs when lift fails and gravity simply pulls the flying object—whether it be a kite, a 747 jet plane or a Canada goose—out of the sky. However, the chances for pulling out of a stall and regaining lift are probably better for the jet plane or the goose than for the kite rider, especially if there is enough distance between the point of stall and the ground.

The hang glider must maintain a certain amount of forward momentum to provide continuous lift for his craft. This usually is accomplished by ascending or descending at the correct ratio of vertical change per linear distance traveled. The kite rider who, for example, tries to climb faster than is aerodynamically possible for his kite or glider is likely to stall and drop to earth like a rock. A kite caught off balance

Hang gliding is an exhilarating new kiting sport—and a beautiful subject for the photographer. (*John Wellsman*)

by a sudden wind gust also can stall if the center of gravity is shifted beyond the critical point for the particular craft; the effect is like that of a boat that capsizes when suddenly upended by a huge wave.

If any reader doubts the importance of aerodynamic efficiency in kite riding or hang gliding, he should be reminded that in the design of passenger gliders even the screwheads must be recessed and the airfoil surfaces polished to eliminate any tiny drag effect. Even a layer of dust can produce unwanted turbulence on an airfoil surface, with the result that linear distance traveled per foot of vertical drop will be reduced. And this is what hang gliding is all about—traveling as far as possible on the forward momentum of the hang glider without touching the ground.

Some knowledge about controlling the airfoil in and near updrafts is essential, also. There usually is a bit of turbulence in the air about an updraft, a good sign for the kite rider that he is entering an upward flow of air. Sometimes an experienced kite rider can tell the presence of an updraft by watching for birds that appear to soar upward without flapping their wings. Once in an updraft, the kite rider or hang glider must learn how to bank the kite so that it travels in a circle within the updraft. Leaving the column of rising air is easy enough when the kite rider wants to glide away and drift slowly back to earth. And if he knows his approximate lift-to-drag ratio, including the gravitational effect of his body weight, he can pretty well estimate how far he can glide without stalling. If the ratio is 4-to-1, reasonable but not extraordinary for a Rogallo, he should be able to glide 200 feet from an altitude of 50 feet. A lift-to-drag ratio of 20-to-1 would allow a linear travel distance of 1,000 feet per drop of 50 feet—but so far, this has been achieved only by other, non-Rogallo glider designs.

Although gravity can be an insidious and even lethal threat to a kite rider in a stall, the smart kite rider or hang glider uses gravity as an invisible "engine" to maneuver the kite on downward glides. It is gravity, after all, that provides the forward momentum for the lift needed in gliding.

Learning to fly is not too difficult, but the obvious dangers of making a mistake while one is well up into the air make it clear how important it is to learn well. One has to learn about the various sorts of wind conditions that can occur; the flight characteristics of the hang glider he wishes to fly; how to plan his flight to take into account wind, glider, terrain, potential obstacles (such as power lines) and landing sites; and how to take off, land and turn.

It is always good to have the benefit of the instruction and advice of experienced fliers. There are local clubs springing up everywhere (see Appendix I), and these can help the beginner find advice and give him friends to swap stories with as he develops his skills.

Although the most glamorous flights are those that begin with a leap from a cliff or mountain, they are not recommended as the sort of flight to learn on. The novice usually begins by reading a bit about hang gliding, watching others fly and then taking a good run down a gentle hill with his kite. After a couple of tries, he lifts off and glides to the bottom of the hill, a couple of feet from the ground. It is a fantastic sensation! Gradually he can develop his skills and eventually move up to the thrill of his first jump off a high hill. Although this sport can be dangerous, if one uses his head, learns well and does not try to fly under conditions he cannot handle, such as heavy winds, he can fly safely and enjoy the freedom of self-powered flight. Then the

Gary Cook, 28-year-old hang kiter, starts his takeoff run from the South Street Seaport Museum in lower Manhattan, New York. South Street is more used to the passage of square-rigged sailing ships than to a man dressed in a wetsuit, helmet and goggles, hanging onto a kite and being pulled by an outboard motorboat.

Just after takeoff, Cook soars under the Brooklyn Bridge on his way to making a complete circuit of Manhattan Island. He suffered six dunkings in the murky waters of the East River in this stunt, which took a total of three hours, fifty minutes.

sky becomes his limit. For example, one flier took off from Mont Blanc into a 25 mph wind and descended 13,142 feet. John Hughes stayed aloft for as long as ten and a half hours over Hawaii, while another expert traveled for fifty miles on one flight in New Zealand.

David Kilbourne was among the first hang gliders to make a glide from a balloon, using the newer equipment. In one demonstration of kite soaring, he launched himself from a balloon at an altitude of nearly 10,000 feet over the Pacific Ocean. Although the city of San Diego was just barely on the horizon from Kilbourne's two-mile perspective, he glided safely to shore. Other untethered kite riders have made a practice of gliding gently into Death Valley from the tops of nearby 12,000-foot mountains or zapping down a high Western ski run with a kite in hand until the relative air speed lifts the kite and the skier high above the snowy ski slope. More and more, meets are being held all over the world, with hang gliders matching their flying skills with those glider experts or "sky surfers" from other lands.

Hang gliding by no means exhausts the possibilities of manned kite flight. In Holland, a professor at the University of Leyden named Hagedoorn is incorporating a Jalbert parafoil into his experimental "sailless and boatless sailboat." The airborne sailor—Hagedoorn calls him an "aquaviator"—hangs like a parachutist from his kite a few feet above the water. He is prevented from being blown up and away by a tether line attached to a floating device that roughly resembles a shallow umbrella opened upside down underwater. By manipulating the shroud lines to the kite and the tether line to the floating device, the aquaviator can maneuver just like a yachtsman—only at speeds much higher than conventional sailboats can obtain.

It looks as if modern man is more determined than ever to free himself from his earthly bonds and take to the skies. Originally I was against kite riding. Interviewed by *True* magazine on this phenomenon in kite sports, I was quoted as follows: "I do not want to be the bravest kite flier; I want to be the oldest."

Although that statement still stands for me, I have changed my mind about kite riding for others. I feel that with the better riding kites now in existence and better and more responsible instructors, hang gliding has a great future for the young and daring.

10 KITES AROUND THE WORLD

Kite flying in India means fighting to the death—kite death, that is. In Thailand it's a major sport, as seriously played as is American baseball. Japan has a big league of kite flying, and in Taiwan a schoolteacher spends a month preparing a 95-foot-long kite that the entire city flies. Throughout the Orient kite flying is taken very seriously. Furthermore it is indulged in by adults, not just kids.

In my kite visit with the maharajah of Bharatpur, described in the opening chapter of this book, I was treated to my first sight of a kite bearer.

In Thailand a kite-fighting fever grips the nation. The greatest contest of the nation takes place on the huge green surrounding the area of the Grand Palace, the

Before the world championship match against the maharajah of Bharatpur, described earlier in this book, the author gave an exhibition of his kite-flying prowess at the Red Fort in Calcutta, India, using the first nonrigid kite ever seen in that part of the world. The Indians were in awe of this new kite and the author's rod-and-reel techniques.

University and the Ministry of Justice. When the monsoon season begins, kites flutter out over the city. The battle of the sexes has begun. The male kite, called the Chula, swaggers into the sky, a huge star-shaped monster. The smaller kite, female, called the Pakpoa, follows soon after, trailing a white streamer tail. The purpose of the male kite is to cut down the girl. The gamblers always give odds to the male—five to one. If the male wins, which is usually the case, it is no disgrace to the feminine kite. But if the female wins, the crowd becomes hysterical and parades through the city with the victor aloft. Some of these kites cost $50 and $75 to make.

May in Nagasaki is typical of Japan's kite craze. In fact so popular has kite flying been in Japan that it was legislated out of existence at one time so that the people could keep their minds on their work. Like our own Prohibition, it didn't work well and disappeared through neglect. Thousands of contestants flock to the hills surrounding the port city. Most of them carry three-foot kites on which the lead line is similar to the glazed string of the Indian fighting kite. The gambling spirit is not as great here, although the fighting is just as keen.

The Nagasaki flights have a long history, some say as far back as the middle sixteenth century. The kite fever had so taken hold here that the sport was once banned because kiters were ruining the newly sown crops by chasing their kites.

The terrible bomb on Nagasaki during the end of World War II failed to stop the spring sport. It sprang right up again after the war, and it's more popular now than ever. The kite festival lasts about a month.

Boys' Day, which runs from May 1 to May 5, is an annual celebration in Japan dating back to 1550. One of the main events is kite fighting—with challengers competing with one another to cut the lines of opposing kites. (*Japan National Tourist Organization*)

In Japan it is the hope of all parents that their sons will grow as strong and graceful as the carp, shown here "swimming in the sky." (*Japan National Tourist Organization*)

During the Boys' Day celebration, the Japanese commemorate the completion of the strong banks that contained the roaring Nakanokuchi River, over 300 years ago, with a parade of kites flown down the river. (*Japan National Tourist Organization*)

In Kazu, Japan, traditional craftsmen design and make carp kites for the annual kite festivals throughout Japan. (*Japan National Tourist Organization*)

In the Republic of China, the ninth day of the ninth month (Double Nine) is designated as National Kite Day. This is observed more as a children's holiday and general sports day. Fireworks and athletic contests of all sorts are featured on this day. The Chinese kites are probably the most ingenious in the world. The musical kite is a specialty of the Republic; such kites are built with perforated bamboo reeds, which emit a plaintive series of notes that can be heard for astonishingly long distances.

Taiwan also has some of the world's largest kites, including one that is 95 feet long. This one, in the form of a dragon, takes a team of men to operate on a strong wind. The builder of this monster, Mr. Chen Shih-fung, is a schoolteacher who specializes in these flying monsters. His pride is a 65-foot-long centipede which has whirling eyes and at night carries a lighted candle. So cleverly done is the centipede that it can be folded into a small bundle and carried about from one flying site to another on a bicycle.

In 1967, I started to make another kite-flying tour, this time through the South American world of kite fliers. And in South America, I was told, are the greatest fliers in the world. Even greater than in India, where I had won the world's championship from the maharajah of Bharatpur.

The tour of South America was to be climaxed with a man-to-man confrontation between me and the Papagaio fliers on Copacabana Beach in Rio de Janeiro during carnival week.

A Pan Am pilot, who asked that his name not be used, made it possible for me to carry my kites aboard the plane so that I could take them out of my bag and fly them at airport stops between here and Buenos Aires. Otherwise, I would have had to go to the luggage compartment each time and try to frisk out a kite from the general cargo. It happened like this:

I was stopped at the check-in counter in New York when I asked to carry my kites aboard the ship.

"Nothing doing," said the clerk politely. "We don't take any kites aboard our planes because the regulations forbid anything but carry-on bags."

"I need my kites with me at all times," I pleaded. "I give kite exhibitions to the local people. They expect me at each airport—hundreds of members of the International Kitefliers Association. I'm president of it, and how would it look when I get off at an airport without a kite in hand to greet them, as they greet me?"

The clerk was adamant. I pleaded with the chief clerk. He was adamant. I asked him to appeal to the pilot, whom I knew to be a member of IKA.

"I am a flier and your pilot will understand," I explained, without telling them that I was a simple *kite* flier, and had never piloted a plane in my life. I have flown kites, however, that were as big as some of the early planes.

The pilot, who happened to be nearby, made a ruling based on the fact that I was a "flier," and he explained to the clerk, "Professional courtesy, you know." This satisfied everyone and I brought my army duffel bag full of small kites aboard the magnificent Pan Am plane. I was a professional flying with pros.

So, the first part of my kite flight was safely negotiated.

In my duffel bag I had the following armament of kites: A Rogallo nonrigid wing, the kite that was developed practically under the aegis of the National Aeronautics and Space Administration in their own wind tunnels at the Langley Field facility in Virginia.

My second kite was a so-called bird adaptation of the French military kite, which the French used in the Franco-Prussian War to signal troop movements. This kite, made for me by the Alan Whitney Company in New Haven, Connecticut, is one of the best lifting kites in the world.

A third kite was a special, made for me by Frank Mots, an ingenious kite maker of Milwaukee, Wisconsin. Fine commercial kites made by the Gayla Company of Houston, Texas, and Hi-Fliers of Decatur, Illinois, rounded out my main inventory.

I had been warned about the "soft" kites. In South America I found various shaped kites, as in the United States. Somehow in Spanish they sound more romantic than do our kites, although ours seem to be hardier. The Estrella is an octagonal kite, three stick. The Corona is a round three-stick kite. The Bomba is a huge three-sticker, also round. The Cometa is our own beloved Eddy kite, the two cross-sticks with a diamond-shaped skin. All fly.

I was ready. A wire service sent out a story to the effect that I was going to defend the title I won from the maharajah of Bharatpur. It added that I was also recruiting a kite-flying team for the next Olympics. And then it closed the report with the astonishing news that "Yolen stated he was in training for this trip. He's given up the fifth Martini to keep in shape."

Well, that certainly put all the South American kite fliers on their mettle—or at least they were mettlesome when I was greeted on the route.

"You better get back to the fifth Martini," exclaimed one Chilean in Antofagasta, where we stopped for fuel. His remark was occasioned by the fact that he had read the story in his local Spanish paper and thought that no one could raise a kite in the awful humid heat prevalent at the airport at the time. "At least you'll get a drink out of it," he scoffed.

In Buenos Aires, Argentina, the great editor Gainza Paz, of the newspaper *La Prensa*, greeted me: "You're the kite-flying champion I've been reading about." With that he picked up the phone and called his sports editor. "I want you to put your best kite writer on a story." You could hear the sports editor explode over the phone with "Kite flying! We don't have kite writers, and besides, kite flying is not a sport."

There was a shocked silence. "What do you mean, kite flying is not a sport," said Señor Paz. "It is a great sport and I have the world champion sitting right here in my office."

Needless to say, *La Prensa* carried a story and picture of me flying kites next day. We won a friend and recruit in Paz, but I'm afraid that the motto of IKA, "Worldwide Friends Through Kite Flying," was not fully realized in the sports editor of the paper.

The highlight of the tour was the "kite-in" at the beautiful American embassy in Buenos Aires a few days after my arrival there. Carter Burgess, distinguished American businessman who became American ambassador to Argentina in 1968, had invited me and other Americans in Buenos Aires to his Wednesday morning breakfast sessions. These were lighthearted get-acquainted sessions in which Mr. B. delighted to tell stories and listen to others' experiences in the business, political or social world.

Traveling around the world on his goodwill kite-flying missions, Will Yolen never fails to draw a crowd. Here, swapping expertise with an Argentinian kite flier in Buenos Aires.

In the early morning visit I presented myself to Mr. Burgess, who seemed fascinated by the kite stories and asked me to come back Friday noon to give an exhibition of kite flying to his staff and friends.

"Can I bring my family?" I asked.

"Sure, bring the family," said the industrialist-ambassador. "My family is going to be there also." He quipped: "The family that flies together, stays together."

Friday noon I arrived at the embassy and there was a party in progress—and television cameras, reporters, photographers.

"Well, is this some sort of a world news event?" I asked.

"Yes, and you're it," a newsman said.

I started to fly my kites in a nimble demonstration. The press urged the ambassador to participate so that they could make pictures. The cameras rolled. The space was limited and the sun was blazing, but I managed to get a French military kite in the air and over the trees. The ambassador, a tall man, towered over me and, at the urgings of the press, took hold of my fishing rod and reel on which I was casting my kite and it immediately came down to the ground.

"Get it up, get it up," screamed the TV men. "Give the kite to the ambassador," the reporters shouted.

The ambassador's twelve-year-old son stepped in. He wanted to fly the kite. We were getting somewhat crowded. I gave the kite to the junior Carter. He was great with it. I changed over to a Rogallo nonrigid wing kite. Young Burgess loved it. The ambassador beamed. I pumped the kite into the air, there being no breeze at all. I practically hoisted it by hand, casting it back and forth on the fishing rod to give it some loft. It took off on a wispy current of air and we were airborne.

At the American embassy in Buenos Aires, Ambassador Carter L. Burgess hosted a kite-flying party on the lawn. The Argentinian newspapers, radio and television stations reported the event as a breakthrough in inter-American relations, and Mr. Burgess made the front pages for the first time in his career in that country.

After the press had left, the ambassador invited me to visit. "I've not had such fun since I was a kid," he explained. "I didn't know that this would be part of my job as ambassador or I would have taken it sooner," he added.

The next day all the local papers had stories on the wonderful new spirit at the American embassy. One paper editorialized that it would be good if all embassies would open themselves to the people and cited the kite-flying event as one of the friendliest gestures any government could make. And there was a picture on page one of all the papers, showing the ambassador, myself, his son flying kites.

Next day he called to say that it was the first time the American embassy had been on so many page ones and had had so much good press and TV coverage. People come to the embassy for a variety of reasons, said Mr. Burgess, but one of the biggest reasons is that they want to hear the sound of American voices.

My official title in Argentina was "Campeón Mundial de Remontadores de Barriletes," or roughly, "world champ, kite flying." This is a big responsibility. It is everywhere but has a real meaning in South American countries where they take their champions seriously. You can't be half a champ or a "cheese" champ or a middle-size champ . . . you have to be a champ all the way, and you have to act as one.

The press referred to me as such and expected me to act as such. That's why they treated me with the respect due to a champ, even if I were only the champ of tiddlywinks. In a Latin country there is a great deal of "machismo" connected with being champ, which is appreciated everywhere in the world but much more so in

Latin America. The kids admire you and so do the men and women. It means buying drinks for everyone, and it means answering a challenge no matter what time of day or night. And you can't talk your way out of anything. If you fail to answer a challenge, you have as good as lost the bout right then and there.

This could have been fun when I was a young sport myself, but when at age sixty-one you get phone calls in the middle of the night to come out of a cool air-conditioned room, it takes a lot of machismo to respond to the challenger.

Therefore, I had to answer to challenges at dawn's early light twice when I should have been sleeping off some parties that were thrown in my honor as former president of the Overseas Press Club and current president of the International Kitefliers Association.

One eager challenger sat at my door all night at the hotel and was waiting for me with kite poised when I opened the door to let in the room service waiter with my breakfast.

As an old world gentleman, I invited my challenger to have coffee with me. He responded graciously and offered me brandy from a flask he carried wherever he went, he explained, on every field of honor, whether it was kite flying or swordplay. He explained that it didn't matter which he was engaged in. Honor was the important thing.

I told him that I would gladly satisfy his honor, but only on the field of the kite. As the challenged, I could name my weapon. I suggested the French military kite at 100 paces.

Obviously disappointed, but a good sport, he went out to the field with me carrying a shabby kite alongside his sword scabbard. No untoward aspect of honor was breached as he released a scruffy type of butterfly kite which didn't have a chance against the French military kite. I quickly destroyed my opponent as he flew with one hand on the kite string and the other hand on his scabbard, as if for support of his honor.

He went off the field of honor with a bow to me. I never saw him again. A friend of ours who had acted as a second, or a "third" as he called himself, explained that this man was a nut on honor and challenged anyone who came here to visit.

He has never won a contest of any kind in his life, explained my friend. He challenges everyone with any reputation. He's a sort of George Plimpton of South America and will enter every contest and compete with the champs of every sport. He has never entered a sword contest, however, so no one knows how good a swordsman he is.

One of the highlights of the Buenos Aires flying was my meeting with a ten-year-old flier who I thought should be the South American champ. We met first on a TV show in which I was interviewed. This ten-year-old, Alejandro Victor Teckarek, had won a kite contest the previous year and was brought to the TV show to be interviewed with me. He showed me his kite, which was a sophisticated vehicle of bamboo and cloth shaped like a ballistic missile, including a nose cone.

To my surprise and gratification he presented the kite to me, a kite that probably cost him many hours to make. At first I started to refuse, but his uncle urged me to accept because it is a breach of good manners to refuse a gift in Argentina. Alejandro made a presentation speech and I made a stammering speech of acceptance. Then I gave him a life membership in IKA and one of my French military kites.

Later, on the field, we tested our kites. His French military kite whooshed into the air. My presentation kite couldn't get off the ground. I apologized by claiming that my fishing line had backlashed and I couldn't begin to experiment with his delicate kite at this time.

We parted with expressions of goodwill. The uncle asked me if there were any contests in the United States that his nephew could attend. I told him of the ones in San Diego, California, New Canaan, Connecticut, in the Sandcastle in Sarasota, Florida. I offered to sponsor his coming to the States to attend these flights, many of which I judge. He promised to attend the Sandcastle, Sarasota, flight—if and when I sent him the tickets, one for him and one for his nephew.

I failed through translation to convey the idea of kite flying in America: that there are no professionals and that everyone pays his own way and no paid fliers. I also emphasized to him that I do not manufacture kites or sell them. I don't even endorse them, although I have been asked by manufacturers to endorse many a kite. Argentina has little or no tradition of kite making. That's true also of most of the Latin American countries, except Brazil. There is some home kite industry, unlike the United States where there are more than 75,000,000 kites a year manufactured by commercial kite makers. In South America, kites are made at home.

But in Buenos Aires a couple of brothers founded a small kite-making plant where they made an imitation Brazilian Papagaio. They started this business about seventeen years ago. Both brothers, Florencio and Jaime Bouturaira, started to make kites of paper, glue and sticks in the shape of birds. They made their kites to sell to their fellow students in the local high school. This paid for their early education. Later the brothers made enough to go to dental technical school. Today they are dental technicians. While Jaime stayed on in Argentina with his father, Florencio is practicing his trade in Los Angeles, California. Today, the father and sisters carry on the kite-making business in a limited way. They make them only in the windy seasons, from September through December.

Once in a while Jaime sends some of their kites to his brother in Los Angeles. Florencio sells all he can get. But the production is too slow. Someday, according to the father, Julio, they will try to put their kites on a production basis similar to the way it is done in the United States. Meanwhile, they supply two kite stores in Buenos Aires.

So popular is kiting in Buenos Aires that I was invited everywhere. One morning I promised an exclusive show to a TV news outfit, who said they would pick me up in the hotel lobby the next day. At 9 A.M. a telephone call said that the TV camera crew was in the lobby and would I please get ready. In broken Spanish to the caller's broken English I said I would. I didn't understand why they were there an hour earlier than expected. I had already had my breakfast, so although I grumbled a bit, I went down to the lobby, where I met a camera crew and they took off with me to a nearby park where I was to do some flying.

My first attempt to lift a huge kite on my light reel and rod snapped my small rod. Disaster! However, the leader of the camera crew claimed he knew where I could get it fixed pronto. Well, we got it fixed pronto but not before twelve noon, when I gave a half-hour show for the camera crew and was then brought back to the hotel with many thanks for my willingness to respond so spontaneously.

I didn't quite understand what the crew leader, Manuel R. Botta, meant by spontaneous, but I found out soon enough when my wife met me with the news that a camera crew had been seeking me for the last two hours.

"I met them in the lobby and we went off to fly kites in another part of the city where I had my rod repaired," I explained.

"Wrong camera crew," my wife explained.

"The road from Asuncion to Iguazu Falls is lined with the graves of pilgrims and giant anthills." This was the lead in a UPI story written by my son, Steven. It was a colorful trip with a driver who knew every inch of the road and hit every bump in it. He also hit a pig and nearly got a pilgrim who was walking on his knees to one of the roadside shrines where they sit down and wait for death to overtake them.

I bemoaned the fact that there was so little kite flying in Paraguay, when out of a dirt driveway a seven-year-old boy darted clutching a kite string to his chest. Overhead his homemade kite was soaring. I felt my visit to Paraguay was justified, not in my mission to fly kites through the Iguazu Falls, but because I had witnessed some real kite flying. And it was the first time in my life I had witnessed kite flying at seven o'clock in the morning.

When I asked the driver to stop so that I could take a picture of the early kite flier, he stated flatly that he would rather show me a church down the road a piece. While the discussion was going on, he traveled another couple of miles, out of sight of the kite. When I finally persuaded him to turn back and find the child, it was too late. The kid had disappeared.

As I was the only one who had seen this child flying a kite, my companions, including the driver, insisted that I had seen an apparition. The native driver insisted that there was no Paraguayan kite flying. All agreed that I had witnessed the first kite-flying mirage in history.

On the road, with all those shrines and giant anthills, who knows? They may be right.

The ride from Asuncion to Iguazu Falls is a spectacular auto trip. It took us six hours in a Mercedes which broke down at a toll booth handled by the Paraguayan police. The auto went back to a small station a mile down the road and the driver made us comfortable at the toll booth. The police there seated us on a bench right alongside the main road from Asuncion to Iguazu Falls. It being Sunday, the Paraguayans were on the road to the churches and cemeteries, shrines and general sightseeing. We made a curious picture sitting there alongside the road, dressed in tourist clothes, my beautiful blond daughter-in-law looking like a movie star and me carrying a kite at the end of a fishing rod.

The native trucks and buses stopped at this wondrous sight and babbled away in rapid Spanish which my son translated, "They're entranced with this sight of the friendly Americans who are putting on this show for them on the holiday." Some of them did applaud, especially when I flailed my kite in the heat to get it aloft. They thought it was a new type of fan.

Soon the car returned all repaired and we were on the road again. It was hot, very hot. I was determined to fly a kite through the Iguazu Falls. I had heard the story of the swallows flying through the falls and nesting in the cliffs behind the crescendo of water. I wanted to shoot a kite through the falls, never before done.

I could use my nonrigid kite, made of a fine steel sheet; it used shroud lines instead of sticks or spars. This collapsible kite could shed water and on a favorable wind or updraft could drive right through the thin sheets of water that were part of the Iguazu Falls at the highest points that could be approached.

The falls, when sighted in the early afternoon, were a beautiful cascade of wedding veil and shaped in horseshoe style something like the Niagara at its Canadian side. I descended to the bottom of the falls with my guide. The humidity was terrific and the heat was at 110°, and no shade. There wasn't a breath of air. We then ascended on stone stairs which circumscribed the tremendous falls but couldn't find a breeze on which I could send my kite through the falls. The visitors at the falls thought I was a fisherman trying my skills with rod and reel but were puzzled when they saw me cast a kite instead of lures.

On top of the falls I tried to send the steel kite through. I succeeded in getting it to the lip of the cliffs but failed to drive it through. I changed to a position on a tower just above the falls and then began to cast the kite, catching downdraft air currents. I was using a light, ten-pound-test line on a small reel that was as sensitive to my handling as though it were a surgeon's tool. And believe me I needed that delicate touch as the water kept pounding down the side of the cliffs.

Just then I saw a bird going through the water. My kite shot out at the same time. Both the bird and my kite seemed to go through the water at the same time.

My reel sang as though taken by a huge fish. The crowd watching the performance gave a cheer. They had finally recognized what I was trying to do.

I finally pulled the kite out from behind the cascading sheets of water. It was a frazzled looking kite but it had done the job.

The fulfillment of a dream—to fly like the birds through the Iguazu Falls in Paraguay, on the Argentine border. Here, the swallows reach their nests behind the falls by flying through a veil of tumbling water. I failed to simulate this flight with a military kite, but succeeded with the nonrigid kite.

My guide looked at me with new respect.

"Sometimes the birds don't come out of there," he said.

"Sometimes mine doesn't come back either," I replied, remembering the many times I've lost kites to such simple enemies as kite-eating trees.

"But this kite is a champ," I explained to the guide.

In São Paulo, Brazil, there is not much tradition of kite flying. Nevertheless, there is the beginning. Strangely enough kite flying in São Paulo was born in the United States.

Several years ago in Connecticut I attended a party given for a visitor, Elliott Dranoff, a young Portuguese-speaking American businessman of São Paulo. With him were his Brazilian wife and three children. The oldest son, Mike, was fascinated with my kite flying, which I did on the lawn of the house we were visiting. Mike was enchanted and insisted on helping me fly kites. I asked him about the Papagaio of Brazil. He didn't know anything about it. He wanted to fly my American kites. I showed him how to put together one of my kites, a cross-stick type of kite, and he was flying it in a second.

When the party was over his father politely offered the kite back. Mike was in tears. He offered to work for me for a year if I would let him keep the kite. I let him keep it without taking up his offer.

Three years later I telephoned Dranoff in São Paulo and reminded him of our meeting in the States. He invited me to attend a dinner his father-in-law had arranged. His father-in-law was Dr. Mendel Diesendruck, chief rabbi of Brazil, who wanted to meet me and give his blessings for having introduced his grandson to kite flying.

That evening son, father and grandson were installed as members of the kite club. A prayer was spoken by the rabbi into the sky, and we all marveled how such a simple thing as a kite could cross barriers of age, background and even language to be meaningful to everyone. And the kite was the same two-stick cruciform.

The Papagaio, the kite against which I was determined to achieve my greatest victory, is a strange creature. I had been under the impression that it was an old and traditional kite, derivative of the kites developed by the natives of the Melanesian Islands who had molded huge leaves into wings, which they mounted on the tree-limb frames. They used vines for lines or ropes. This, history tells us, is what the Melanesians did. Because the Papagaio seems to have the outward appearance of the bird kite—the "barrilete pajaro" of Argentina—I assumed that it was an ancient flying vehicle.

Instead, I found that the Papagaio, the kite that had revolutionized kite flying at least in Brazil, was never seen before twenty-five years ago when the Cariocas of Rio began to handcraft it and sell it to tourists. That they had stumbled on a great art form never occurred to them. Like the English of Shakespeare's time who didn't know they were speaking noble Elizabethan language, the natives of Rio didn't realize they were creating a great kite form and style. Its manufacturing history is lost in the mist of twenty-five years. No one at the beach or in the libraries knew anything about the Papagaio, although they knew about the other native kites, most of which followed the pattern of the American home-made kites, including the fifteen-cent diamond-shaped and the sled kite, which looks so much like a sled because of the two wooden runners that give it shape and stability.

One of the advantages of the Brazilian kite is that it can be assembled so easily—in seconds, in fact. But making one is impossible for the average hobbyist. Furthermore, even the men who assemble them on the Copa Beach where they achieved world renown, do not know how they are manufactured. And the few manufacturers will not reveal the secret to outsiders.

These kites are built to withstand extreme air turbulence. The inventor of this kite was modern enough in his craftsmanship to insert metal bushings in the two wing spars where they join the center spar. No such modern kite is made anywhere else in the world.

Time after time American toy manufacturers have tried to mass-produce these kites. They've invariably failed. One manufacturer lost a quarter of a million dollars before he gave up on it. There is something about the cloth and wood used in this kite which fails to respond to mass-production methods. Furthermore, it seems that nowhere outside of Rio does this kite fly as it does in its home air currents. Of course, the wood in the frame of the kite is grown only in Brazil. Even in Saõ Paulo they do not fly this kite or make it. They'd rather import it from Rio, 200 miles away, to use for decoration or mobiles.

The maneuverability of this kite is amazing. The Cariocas place fishhooks on the kite's tail and swoop it to the ground to pick up pieces of paper scattered on the beach sand.

This I promised myself was to be more exciting than my combat against the great Pablo Diablo in Central Park in New York or against the kite-flying prince of India.

Never did a pilgrim approach Jerusalem with more reverence than I approached Rio de Janeiro. This was the city of lights, the most beautiful city in the world as far as I could remember, and I had been in all the great cities of the world.

And it was carnival time, a carnival that lasted four days and lived day and night to the samba beat. The drums were banging away and the guitarists were strumming even as the Pan Am plane approached the scenery which looked like a prop city, set up only for carnival time.

The city was in an atmosphere of a feast, a feast that was a combination New Year's Eve in Times Square, Guy Fawkes Day in London, Christmas around the Christian world and a dash of a Bar Mitzvah.

The big prize was the diadem that goes to the winner of the contest of the Escolas de Samba, the dance schools. Almost every Carioca participates in the great dance band tournaments or in the costume balls. And on the beach I could see the Papagaios being flown by merchants all over Copacabana Beach, a two-and-a-half-mile strip of the most beautifully framed beach, with the statue of Christ hovering over it on a nearby mountain top.

The beach is oval-shaped. The hotels are across Copa Boulevard. The sky was blue, the breeze just murmuring enough to keep the kites in the air. I couldn't wait to get my hand on my kite bag and rush to the beach to contend against the first kite flier I saw. I knew they were waiting for me. The Rio magazines and newspapers, TV and radio had sent word ahead. I had to turn down an invitation from the Brasilia Kite Club so that I could be in Rio where the kite fliers were dedicated to pure kite flying.

It was there I heard that a famous or infamous antagonist of mine was lurking to take a shot at me with his razor-studded kite. He also carried a glazed string, glass encrusted, and ready to rip apart anything it touched.

My first bout was dedicated to the Brazilian beauty Miss Universe of 1969, Martha Vasconcellos, who was on the same Pan Am plane. In the flight to Rio I had installed her as a member of IKA. She had already been honored with the role of queen of the carnival, so she wasn't exactly overwhelmed by this honor. Nevertheless, she graciously consented to let me wear her colors. She warned me she was accustomed to winners. I assured her that I would not only bring her honor but present her with the winning kite.

So again my kite-flying activities had fulfilled the promise of the club's slogan, "Worldwide Friends Through Kite Flying."

She promised she would attend our next convention wherever it might be and fly a kite with us in memory of our lovely Pan Am flight. I blithely kissed mademoiselle's hand in Continental style, bid her a gallant goodbye and promised to invite her to our next bash, which would be in January at the Sandcastle in Sarasota, Florida.

So far so good.

Instead of the kite fliers greeting me, there was nothing but a group of kite merchants. No one was flying kites for fun. At every street entrance to the beach, in front of every beach hotel, there was a stand of Papagaios with a busy merchant selling them to tourists.

"Come fly with me," I challenged one of them.

He paid no attention. He was busy selling a handful of rolled up kites to a tourist, an American who exclaimed gleefully that this was the best souvenir of his trip he could possibly find.

"Sure beats postcards," he exclaimed as he plunked down $10 in cruzeiros for five kites.

I unfurled my kite and challenged the tourist. "No, sir," he said. "I just want to look at them, I can't afford to break 'em up. I don't fly kites, I want to bring them back to my nephews and nieces. Aren't they beautiful?"

He wouldn't fly against me.

I wandered up and down the beach flying my Rogallo wing and a French military kite, one in each hand. I tried to bait every kite seller on the beach. No one would respond and my lack of Portuguese handicapped me somewhat.

Undismayed, I kept myself in shape by flying my kites waiting for something to happen. The beat of the drums and the shouts of the revelers and the sound of the surf hypnotized me. My kites were in the sky. My mind was wandering.

A couple of kids were flying kites. Not Papagaios, but plain, simple paper kites, which they had made themselves. They greeted me. I greeted them. They gazed at my bag full of kites with wonder.

"Come fly with me," I suggested.

"Yes, yes," they responded in Portuguese. We were airborne in a few seconds. The fun had returned to kite flying. The disappointment of finding no competition was gone. The beauty and fun of kite flying are that it doesn't have to be competitive. It doesn't have to have body contact or physical exertion. So here I am, flying thousands of miles away from home with kids who are decades younger than I. And when the people on the beach saw me flying with the kids they seemed to open up and cheer us on. I traded kites with the two young Brazilians, and they used my rod and reel. I used their hand-over-hand reel, pretty primitive according to our standards, but fun nevertheless. I have become so accustomed to flying with rod and reel, I had forgotten the joy of holding the kite string in hand and feeling it slide through my fingers, sometimes burning them when a strong gust took the kite by the throat.

I forgot the tensions of trying to be a big-time kite champ. I just stood along the water's edge, with the kite string in my hand, my eyes in the sky, and thrilled to the feeling that I was in touch with the infinite.

My two companions, João and Sergio, meanwhile were having a fine time with my kites, one with the Rogallo wing, the other with the French military kite. One of the bathers came up to me and asked to see how the French military kite was made. Another bather joined him. A pretty girl joined us and helped herself to one of my kites in my nearby duffel bag. Another joined us. I began to break out some of my other kites and showed my new friends how to fly them.

I had about fifteen kites out now and people were scampering along the beach with my kites. I was having a wonderful time myself, although it was difficult to keep track of all the kites that were out now. Some of the kites were diving into the water because of experiments being carried on by boys and girls who had not handled this type of kite before. I ran from one to another shouting words of encouragement and helping to sort lines out.

I sure was making friends.

I was having such fun that I forgot to keep an eye on João and Sergio. They were struggling to keep the Rogallo wing kite under control and, of course, finally they could not. The silver kite streaked to the ground and smashed into a row of Papagaios where the first kite merchant I had tried to lure into the battle had set up shop. It busted two of them.

The kite vendor rushed over to the two little boys and started cuffing them. I intervened. He did not dare cuff me, although I could see he wanted to.

"You're responsible for this," he said, flapping the two broken Papagaios in my face.

A beach cop came over, attracted by the ruckus. He was a friend of the kite salesman. In fact, I found out he gets a percentage of the profits for allowing the vendor to set up along his sector of the beach. The salesman explained to his friend what had happened, that a kite had broken two of his precious Papagaios, which he called "gaivotas." The cop, a big, handsome man, came over to me, after cuffing João and Sergio.

"Buy them," he commanded, pointing to the two broken kites.

I did not see much alternative. An unfriendly crowd had gathered and the cop was clearly ready for trouble. He was flexing his muscles.

So I bought the two gaivotas. I gave them to João and Sergio. They were delighted. They knew where to find replacement wood for the two broken cross-spars, the only parts that had been busted up in the crash. They discarded their little paper kites and ran away joyfully.

I flew only once more in Rio, a week after my incident on Copacabana. I had in the interim been caught up in the carnival happenings, dancing in the streets with the Escolas de Samba and doing all of the things that tourists do in Rio, visiting the Corcovado Christ, Sugarloaf, the many boîtes in the city. It is a truly fun city.

The day before I was to leave, I saw two gaivotas dancing about fifty feet off the ground together, on the beach, and I thought that peculiar, for the kite vendors usually flew their wares singly. Going down to investigate, I suddenly heard a merry shout of "Wheel, wheel."

There were João and Sergio, back on the beach flying kites, but this time with their new kites, the fancy gaivotas I had bought for them. They had replaced the broken parts and now had put them together as good as new.

I ran back and got my Rogallo wing and fishing rod. We flew our kites together on the beach, and I finally fulfilled my desire to fly with the gaivotas. And not against a kite merchant who knew no love of kite flying.

I was flying together with two more members of the brotherhood of kite fliers, the fellowship that knows no barriers, be they of space or distance. Or age.

Kite flying in the Middle East can be a tricky business in these sensitive times. During a recent trip through Egypt, Syria, Jordan, Lebanon and Israel, encounters with other kite fliers were frequently unusual, to say the least. One of these encounters took place in Beirut, Lebanon, where a newspaper reporter from Wilmington, Delaware, Bill Frank, and I went out on the town to take some photos of kite flying at the Eagle Rock Beach. Bill had gone down ahead of me to engage a cab for two hours; I followed ten minutes later carrying a duffel bag full of kites.

Arriving downstairs, I was taken aback by the taxi driver, who, seeing me and my bag full of colorful kites, began an ululation of such intensity that I began to retreat. Instead, the cabbie rushed to me and took my kites and began to scream, "Remember me, remember me, I am Abdul . . ." Sure enough, it was a cab driver named Abdul who had taken me on a kite tour of Beirut in 1960 when I had been on a kite-flying junket for my first book on the subject and for a series for *Life* magazine. At first I thought Bill had put him on to this, but Abdul looked familiar and showed me a clipping describing the event in his "Book of Notables" which he kept in the cab. I was in it all right. Abdul admitted that he didn't recognize me at first. But when he saw my kites, it all came back to him.

Thus are all kite reunions and cab drives arranged by all-seeing Allah Akbar.

Takieddih Al-Solh, the prime minister of Lebanon, a cherubic, grandpappy type, carries his IKA card around with him through successive press conferences. When we left, he held our hands in traditional Arab style and whispered, "Will this kite card get me through New York traffic?" I assured him that if I got through Beirut traffic, he could get through New York traffic. A friendly man, he asked me questions about New York, rather than America as a whole. I told his press officers that he would make a lot of friends for the cause of Arab-Israeli peace if he would come to New York. The Overseas Press Club could give him an audience, I suggested. This startling new idea in kite diplomacy was greeted with enthusiasm.

Weeks later, in New York, at a meeting with some Lebanese notables, the suggestion was discussed again.

"He's too old to leave the mother country for a Western tour," it was explained. I

On a tour in the Middle East, I taught my cameleer, Mustapha, how to fly kites on a rod and reel. He paid me back by making me take a seven-mile camel ride to the Pyramid area in Giza.
(*Ray Shaw*)

still remember, however, how much he wanted to break away from the old patterns of hate as he wistfully asked, "Will this kite card get me through New York traffic?"

At a dinner meeting in Tel Aviv, Israel, I installed the new minister of defense, Shimon Peres, as a member of IKA as well as the American Kitefliers Association in New Mexico, where he had once visited the atomic facilities. I had recited to him a story about the way the ancient Chinese had scared off an invading army by sending up firecrackers on huge platform kites over enemy lines.

"Please draw up these plans," he urged me. "We may have to resort to such methods," he explained, "because of the slowness of getting additional arms after the October war."

The *Jerusalem Post*'s Ernie Meyer story on my tour of the Middle East battle areas with other newsmen went to great lengths on our observations of the area, but quoted me only on my kites: "The motto of his flying club is to soar high into the clouds, while keeping one's feet on the ground." Which he later adjured his country-men to do likewise.

The author flies a French military kite over Haifa, Israel, in 1973, soon after the October war. (*C. Eischen*)

"Don't send up any kites in this area," the Israeli lieutenant joked, "You'll raise enemy fire." We were on a rise in the Golan Heights, facing Syria in the distance, three or four miles northeast of our position. "Let's test it," I replied. With that, I sent up a silvery Rogallo wing. It flashed in the sunlight, fluttered, rose again. Not a shot was fired.

There was a stillness in the air. Some of the Israeli soldiers cheered the kite on the wing.

Later in the day, we descended the Heights at the staging area where a Swedish contingent of UN troops was getting ready to take over the Israeli positions the next day. We were allowed to talk to the UN "observers," as the troops were called.

I still had the Rogallo kite on the end of my casting rod and reel. The soldiers asked me to fly it. When I did, they exclaimed (via an interpreter), "That's the bird, that's the bird."

An English-speaking Swedish soldier explained that his men had gone through the Syrian lines early in the day and had observed the kite flashing in the sun. The Syrians thought it was a signal for a fire fight and began preparations to return the fire when the Swedish officer halted them.

"That's not a signal for enemy action," he explained. "That's a bird of peace."

Thus a border incident that may have started another round of firing was settled on the wings of peace. Kite diplomacy had done it again.

Kite flying is so well established as the Bermuda national pastime that children often learn to construct and fly tissue-paper kites before they learn to read. As Bermudians grow older, their kites tend to grow larger, as this traditional round kite illustrates. It requires over 200 feet of tail. (*Bermuda News Bureau*)

Ulku Imset displays her classic, starlike Turkish kite at the annual kite carnival in Washington, D.C. (*United Press International*)

11 CONTESTS, TOURNAMENTS, JOUSTS AND GYMKHANA

The climax of a kite flier's existence is the contest—that is, if he is not a contemplative. There are no real kite jocks in this world, but there are competitors, usually low-keyed individuals. No screaming audience cheers on the contestants. No pretty girl cheerleaders whirl their short skirts and twirl their batons to rouse the players or audience.

Most contests, says Jan Nordheimer of *The New York Times*, are a "demonstration of torpor." Kids with running noses keep whining throughout, crying for their parents to help untangle their strings.

Nevertheless, there are some highlights in the life of a contest if it is run right. For this reason and against the advice of the venerable head of the American Kitefliers Association, Bob Ingraham, some basic contest rules and procedures are set forth here.

As in all airborne competitions "SAD" is the basic tenet of kite contest:

Speed

Altitude

Distance

or any variation of these three elements.

Generally speaking there are four classifications of kites eligible.

1. Plane surface kites, or those having tails.
2. Bowed or tailless kites.
3. Box kites or combination kites.
4. The nonrigid kites, the kites that have no sticks. None of this last breed are being seen enough to have much impact, but it is the kite of the future, according to contest masters.

In addition to the preceding categories, there is virtually no limit to the classifications that may be set up: (1) largest, (2) smallest, (3) most beautiful, (4) most unusual. But there is nothing to prevent you from a setup such as (1) most comical, (2) most newsworthy (if made from newspaper), (3) most ingenious, etc. The basic rule

A delightful old print depicts various aspects of a turn-of-the-century kite-flying contest—"at home" at Malta.
(*New York Public Library Picture Collection*)

must be enforced: The kite must fly and stay in a stabilized position for at least 30 seconds.

Today it is no longer possible to have a contest for "homemade kites" only. Store-bought kites may be entered. However, there should be at least one category for homemade kites. Some of the older contest towns, such as Huntington, California, insist that only homemade kites be entered. But this rule has been waived lately even in the most conservative contests.

One assistant per flier is usually allowed. However, if the giant jumbos are in the contest, more than one assistant may be permitted. After helping launch the kite, either by lead-out or by over-the-head launching, the assistant must retire. This is a good rule, because the tendency of the helper is to seize the line himself when the kite flutters a bit, thus taking the initiative away from the kiter. This has happened many times and has busted up friendships of long standing.

A *messenger* race may be run with any kind of kite, but the lines must be measured—not only measured but must be of the same quality and degree of smoothness.

Banner Raising: This can be a contest within a contest. Not only is it a test of ingenuity in kite flying but it is a test of banner writing. It is the beginning of sky writing.

The rules: Mount a banner, with whatever message you want, on the kite line. To qualify the banner must be raised at least 50 feet and the words on it must be legible from the judging stand after the banner is in full flight.

Largest Number of Kites on a Single Line: This is one of the great contests and may be the most frustrating to perform. This event should be held in a side field and

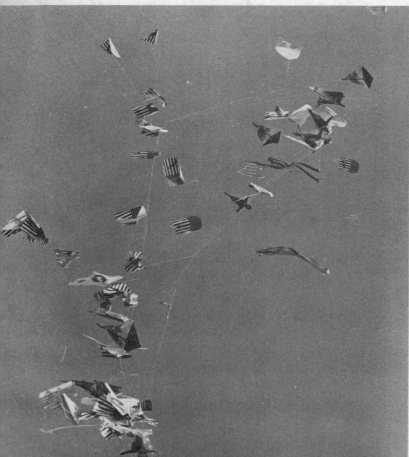

Thrill of thrills . . . Winning a prize? No, setting a record! At the annual Sheraton Sandcastle kite-flying contest in Sarasota, Florida, the author sets a new record of 57 kites flown on one line in 1973. (*Stuart Sellers*)

In 1974, the author set a new record of 178 kites on one line. (*Barney Stein*)

Members of the Rio Vista YMCA Apache Tribe attempt to launch a giant kite in 1962 at the annual kite-flying contest. The kite, 400 feet square, was as big around as a swimming pool. (*United Press International*)

A real stopper—the huge delta-wing kite that flew successfully in Central Park's annual kite festival. (*Caleb Crowell*)

away from the main action. Ground rules should be immediately established on raiding other kites. Some permit this; others do not. Only the kites you put on your own line are counted in most tournaments.

In the great Sandcastle tournament in Sarasota, Florida, I had 50 kites on my line, including 10 that I had bravely swept from other fliers, only after 15 of my kites had been ripped off my line by sky pirates.

The "Go Fly a Kite Contest" which is run by Andrea Bahadur with the help of the New York Parks Department is a good standard for single heats in half-hour intervals as follows:

1 P.M. *Highest Flier:* All contestants will take assigned positions on the field. At the signal all the kites will be launched. At the end of 3 minutes the highest kite will be declared winner.

1:30 P.M. *Smallest Kite:* Contestants in this event will bring their kites forward for inspection by the judges. Then the judges will enter the field to seek out the tiny kites in flight, which must fly out 25 feet of line to qualify.

2 P.M. *Largest Kite:* These jumbos must prove air-worthiness by attaining an altitude of 75 feet. Limited to 3 persons per kite. Contestants will be allowed unlimited running space within a 5-minute time limit.

2:30 P.M. *Most Beautiful:* Open to homemade kites only. In this gorgeous event the emphasis will be on decorative qualities, but they must fly, of course.

The Poster Kite Contest in New York City's Central Park has a "walkout" as it commences on the field.

3 P.M. *Most Kites on One String (flying in tandem):* Limited to 2 persons per entry. How many kites can you fly on *one* string? You'll have half an hour to get your kites up.

4 P.M. *Most Maneuverable:* Above all others, this event requires the trained hand of an experienced kite flier. Helium balloons will be placed around the field, to be brought down by your maneuverable kite.

4:30 P.M. *Fly-In:* Everyone is invited to fly kites. Free kite instructions will be given by the "Go Fly a Kite Team."

Here are some basic *contest rules:*

1. Wire lines are taboo. A flat rule is as follows: No wire lines may be used, period.
2. A line entangled in a power line or any electric line is automatically out of the contest. Furthermore, no attempt should be made to retrieve the kite. (This presupposes that the contest people have been stupid enough to set the contest in an area in which there are power lines.)
3. The contest should be held in an area free of roads or public highways which contestants have to run across. This may seem like an obvious no-no, but there are many such contest sites and more to come as more roads are being built.

The Field:

The field should be limed on the day of the event; otherwise overnight wind or rain will wash it out.

Depending upon the wind conditions, set three lines (white lime) at right angles to the direction of the wind. These consist of:

1. Boundary line, back of which starters may not run in working their lines into the air.
2. Start and finish line, 100 feet from the boundary line in the direction toward which the wind is blowing, on which line the flier will stand at the start of the event and to which he must return for the judging.
3. Helper's line: 50 to 100 feet from the starting line on which the helper holds the kite and projects it into the air at the start of the event.

Measuring the Flight Line:

Kite lines must be measured in advance. This is only if line length is critical in the contest. In free flight or highest distance, obviously measurements are a waste of valuable time.

In addition to the categories listed in the NYC festival, here are some more suggestions for contests:

Kite Fight: Contestants are given a time period in which to bring down an opponent's kite. Under no circumstances may cutting string or razor blades be allowed. There will always be a wise-guy kite flier who shows up with a killer kite, with razor blades studded in the frame. Throw him out fast and get the cops to keep him out of the area. He is a menace; there is usually a statute on the local books that

The gigantic tetrahedron was flown by Carl Jewell of Baltimore with a team of assistants, and it took grand prize at the 1972 Maryland Kite Festival. (*Anneke Davis*)

Judging for craftsmanship at the Maryland Kite Festival. (*Anneke Davis*)

says he can't make a public nuisance of himself. Or break his kite. Show no mercy or he will steal the show, not to mention that he will frighten most of the kids out of competition.

The Maryland Kite Society runs many contests throughout the year. One of the highlights of its contesting schedule is a real jousting tournament. This type of tournament has its own vivid rules, and instead of knives or cutting strings, it uses red lipsticks to mark the points where contestants hit each other.

Here are the rules for this contest:

Elements of the Tournament:
1. A kite chosen and furnished by the contestant.
2. A contest regulation flying line, #8 pound cotton, issued by the Scorekeeper and armed with 18 inches of lipstick by the contestant.
3. The field of honor, a 50-foot chalked competition circle in which the contestants must remain during the duel.
4. A jousting referee, a starter, a field judge, a scorekeeper.

Procedure for Contestants:
1. Report to the Scorekeeper to get time and opponent assignment. There is a limited number of times available, so it is first-come-first-served.
2. Report to the Starter at least 10 minutes before you are scheduled for combat. Your kite should be properly adjusted and tested and your own line detached at the towing point when you report.
3. Get your contest line from the Starter and attach it to the bridle of your kite.
4. Arm your kite with the "kiss of death," 18 inches of lipstick, bridle line.
5. The Referee will call you to the center of the ring and explain the rules. Shake hands, pace off 10 paces, and prepare to launch your kite.
6. On signal from the Referee you will launch your kite. (You may use your Second or a Field Judge to help you.) Raise it to fighting height, at least 50 feet of line out. When both kites are airborne and ready, the Referee will signal the beginning of the Match. The Match will run 10 minutes, at which time the Field Judge will signal the end of the Match. No scores will count after the final whistle sounds.

Scoring:
Contestants will be given points on the following basis:
Touch (lipstick marks on opponent's line) . . . . two points
Foul . . . . minus one point

Fouls:
1. Engaging your opponent before the starting signal or after the final whistle
2. Tripping or shoving your opponent
3. Touching the ground outside the field of honor with any part of your body or your kite

Tony ("The Kiteman") Ziegler is a living example of the wonderful people involved in this non-professional, nonpaid sport. A sort of Pied Piper of kites, Tony has turned his backyard in Monroe, Michigan, into a kiter's paradise, giving instructions in kite making as well as flying. He also demonstrates dropnik techniques (see Chapter 7) with a parachutist almost as fearless as Bob Ingraham's "Fearless Fosdick."

4. Profanity
5. Unsportsmanlike conduct on the field

Disqualifying Behavior:
1. Failure to launch your kite within a reasonable time
2. Failure to relaunch your kite *without assistance* within the count of 20 if it grounds during the Match
3. Failure to report on time for assigned combat

In case of disqualification of a flier, his opponent is decreed victor by default, except that both may be disqualified if neither kite flies. At the discretion of the Referee, in case of unfavorable wind, the Match may be postponed with no fault.

Tallying the Score:
At the final whistle, contestants will ground their kites. The Scorekeeper will count Touches, discount Fouls, and declare a Winner. The contestants will disconnect and rewind their lines, to be kept in case of challenge for a statute of limitations in such cases of not less than 24 hours.

One of the continuing controversies in the kite field is the matter of the judge. What is his role? Should he be a participant as well as judge?

The Maryland Kite Society scoffs at the idea that judges can't compete. Of course they can; otherwise they wouldn't be judges, says one distinguished judge. Kite fliers are fliers first and judges second. One factor keeps their passions from overruling their judgment: judges may not score their own kites.

In the 1973 "Go Fly a Kite Contest" in Central Park in New York, one judge and one timekeeper competed against the general field. Neither one scored. As a judge myself in this contest I maintained a judicial calm; first, by restraining myself from joining the contests; second, by voting for everyone other than the other judges or park employees and officials who were foolhardy enough to enter the contest in the face of my incorruptibility as a judge.

AKA handles the problem in the usual Executive Director Bob Ingraham subtle manner: no contests.

A contest especially for children should have the following elements:

1. Judges drawn from the ranks of schoolteachers, city government and local sports notables.
2. A weather expert who can determine in advance the best (windiest) period favorable for a kite contest.
3. Sponsorship by local merchants and business leaders.
4. Nothing fancy or difficult for kids, please. An altitude contest is simplest to operate.
5. The contestants should be divided into the following age groups:
    6–8 years of age
    9–12 years of age
    13–14 years of age
    Parents of contestants

Team flights (if huge kites are used). A team consists of two or more members. In all categories, the children get help.

Bermuda's "Kite King," Vincent Tuzo, proudly exhibits his battered but still airworthy round kite, which set two world records for endurance. He set a world record of 49 hours 40 minutes in 1972, and then eclipsed his own record by flying the kite continuously for another 61 hours, 21 minutes in May, 1973. (*Bermuda News Bureau*)

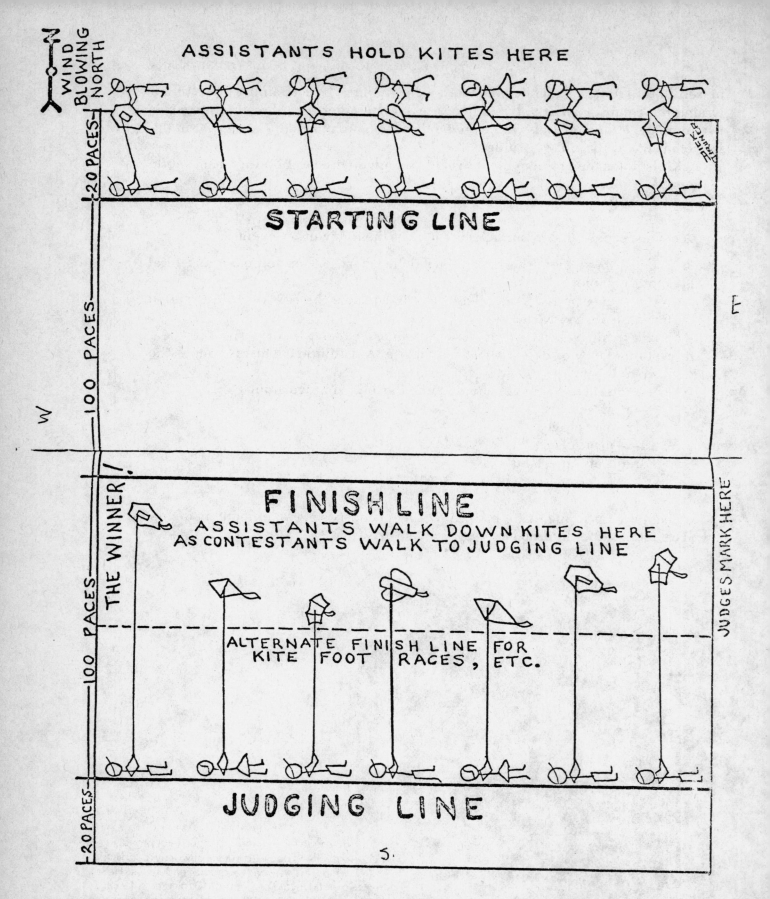

ASSISTANTS HOLD KITES HERE

WIND BLOWING NORTH

20 PACES

STARTING LINE

100 PACES

W

E

THE WINNER!

FINISH LINE
ASSISTANTS WALK DOWN KITES HERE
AS CONTESTANTS WALK TO JUDGING LINE

JUDGES MARK HERE

100 PACES

ALTERNATE FINISH LINE FOR
KITE FOOT RACES, ETC.

20 PACES

JUDGING LINE

S.

The simplified contest field, a blueprint for school yards, fields or (for certain kite festivals) shopping centers. It can be expanded or constricted to a shoreline, as in front of the Sheraton Sandcastle, in Sarasota, Florida, where there is a kite-flying contest every year on Benjamin Franklin's birthday.

A. The contest should be of no more than 5 minutes of air time in each category. Do not allow contestants to take time out to have a solo flight of their own fancy. It'll clutter up the succeeding groups of contestants. In other words, the sky should be clear of all kites at the beginning of each contest. Judges should be firm in clearing the sky of kites.

B. Each contestant may use a "lead-out man," that is, a helper who can lead the kite out 50 feet for the flier.

C. Establish a starting line at the end of the field (chalk line will do) so that the contestant can run into the wind.

D. On a signal from the starter (who may also be a judge), the helper tosses the kite into the air against, not into, the wind. Or if no helper is involved, set up a 50-foot launching pad.

E. Contestant runs into the wind, letting out line up to the limit of his spool, which should be no more than 200 feet. Fishing rod and reel may be used to launch the kite, or any hand-over-hand reel.

F. Contestant's line must be fully out when he crosses the finish line. Do not allow a foot race to develop. He can walk or run but must not, *repeat, must not,* cross the finish line until his entire 200 feet of line is let out.

G. Only then do the judges look for the kite which is highest. Tag the contestant immediately for altitude. However, he must now bring the kite in gracefully, right up to his hand without his kite touching the ground at any time.

H. Do not allow more than 25 contestants at one time. Run a number of heats, if necessary, but do not clutter up the field with too many contestants.

After the official contests you may have a free-for-all, and everyone may fly to his or her heart's content. But during the course of the tourney, you must maintain tight control. Your judges and officials should police the area at all times to check wild fliers out of the area.

Do not mark the area off with string lines or fences. Use chalk or white lime markings. Otherwise, the fliers will be stumbling into lines or fences.

The accompanying diagram of a contest field may be simplified so that only single fliers participate. The trend now is for the single flier who must get the kite up on his own power, without a helper.

In order to keep the contest in some semblance of sanity, it is recommended that a kite hospital be set up in one corner of the field so that injured or busted kites can be readily repaired. This does not relieve participants from bringing extra spars and lines with them. There is no excuse for running out of sticks or string when engaged in a contest.

The "kite doctor" is usually the person or persons who run the local toy store and know a bit about this type of repair. Usually the repair work can be done with some tape of one kind or another.

Be sure to establish a rain date—usually the following week, same time and same place.

12 KITES, THE LAW AND SAFETY FIRST

December 8, 1965, *The New York Times* ran the following story:

> Will Yolen, a prominent kite flier, appeared in Criminal Court yesterday, accused of violating the air space over Central Park with an eight-foot-long "Vote for Lindsay" sign that floated from one of his kites.
>
> The blue-eyed, ruddy-faced, gray-haired Mr. Yolen, 57 years old, of 50 Sutton Place South, is founder and president of the International Kitefliers Association. He is a publicity man, who also wears the rosette of the Adventurers Club in his lapel [and the Explorers and Players Club ties].
>
> Last Nov. 2—the day he received a summons for displaying a banner for political purposes in a city park—was, he recalled outside the courtroom yesterday, "beautiful kite flying weather."
>
> The New York Civil Liberties Union is defending Mr. Yolen on the grounds that his constitutional freedom of expression is being abridged. Yesterday its lawyer filed a brief with Judge James L. Watson, who reserved decision.
>
> Mr. Yolen said only two words. The judge wanted to know if he used a spinner reel on the fishing rod that held the line and that held the kite.
>
> "Regulation reel," said Mr. Yolen.

This was the beginning of a fight for freedom for kite fliers which earned the author the title of "Peter Zenger of Kite Fliers."

Judge Watson ruled for the defense and thus opened all the parks in New York.

Now white-haired, no longer ruddy-faced though still blue-eyed, your author has helped other communities develop sensible and legal kite-flying areas. He is now in position to advise other kite fliers how to fly kites within the law and with safety to participants as well as the people watching.

It is foolish to argue that kite fliers should have access to any flying area they wish. It is no more logical than crying "Fire" in a crowded theater when no such fire exists, just for kicks. Therefore, it is no use trying to get legislation to fly kites in and near airports, or near power lines, just because it is an inherent right of fools to kill themselves.

Members of the cast of the Broadway show "Hair" mingle peacefully with New York City's finest after Will Yolen led the fight to repeal the ban on kite flying in Central Park.

If you have legislation problems in your area, herewith is reprinted a letter used by the Maryland Society to get its point across to the city fathers. This letter could well be adapted to your region:

OPEN LETTER to
City Council of Baltimore
City Hall
Baltimore, Maryland 21201

Dear Honorable Councilmen:

The Maryland Kite Society wishes to go on record in support of repealing the city ordinance against kite flying in a city street or alley.

Where kite flying is concerned, is it fair for the law to penalize a person who flies a kite over a yard while standing in the street, yet permit another person, advantaged with a yard of his own, to fly a kite over the *street* while standing on his own property? Isn't it his constitutional right to do so? We would suggest that the law as it stands threatens a breach of rights, and takes an unnecessary plunge into the deep and muddy waters of legal and moral rhetoric that could keep a City Council going for days.

The issue, really, is safety. We are all for safety, but there is no point in levying a $5 fine for risking a broken neck. A broken neck is bad enough.

We feel that such laws are unnecessary, however, and that voluntary efforts such as ours can do more for safety in recreation than obscure, repressive laws not balanced against the positive values we emphasize in our program. Kite flying, with its unique benefits, is more to be acclaimed and properly guided than merely to be censured for its hazards.

We believe that the good of kite flying far outweighs the bad. Kites are only superficially trivial. They have a long and honorable history in science, war and legend. They are a craft project, a study tool, an aesthetic experience to families, groups, individualists, young and old. They continue to hold out an aerodynamic challenge to innovators, while remaining always a true form of re-creation, as tensions blow away with the wind.

     With these truths in mind, the Maryland Kite Society takes justifiable satisfaction in encouraging everyone to Go Fly A Kite!

Respectfully yours,
Valerie Govig
(Mrs. Melvin E. Govig)
Executive Secretary
MARYLAND KITE SOCIETY

COPIES TO:
City Council of Baltimore
Editor, morning *Sun*
Editor, *Baltimore News-American*
Editor, *Windy Notice*, publication of the Maryland Kite Society
President-Editor, International Kitefliers Association

    The *Washington Star*'s Jim Fiebig commented as follows when kite flying left Washington for Maryland: "Finally progress is being made . . . dope pushers, hold-up men, rapists and murderers . . . abound . . . but those damned kite fliers have been run out of town." This was a comment on the fact that Washington kite fliers went to Maryland when their contest was banned at the Washington Monument.

    Later in Washington, D.C., the kite community, under the leadership of Paul Garber, took the anti-kite legislation off the books in certain areas. The late John Kennedy having been an ardent kite flier may have helped the situation somewhat.

A park policeman helps demonstrators get their kites airborne on the Washington Monument grounds as thousands turn out in the spring of 1970 after the repeal of a nineteenth-century anti-kite law. Police handed out 2,500 kites to promote the "Summer in the Parks" program. A few weeks earlier, several kite fliers had been jailed for cluttering up the capital skies. (*Wide World Photos*)

Former Secretary of the Interior Walter Hickel, the late President John Kennedy and New Jersey Congressman Frank Thompson, Jr., set up legislation to help kite flying in Washington. Mr. Thompson's bill H.R. 7643, which finally overturned D.C. statutes, reads as follows:

> A BILL: To repeal Section 4 of The Act of July 29, 1892, relating to the prohibition against kites, balloons or parachutes in the District of Columbia.
> Be it enacted by the Senate and House of Representatives of the United States of America in Congress assembled, that Section 4 of the Act entitled "An Act for the Preservation of the Public Peace and the Protection of Property Within the District of Columbia," approved July 29, 1892 (D.C. Code, Sec. 22-1117), is hereby repealed.

Paul Dickson, a writer of perception, in the magazine *Washington Monthly* noted that kite flying has long been a humble but clear symbol of individual freedom; suppressing it for whatever reason is a signal of repression. Thus, he states, there is a body of politics of the kite.

For example, in Japan, "where kiting is both an art and a national pastime, kites have been banned twice: once during the pre-World War II buildup so that people would keep their minds on their work and then again at the end of the war by the American occupation forces because kites were judged to symbolize Japanese nationalism."

Kites have been banned in ancient China for economic and agricultural reasons because kite flying and seed sowing came at the same time in the spring. The Chinese emperor banned kite flying because the fliers ran over the newly sown fields and devastated them. The penalty for this kite flying was death. Some people at beaches who dodge heavy kite traffic do not believe the emperor was overly cruel.

Recently, kite flying has been banned again in China because it is a symbol of the counter-revolutionary movement.

Undoubtedly the first example of a civil rights demonstration, this group of Japanese kite fliers in ancient times proclaim their rights to fly kites, despite laws that invoke the death penalty for destroying newly sown rice paddies during their spring kite-flying madness.

Early in the nineteenth century in France (1836), a wave of kite contests created such rioting that the king banned them—contests, not kites. The Revolution swept the ban away but kite-hating Napoleon proscribed kites in the army.

In England there is still a ban on kites flying more than 200 feet high.

In San Francisco, Howard Levy wanted to follow the law carefully. Therefore, he applied for permission to fly a kite, as provided by the city code. An officer of the court called on him and questioned him as to motives. Permission still has not been granted because of the red tape involved. Mr. Levy has found other ways to occupy his time. Thus are great kite fliers lost to the world.

The nearest thing to a possible airplane-kite collision on record took place at the Honolulu Airport in 1962 when a United Airlines pilot spotted a "hazard to air navigation" on his screen and reported it to the control tower and zoomed off for another landing try. The tower spotted Mr. Pablo Cannote, 67, calmly flying a kite at 4,000 feet over the airport. He and kite were hauled in by police and told to "go fly a kite" but elsewhere than the airport. Pablo went away quietly.

Rarer still is a seagoing or undersea kite hazard. Nevertheless, there is a record of a kite snagging a submarine. The submarine *Raton*, returning from a weekend cruise to its San Francisco base, found a kite snagged on its periscope. The crew kept the kite as a trophy.

Intrepid author, Will Yolen, who otherwise preaches law and order, defies the "No Kite Flying" sign at the Buenos Aires Airport. This is the only known billboard in the world banning kite flying. (*Argentina News Bureau*).

Kite messages are as much at fault as are the kites themselves, and here is an example: A Detroit man was arrested for flying kites decorated with dirty words. A high court vindicated him on the grounds of constitutional freedom, according to Tom Tiede, columnist for the Newspaper Enterprise Association.

Kite flying is a crime in Newark, New Jersey, with a $500 fine or 90 days in jail still on the books.

Competitions for highest fliers, best decorated, loudest hummer and kite fights were banned in North East Malaya only recently because they engendered ill feeling. This ill feeling might lead to mayhem, it is explained, especially in the town of Kota Bharu, notorious for its short-tempered kite fliers whenever the heavy winds blow in the spring.

In Amman, Jordan, the sight of kites in the area is an indication that the fighting has ceased between the regular army and the Arab guerrillas or the watchful Israeli border troops.

SAFETY

The subject of kite safety is approached warily by most manufacturers and kite merchants. The occasional kite flier injured by violating simple rules makes kite headlines. And well he should. There is no excuse for anyone to get hurt flying kites. Statistics show about one person killed per year, few hurt. No kiter should be killed or hurt.

Adding to these statistics are the kite riders, drawing national attention with the kite glider death of Robert Kennedy of California, who died entangled in the shroud lines of his parachute in front of the Transpo '72 site in Washington, D.C. The death was spectacular enough, but as luck would have it, Senator Proxmire condemned the exhibition's alleged misuse of $5,000,000 and thus drew even more attention to the cruel death.

Many companies today have taken an interest in kite-flying self-defense, especially the utilities, which are very much involved in overhead wires. One of the leaders in espousing safety rules for kite fliers is the Pennsylvania Electric Association, which in cooperation with kite organizations has developed a code which should be helpful to all.

Herewith is a safety code acceptable to the major kite-flying organizations.

KITE FLYING SAFETY CODE

1. Do not fly in the rain.
2. Observe local flying rules posted by the parks department.
3. Do not fly across roads.
4. Do not fly near or across power lines, nor try to retrieve kites from same.
5. Do not fly live fireworks other than sparklers.
6. Do not fly on crowded beaches.
7. Do not use glazed string or razor-blade-studded kites.
8. Do not fly too close to airports or during low visibility.
9. Do not fly kites that have metal in the frame or tail.
10. Do wear gloves when flying kites that are more than five feet wide.

Appendices

I ORGANIZATIONS

Kite organizations in the United States are, with the exception of the AKA and the Maryland Kite Society, not very well organized. Most of them consist of friends who just like to go out and fly some kites around and make out they're getting fresh air.

Most of them seem to have taken their cue from the now defunct ABCD Kite Flying Club of Terryville, Connecticut, near my hometown of Waterbury, founded in 1887 by a jolly bunch of cutups whose aim in performance of their recondite art was to get higher than the kites they flew.

The chief item in their formidable kite armament was a vehicle 16 feet tall and 12 feet wide, made of cloth and with a tail 104 feet long. The kite weighed 50 pounds. The frame was of spruce fastened with iron bolts.

"A good number of unrepentant Terryville sinners looking above in unprepared astonishment, entertained the horrible suspicion for an instant that the avenging angel was sliding down into the village and would blow his horn in about a minute as it flew above the steeple of the Congregational church," *Yankee* magazine stated soberly in reporting on it.

The kite was named "Sky-Scraper" long before the high-rise buildings were invented. Sky-Scraper was engaged in some winsome local capers, including being dragged through the swamp surrounding that little factory town at that time. The club scared the local gentry by flying a lighted lamp one dismal night, with the result that the church got a lot of converts. The club sent up a pet animal on one flight, thus anticipating the Russian Sputnik that carried an animal on the first space flight. Furthermore, still using Sky-Scraper as the pulling force, the ABCD boys of blessed memory also pulled a wagon. In the Bristol *Herald* Burton Andrus claims that only one person was actually in the wagon, though the legendary feat was at the time reported much more dramatically than that (see illustration on page 63).

Even earlier than the ABCD Club, there was a gentlemen's kite club in Philadelphia, according to William J. Rhees, once chief clerk of the Smithsonian Institution. The name Franklin Kite Club was adopted and the following description and activities of the club were inscribed in the organization records:

In 1835–36 several gentlemen formed a society with the name of "The Franklin Kite Club" for the purpose of making electrical experiments. For a considerable time they met once a week at the City Hospital grounds (in Philadelphia) and flew their kites. These were generally square in shape, made of muslin or silk, stretched over a framework of cane reeds, varying in size from 6 feet upward, some being 20 feet square. For flying the kites, annealed copper wire was used, wound upon a heavy reel 2 or 3 feet in diameter, insulated by being placed on glass supports. When one kite was up sometimes a number of others would be sent up on the same string. The reel being inside the fence the wire from the kite crossed over the road. Upon one occasion as a cartman passed, gazing at the kite he stopped directly under the wire and was told to catch hold of it and see how hard it pulled. In order to reach it he stood up on his cart, putting one foot on the horse's back. When he touched the wire the shock went through him, as also the horse, causing the latter to jump and the man to turn a somersault, much to the amusement of the lookers on.

The club used mostly decorative kites imported from China. In cold weather sleds were drawn by kites.

Dan Beard believed in kite clubs for the Boy Scouts. In his book *The American Boys' Handy Book*, Uncle Dan posited that in the kite field, boys (not girls) had many opportunities for originality and ingenuity almost unbounded. "If some enthusiastic, energetic boy will take the initiatory steps, kite clubs might be formed throughout the country with appropriate names, rules and regulations, which, during the kite season, would have their meets and tournaments, and award prizes to the steadiest stander, the highest flyer and the most original and unique design besides the prizes awarded at the jousts of the war kites." This is a pretty good description of what a contest is all about, as well as a description of how to get an organization started.

Uncle Dan should know. He founded two organizations, "The Sons of Daniel Boone" and "The Boy Pioneers," both of which later were absorbed into the Boy Scouts of America.

Footnote to history: The boys at one time issued an Eagle award for kite making. This award has been discontinued for lack of entries. And *The American Boys' Handy Book* by the late Dan C. Beard is today printed in Japan for distribution in the United States.

The greatest of the organizations today is, of course, the American Kitefliers Association, headquarters of which is in Silver City, New Mexico, and in the heart of its founder and executive director, Robert Ingraham. A retired newspaper columnist and entrepreneur of lost causes, Ingraham's devotion to kite flying has created the one unifying force in this emerging sport on a national basis. The quarterly publication *Kite Tales*, the entire corpus of contemporary kite lore, is delightful reading and comes with a membership in AKA. The dues are $4.00; write P.O. Box 1511, Silver City, N.M. 88061. Only adults are recruited. Children get in the way of AKA fliers.

AKA's policy is simply stated as an "organization of kitefliers who are interested in kite design, building and flying in the interest of sport, recreation and scientific study of aerodynamics." There is no more dedicated membership, nationally and internationally. I am a life member of this club, the first, if not the only one. My daughter, Jane Yolen, author of *World on a String*, is also a member.

The Maryland Kite Society has a periodical, issued on a whimsical schedule, called *The Windy Notice*, edited by Valerie Govig, who is also the society's executive secretary emeritus. Membership costs $1.00 and includes *The Windy Notice*. I am also a life member of this organization, which puts on some of the great contests in its area. Address of the society is 7106 Campfield Road, Baltimore, Md. 21207.

The International Kitefliers Association, of which I am founder and president and total angel and sole support, is not incorporated, no dues, no meeting. From time to time we sponsor kite contests and certify records. Membership cards are issued at world headquarters, 321 East 48th Street, New York, N.Y. 10017, if stamped, self-addressed envelope is sent. Motto of IKA is "Worldwide Friendship Through Kite Flying."

Free memberships may be had from other clubs such as the ones who are in retail business or manufacturers.

Go Fly a Kite store, 1434 Third Avenue, New York, N.Y., 10028, retails kites from all over the world and has shaped up a club called Go Fly a Kite Assocation, which issues cards on request. The association is now run by Andrea Bahadur, widow of the kitemaster Surenda Bahadur.

The association legend reads, "Members have the privilege of joining and cooperating with other members in promoting kite flying as a clean healthy outdoor activity and improving kite-flying techniques."

One of the more enterprising promoters of kites is David M. Checkley, who runs the Kite Factory at 678 West Prospect, Seattle, Washington 98119. Members of Mr. Checkley's club get together once a year under his sponsorship and charter a plane to take them to the more exotic kite-flying bashes in the Far East. Last year the organization went to kite festivals in Bangkok, Thailand; Taipei, Taiwan; Hammamatsu and Tokyo, Japan.

Checkley, himself, started his career in kite flying in Connecticut, from which he commuted to New York City to his job in an architecture office. Now retired, he manufactures some and licenses other kites on which he makes improvements based on his architectural skills.

One of the most unusual kite organizations is the Nipon No Tako Kai (Japanese Kite Association), which was founded in 1969. Founder and historian of the JKA is the University of Denver Professor Tsutomu Hiroi, who has written the definitive book on Japanese kites. JKA has members all over Japan. I am the sole American member so far through the courtesy of the kite-flying prof.

Twice a year the association publishes a pamphlet of activities, which consist of flying meets and exchange of information on various kinds of kites. Also they have an annual exhibition of kites and kite making as well as flying, at which time they receive donations with which they purchase kites to give to children.

Dr. Hiroi is on leave from Tokyo Gakugai (Teachers) University, where he teaches art, with emphasis on kites, because, he says, "I hope my students will teach the art of kite making and flying in the classrooms."

The address of the Nipon No Tako Nokai is Taimaiken 103, 1-12-1 Nihonbash, Chuo-Ku, Tokyo, Japan. The association does not have membership cards, and membership requests have to be submitted to the association.

In India, the leading organization is the Kite Flying Association of India, 3126 Lal Darwaza, Bazar Sita Ram, Delhi 6, India.

In France what organization there is is handled by Frank Bauer at Bureau: 24, Place Malesherbes, Paris 17 E, France.

One of the leaders in kite flying in England is Mr. G. H. Pilch, 54 Broomhill Road, Hucknall, Nottinghamshire, England. Somewhat new to kite-flying organizations himself, nevertheless, between his nephews and nieces and neighbor kids, he has managed to put together a group of kite fliers who are always ready to fly. They especially welcome foreign friends. Assistant to Mr. Pilch is his grandson, Steven Wells, whose life-long ambition is to set a new world record of sustained flight.

II CONTESTS AND FESTIVALS

Because of the tremendous revival of regional kite flying, it's almost impossible to keep track of many of the local events. However, you can rest assured that there is a kite event of one kind or another always going on in your area. Although some of the leading events held in the past will be listed herein, it's best that you check in with your local parks and recreation department, chamber of commerce or police department—and even your weather department. Certainly for starters you should check your local parks department. At one time the Recreation League of America sponsored regional festivals and contests but gave it up recently because the main thrust of its operations is in a different if as worthwhile direction.

This list is alphabetical by state, with extracontinental events being listed alphabetically by country.

Arizona

Flagstaff, Buffalo Park, April. See Superintendent of Parks.
Phoenix. A rally of kite fliers in Encanto Park about March 16.

California

Burbank. Early March contest; afternoon at Stough Park. Prizes.
Long Beach. City of Long Beach Recreation Department, Betty Brown and Nancy Jean Kleinhammer, April. Held annually for a half century.
Los Angeles. Drinking and Fighting Club. Although there have only been seven contests, this crazy club insists this is the 23rd annual. James Furlong, coordinator and confuser.
Montecito. Beautiful, colorful "The Day of the Kite," Sunday in middle May, sponsored by Art Affiliates, Tecelotes Book Shop.
Pasadena. March late flyoffs with preliminaries all month of March.
Sacramento. March 18–23 at all playgrounds.

San Diego. Ocean Beach Kite Festival. Early weekend in March. Parade and judging. Write Community of Ocean Beach or Dan McKinnon, Station WSON.
San Francisco. Late weekend in March, Fly A Kite Day. April, middle weekend in Marina Park, Home Made Kites contest. Phone (415) 826-0415 for details.
San Jose. Late February and early March District Meets. Call (408) 279-0526 and mention my name.
San Luis Obispo. All-day meet middle of March at Quintana School, sponsored by Jaycees. If you're a Jaycee, you've got it made.
Santa Ana. Early March flyoff at Centennial Park. Park Department will fill you in.
Sea Ranch. Late March. Kite fliers and watchers annual. Write Recreation Department.
Walnut Creek. Write to Betty F. Bernstein. 1445 Civic Drive, 94596.

Connecticut

Fairfield. P.A.L., Jennings Beach, in spring. Contact Richard Osborn.
New Britain. Al Squillacote, 199 Robindale Drive, 06053. Beautiful local festival by the ubiquitous Al.
Norwalk. Kendall School, Willow Street., Mrs. Merlyn Rogers.

Delaware

Lewes. Delaware Kite Festival, tournament of kite-flying skills, in spring. Write Chamber of Commerce.

District of Columbia

Smithsonian Institution, Washington Monument, early April.

Florida

Jacksonville. Write to the mayor. This contest has been held for more than forty years.

Miami. Phi Delta Theta Fraternity, University of Miami during winter months.

Sandcastle, Lido Beach, Sarasota. Weekend closest to January 17, Ben Franklin's birthday. Contact Harry Galloway, General Manager. It's the best annual of its kind. World record champs seek to set new records. Winds fair, also mild competition for youngest and oldest.

Idaho

Idaho Falls. April 6–7, Freeman Park Fly-In. Write Chamber of Commerce.

Sac City. Open to school children only.

Kansas

Wichita. Thomas Irving, Chairman, and Sam Howell, and say hello for me.

Kentucky

Louisville. Tom DeMuth, manager of the popular station WAVE, sponsored a kite contest which brought all the kids in two separate parks and ended in a tremendous snowfall. Now DeMuth is planning to hold the contest in the middle of summer, not early spring.

Maryland

Baltimore. Maryland Kite Society, Valerie Govig, Ex. Sec., 7106 Campfield Road. One of the oldest and best organized.

College Park. March 18, Kappa Alpha Theta Kiteflying Contest, Fraternity Row.

Joppatowne. Kite festival April 8. Write Maryland Kite Society.

Massachusetts

Boston. The Great Boston Kite Festival is a middle-of-May carnival of joy and unrestricted fun, including hang kiting. Coordinated in the past by Marjorie Waters and Gill Fishman, it is run for simple kite fliers, hang kiters and other strange and wonderful people who just like to fly kites without savage competition. Prizes are given for "lovingest kite," "fanciest kite," "biggest kite flown by the smallest person," "most whimsical kite," and other such mystical categories. One prize is for the kite "which looks most like the person flying it." Kites are given away for one tenth the retail cost, Cokes and beer are practically free, and it's all done to acquaint the public with the pollution fight led by The Committee for the Better Use of Air, 23 Arrow Street, Cambridge, Massachusetts 02138. Other heroes of this festival are Lionel Spiro, Fenton Hollander, Dr. Alvin Kahn, Michael Sands and many, many other beautiful people.

Hingham. Springtime—on and off. Contact the librarian at the Hingham Public Library, 66 Leavitt Street.

Michigan

Detroit. University of Detroit. Architectural Dept. Write to Dean.

Monroe. Tony The Kite Man Ziegler, 966 Adam Street, one of the best kite shows. Tony is superb showman and will put on a show anytime you ask him.

Missouri

Columbia. Spring event. Write the Chamber of Commerce.

Kansas City. Kite Carnival, Cub Scouts, about latter March. Elmer A. Stegner.

New Jersey

Hackensack. A. Alan Leveen, V.P., International Kitefliers Association, Suite 511, 241 Main Street, Hackensack, N.J. Runs a contest when the fancy strikes him.

New York

Brooklyn, Abraham and Straus department store in Brooklyn has held an annual contest for kite builders. Write to the promotion department.

Manhattan. Seamen's Institute of N.Y., 15 State Street, New York, N.Y. 10004, Dorothy Sheldon. Also the Parks Department gives good listings. Every weekend in Sheep Meadow during spring, summer and fall. Sam Samuels of Parks Department will give information on kite flights in other boroughs. 830 Fifth Avenue, New York, N.Y.

Rochester. Longmeadow. Write Dean of Monroe Community College.

Somers. Primrose Grammar School, Mrs. Mary Eagan, in spring.

Southampton. Halsey Neck Lane, Publisher Dan Rattner, Coordinator.

Ohio

Middletown. Recreation Department, in spring.

Toledo. MacDonald Stores sponsor one but dates are vague.

Oregon

Grambs Pass. March 30, annual, at high school baseball field.

Rockaway. First weekend in May. Design competition featured on beach.

Rhode Island

Providence. Radio Station WICE, Crown Hotel, annual, in spring.

Texas

Austin. Annual festival in the spring is run by the Exchange Club in cooperation with the Parks and Recreation Department. This is one of the oldest and should be about the 50th annual.

Dallas. Olla Podrida Shopping Center, April 14.

Washington

Bellingham. April through September. Monthly flyoff by Fairhaven Kite Co., 1200 Harris Street. May 19, Hovander Farm Park festival and contest.

Port Townsend. A Saturday around the middle of August at Fort Worden. Two-day event: original kite design and noncompetitive flyoff. Write mayor.

Seattle. The Kite Factory, David Checkley, sponsor. Any date will do. Checkley also takes parties to Far East. Or write Seattle Center for early May flyoffs in Golden Gardens Park. Early August contests in Volunteer Park. Seattle takes its kiting seriously.

Spokane. Early April, annual, Franklin Park. Call Recreation Department.

Wisconsin

Milwaukee. Washington Park Boat House, Dir. Frank Mots, 2977 Frederick Avenue. Kite designer Mots and lovely wife put this on. Mots gives great show.

EXTRACONTINENTAL EVENTS

Barbados

One of the most colorful of the island contests was established in Barbados in 1960 by the late kite pioneer Frank Weisgerber. This contest is now sponsored by the local newspaper, *The Advocate*. A feature of the contest is a kite made up of over 500 pieces of newspaper clippings. Sometime in the spring.

Bermuda

Marathon kite festival, town of Somerset or St. George. A feature of this event on Easter Sunday is the release of kites by school kids and prayers that ascend with the kites.

Canada

Toronto. Canadian Exhibition Kite Festival. This one is discontinued but survives in a different form. Write to Canadian Chamber of Commerce.

Victoria, British Columbia. Kite Festival Alma Mater Society, University of Victoria, Student Union Building, Bert Weiss, coordinator.

Hawaii

Kapiolani Park, Honolulu. Sponsored by Honolulu radio station KGMB and local business. Helicopter used to judge highest kite. Around early March. Prizes for fiercest, most beautiful, smallest, largest.

Japan

Shizuoka. Early May. Mr. Tatsuzaburo Kato may be reached via Japanese Consulate in N.Y.C.

Tokyo. Saitama Spring Kite Festival, Boys' Day, Prof. Hiroi, Tokyo University, use my name.

Taiwan

Taipei. Write to T. C. Ting, Chinese Youth Association, for information about this organization's springtime flights.

Thailand

Bangkok. Pramane Grounds, daily 4 to 6 P.M., except Saturday and Sunday, when the marketplace takes over. Near Grand Palace. Stop in when in neighborhood, everyone welcome, use my name.

III RECORDS

Keeping records on kite performances, either in height or the number on one string, is a hopeless job. There is no central charthouse. Records are rarely certified because of the lack of a certifying agency. IKA has tried to keep some records, as has the more orderly AKA. There are local records, national records, as well as international records.

There are no unifying rules. By and large whimsy has replaced statistics.

Nevertheless there are some facts and figures that should be placed in this book, as moving targets rather than fixed positions. Records were made to be broken it is said; so let's break some.

One of the more controversial records is that of the number of kites on one line. The only strictly certified records are those of the Sandcastle, Lido Beach, Sarasota, Florida, flights of 50 kites on one line in January, 1972, and 57 in the same place in Ben Franklin's birthday week in 1973. No sooner had these records been certified by local officials and IKA, than in poured other fliers with claims of all kinds, led by William R. Bigge, of Montgomery County, Maryland, with a whopping 151 kites on a single line and five observers who signed an affidavit that they had witnessed this feat. Bigge's kites were 9-by-12-inch, light plastic, Scott-type sleds which fly in light winds or no winds. The Sandcastle kites were twice as big and pulled three times as hard.

The fact is that kites can be chained or set in tandem into infinity if you have enough line and kites of little or no weight or size. Without taking any credit away from Bigge, his flight can be duplicated by hundreds of fliers who have experimented with clusters and coteries of kites running into the hundreds and literally could be ganged into the thousands.

The first Sandcastle flight was a demonstration of unified, large, commercial kites, spaced 50 feet apart, and purposely stopped at 50 so that others could go on from there. Also, 57 went up next year and 57 were retrieved. Fifty-seven kites were all that were available.

Nevertheless, on January 17, 1974 (Ben Franklin's birthday) this author sent up 178 kites on one line at the same site, the Sandcastle in Sarasota, Florida. This flight was certified by a notary public as well as by the mayor of the city. Again Bill Bigge responded with a grand total of 261 kites, a magnificent feat and one that will surely stand in its category for as long as the earth turns, as far as I'm concerned. And yet . . . there is a yen to bust that record sometime soon.

Incidentally, neither mine nor Bigge's record has made *The Guinness Book of World Records* (although *Ripley's Believe It or Not* did recognize my flight). This despite the fact that kite record attempts are referred to me in the United States by the McWhirter brothers, editors of the fascinating collection.

Let Mr. Bigge's record stand. Let someone else challenge it. Let the IKA 178 kites stand separately as a landmark flight, a record of some kind as was the Babe Ruth record of home runs, 60 in one year, as against Roger Maris' 61 in a footnoted year.

Raising multiple kites by anchoring a huge kite first is the best method, according to modern experts. However, early experimenters in this art first sent up a fragile, sensitive, light kite to test the atmosphere at 200 to 300 feet before attaching the larger and sturdier kites, many of which would have to carry thermometers of considerable weight.

Thus they began by raising the smallest kites first, which carried a light line. The second, third and fourth, and so on, kites of greater strength were sent up on their own lines. These were kites with tails so that they had first to be laid out on the ground with an assistant's help. The second line was attached to the extremity of the first line, and the third kite was attached to the extremity of hand position of the second kite. This is not the same as placing 50 kites on one center line. In this method each line carries itself.

Charles Lohsen, 755 E. 18th Street, Paterson, N.J., claimed a record back in 1949, at the age of 75, of 108 on one string. He said, "The leader kite should be larger than the others that follow. Do not use tails on following kites. The kites should be about fifteen feet apart." The lead kite bridle is adjusted to high pitch so that it will easily spill the wind and keep climbing.

More important, if less dramatic, are the records of the longest stay in the air. In 1971, a record 37 hours 17 minutes was accepted by *Sports Illustrated* for a flight made at the Sandcastle in Sarasota, Florida. This flight was made by a team of James Adams, Hall Davidson, Jack Elias and, as captain, the author. *The Guinness Book of Records* expressed surprise that the record was of such short duration and suggested that a new record attempt should be made in Commonwealth Bay in Antarctica "where the winds blow for several weeks without intercession."

Walter Scott is reported to have sustained a kite in the air for 168 hours. Scott never documented it, but his word is so good it will be entered here. One hundred sixty-eight hours means a full week of flying in a moderate breeze. That such a breeze exists for that length of time is improbable. But let it stand.

How high is up?

Bob Ingraham, editor of *Kite Tales*, has a simple formula for measuring height: "If you have 5,000 feet of line out at a 60 degree angle, tell your friends it's at 3,000 feet."

The Weather Bureau claimed a record 23,826 feet on a train of ten kites in 1910; 8½ miles of fine steel wire led this load of kites.

Paul J. K. Donovan of the Paignton *News* of western England contributes some records from his country: a single kite flown 18,000 feet high by a Peter Powell who owns what is believed to be the largest kite in England, 37 feet tall and 30 feet across.

The United Press International checks in with a mystery flight that is a world record: Robert and John Settich played out 10½ miles of special polyester string in two and a half hours in Kansas City in May of 1973. Here is what the Settich brothers said about getting such distance: "Shun all diamond shapes; use box kites and reinforce them at the angles. Varnish the surfaces. Get the largest spools you can find so that you will tie as few knots as possible. Wear gloves and coat them with paraffin to cut friction. It takes two men to fly this distance: one flies, the other tends the line."

Record attempts are best made in moderate winds. The winds in March and April may be too strong. However, you can adjust for the wind by the type of kite you use. Avoid fancy bridles and tails, if possible. Tails are especially troublesome when putting up multiple kites on a single line.

Record size round kite: Wan-wan-Dako, a round kite constructed in 1936 in Naruto, Japan, was 20 feet in diameter, made of 3,100 sheets of light paper, each sheet measuring 16 × 20 inches. The assembled kite weighed 8½ tons. It took 200 townsmen to handle the lines in flight.

In 1969 students of a Gary, Indiana, high school sent up 19 stock kites on 54,457 feet of line which in 7 hours soared to a height of 35,531 feet, presumed to be a world altitude record.

Here is another offbeat record: Bernard Danis crossed Calais, France, to Dover, England, by kite towed by motorboat in 100 minutes. The channel is about 21 miles wide near Dover and unusually rough.

Harry Smith, a California mathematician, has run out a single flier to 8,700 yards—repeat yards.

The largest Eddy Kite on record was first sent aloft on August 21, 1897, in South Bethlehem, Pennsylvania. Its sticks were 25 feet long, 6 inches wide and 1½ inches thick. It was covered with 46 yards of cotton duck and held together by sash cord capable of holding 500 pounds of dead weight. About 1,200 feet of line was sent out on this first flight. A team of men held it firmly. The young boys were tested on it. In a light wind, the kite took the small boys off their feet. The pulling power was estimated at 250 pounds.

According to Guinness the record for solo kite flying is 22,500 feet by Phillip R. Kunz of the University of Wyoming, set in 1967 when I was visiting the Dallas Clinger ranch and trying to fly kites over the Grand Teton near Jackson Hole.

Guinness states that for manned flights, the record was set by Bill Moyes of Sidney, Australia, who descended to earth from a plane-towed kite from an altitude 8,610 feet over Amery, Wisconsin, on October 14, 1971. The greatest free flight descent from a land takeoff is 5,757 feet, set by Bill Bennett, also from Sydney, Australia, from Dante's Peak, 6.2 miles away to the floor of Death Valley, California, on February 24, 1972.

Keep your own records.

Harold Ridgeway, whose *Kite Making and Flying* is a hobbyist's must, suggests the following: Make your own record book. Any old notebook will do. Take a weather reading every day at the same time, 8:30 A.M. and 5:30 P.M. Make your comments alongside the time check as follows:

Date of flight
Base (where kite is flown)
Cloud formation
Wind—direction, speed
Flight—start, finish
Height attained
Kite (type—box, etc.)
Additional comment (e.g., behavior of kite, adjustments to line or tail)

And there you have a complete log.

IV WHO'S WHO

Kite fliers are all amateurs. There are no professionals. It is the least likely sport ever to become professional or commercial. Some sports philosophers believe that it is amateur all the way because the gamblers haven't discovered it. And it's hard to "fix" a kite contest, it being so visible and disorganized.

In all human endeavor a group steps out ahead of the rest to lead by daring example or inspiration or style. So it is, too, with kite flying. But kite-flying leaders, other than the historic ones, have not always been given full recognition. It is hoped that some of the great kite innovators will find a place here in our living Hall of Fame.

The people listed below* have contributed time and effort and love to keep this sport viable and full of fun. Some commercial people are listed because they have gone beyond the commercial aspect to the heart of the sport. Most of the people herein will correspond with other kite fliers, answer technical questions and, if in your neighborhood, even come out and fly with you.

To them we raise a special kite salute, an aspiring flag rising on a thermal in a moderate breeze on a cloudless sky.

Maj. Harold B. Alexander, The Citadel, Charleston, S.C. 29409. Develops exotic kite shapes and provides designs and descriptions of Oriental kites. Writes articles on kite construction methods, where to get materials, etc. Is member of Citadel faculty.

John Aymar, 120 Primo Dr. Beach, Ft. Myers, Fla. 33931, who flew kites with the late William Eddy, has done a lot of work with bow kites.

Andrea Bahadur is the widow of the great master Indian kite flier Surenda. She maintains the Go Fly A Kite Store in New York City which

Where no addresses are given, it is at the request of the subject.

he founded. She carries on his tradition of kite contests annually in New York.

Dinesh Bahadur, Come Fly A Kite Store, Ghirardelli Square, San Francisco, Calif., nephew of the late, great Surenda Bahadur.

Willis R. Battles, 560 Helberta Avenue, Redondo Beach, Calif. 90277. Dedicated to kites and kite devices. Has flown kites for years, mostly from roof of his apartment building. Has invented and marketed line traveler device called the "Astrozoomer," which goes up line and returns automatically and continually. He is a chemist.

A. A. Beach, 452 Locust Ave., Long Beach, Calif., 90812. Builds own kites, including 42-square-foot parafoil, the most difficult of all kite constructions. Flies 30-foot-span delta kites. Works with city recreation department in arranging annual kite fiesta there.

Maharajah of Bharatpur, Uttar-Pradesh, India, the prince of kite fliers of the Eastern World, who spent a honeymoon flying kites with his new bride.

Raymond Biehler, 1597 Ridge Road West, Rochester, N.Y. 14615. Industrial arts teacher in Rochester High School. Is designer and builder of the famed all-metal, demountable "Todd" kite.

William R. Bigge, 5131 Massachusetts Ave., Washington, D.C. 20016. This aerodynamics expert develops small kites and has evolved means to fly multiple kites on one line. He is an authority on aerodynamics.

Benn Blinn, 2879 Wickliffe Ave., Columbus, Ohio 43221. An international kite-flying champion.

Elissa Bludau, who more than ten years ago won a kite-flying contest against a field of boys in Somer, N.Y. Still flies against and with them.

James C. Bowers, 1505 N. Tejon, Colorado Springs, Colo. 80907. Designed and patented drilled blocks and dowels to build various-shaped kites including aircraft configurations, fighter planes, etc. Flies kites over football stadium at Air Force Academy during big games. Is real estate and insurance man.

Wyatt Brummitt (living in Florida for winter). Home address: 215 Westbrook Rd., Pittsford, N.Y. 14534. Authority on photographing kites. Has worked with Ray Biehler and Ed Grauel in giving courses at Rochester schools on kite making and kite flying. Author of *Golden Kite Book.*

Keith B. Capron, 1205 Hermosa Way, Colorado Springs, Colo. 80906. Is retired and regards kite flying as a key to sociability. Has a group of friends who go on picnic expeditions in the Rockies and fly kites.

Lincoln F. L. Chang, Hawaiian businessman of Chinese ancestry, who has been a leader in kiting in the Islands for many years. Is a craftsman in Oriental kites.

Edward Chavez, 142 Tabar Drive, San Antonio, Texas 78213. Has been ardent booster of kiting in his area and active participant in all kite events.

David Checkley, 678 West Prospect, Seattle, Washington 98119. Runs the amazing Kite Factory in that city. He also arranges annual kite tours featuring visits to kite-flying centers in the Orient.

George R. Cook, A Princeton, N.J., banker, who made a box kite which he decorated with bad checks that were collected by his bank.

James R. Cranwath, Kirkland, Washington, an authority on kite construction as well as design.

Caleb Crowell, master craftsman and kite designer. Editorial Director of Educational Design, Inc., 47 West 13th Street, New York. Is one of the most imaginative and ingenious people in the field and has proved it innumerable times with his contributions to this book.

Bernard Danis, crossed from Calais to Dover in 100 minutes, 20 minutes behind a water skier.

Paul A. Dickson, National Press Building, Washington, D.C. 20024, gives journalistic reports on current events in kite flying by way of his *Washington Newsletter.*

Fred Erhardt, of Sac City, Iowa, instructs the neighborhood kids and runs an annual contest there.

Leo P. Eustis, 80 Cherry Street, W. Newton, Mass. 02165. He is an inventor, manufacturer and promoter of new patented aerodynamic products, including a 14-foot spaceship kite he made.

Maynard Faith, 1807 Tecumseh Street, Fort Wayne, Indiana 46805. Retired telephone company worker. Builds exquisite light kites, including the difficult tetrahedron.

Joe Faust, Box 1671 Santa Monica, California 90406. The youngest pioneer in hang gliding.

Paula Fishman, associate director of the prestigious Jacqueline Anhalt Gallery in Beverly Hills, California, who encourages kite flying in arts by making the gallery available to artists who feature kites in their art. Her latest exhibit was that of Tom Van Sant, whose ten kites—one of which could hold four people—were a smash hit in art circles.

Sam Fox, 218 W. Sheldon St., Philadelphia, Pa. 02116. Active kite flyer who helps with annual Benjamin Franklin Day kite event each January and with Al Riederer puts on demonstration. Works with city recreation department in promoting kite events for children.

Paul Garber, 310 N. Jackson St., Arlington, Va. 22201, flight curator emeritus of the Smithsonian Institution. For years he conducted the annual kite flight in Washington, D.C. He is one of the great innovators in kite flying, and there is more on him throughout this book.

Sam Gardali, 914 Stanford Avenue, Modesto, Calif. 95350, is a printer. Makes beautiful bird kites and imprints fabrics with offset printing process, making realistic decorations such as feathers for bird kites.

John Gibson, 625 Steyskal, Bayard, N.M. 88023, is 17-year-old, six-foot five-inch high school senior, interested in unique kites. Developed the vacuum cup idea for releasing payloads from kites and works closely with David Omick in development of parachute deployment systems using kites to carry model assemblies.

Mrs. Aylene Goddard is most enthusiastic of all women kite fliers. She has produced television shows on kiting.

Robert Gonter, 888 E. Pleasant St., Amherst, Mass., inventive developer of kite flying via data processing methods, who is an associate director of the University of Massachusetts Computing Center. More on him in this book in aerodynamics section.

Mel and Valerie Govig, 7106 Campfield Rd., Baltimore, Md. 21207, who operate the Maryland Kite Society and give advice on contests in this book.

Ed Grauel, General Delivery, Borrego Springs, Calif., is the developer of the paper kite which is demonstrated in this book. A retired advertising manager of Eastman Kodak, he has brought kite flying to the forefront with his many tour demonstrations.

Albert Gregory, Ph.D., USC Architectural Dept., University Park, Los Angeles, Calif. 90007. Plans and builds huge tetrahedron-celled kites, some with 20- to 30-foot span.

Mrs. Pat Hammond, 215 Argyle, San Antonio, Texas 78209, is mother and housewife who went to Washington for 1972 carnival and won first prize for flying a homemade, highly decorated delta.

James Hannon, a Columbia, S.C., lawyer, who has developed a method of sending messages in bottles towed by kites across bodies of water.

Ed Hanrahan, eminent Baltimore man about town and creator of the Falcon kite which he adapted from kites flown on the Copacabana, Rio, Brazil beaches where they were called Papagaios.

Edward Harrison, 5540 Queen Mary Road, Apt. 8, Montreal, Canada, frequent judge and contest organizer.

Clive Hart, scholar and historian of kites, whose book *Kites* is a classic and historic survey.

Al Hartig, the "Nantucket Kiteman," has made Nantucket, Mass., famous for kite flying of his great delta-wing cloth kites, some of them big enough to fly a small man across the ocean. His kite store on the fabulous island is a summer showplace, and Al and his lovely wife, Betty are a landmark off the Massachusetts coast. Many of the Hartig kites are so beautiful they are used as decorative pieces. All are individually crafted.

George Helker, 1261 N.E. 112th St., Miami, Florida 33161. Yachtsman and kite hobbyist who has worked for years to promote kite flying. Is friend of Harry Sauls, with whom he collaborated in setting up kite exhibits at annual Dade County (Florida) Fair.

Professor Tsutomu Hiroi, a founder of Japanese Kite Association and author of *Kites—Plastic Art in the Air.* University of Denver.

Ray Holland, Airplane Kite Co., Rosewell, N.M., is a manufacturer who really tries to help his customers on a personal basis. He seeks the perfect kite material as others seek the holy grail.

Bob Ingraham, P.O. Box 1511, Silver City, N.M. Editor of *Kite Tales* and executive secretary of the most prestigious American Kitefliers Association, whose name should have led this list regardless of alphabetic order. He refers to his kites as "aircraft" and navigates them as such. Some of his kites even have landing skids. More on him throughout this book.

Domina Jalbert, Space Recovery Center, 40 N.W. 20th St., Boca Raton, Fla. 33432. One of the greatest innovators in the parakite field. I discovered him for *Life* magazine when working on a story on parachutes which Jalbert was designing. More on him in book.

Tom Joe, Made In Japan Shop, Long Beach, California, proprietor. Makes and flies his own kites.

Tony Johnson, 3 Ross Street, Kew 3101, Victoria, Australia, is leader of kite fliers in Australia and heads club that flies at regular intervals.

David S. Jue migrated from China at the age of 14, bringing his skill in kite making with him as a gift to his new home, the United States. His book *Chinese Kites, How to Make and Fly Them*

is a classic. He now makes his home in Palo Alto, California.

Fred W. Kenworth, 379 Cedarcroft Drive, Bricktown, N.J. 08727. Outstanding senior citizen who, at age 87, remains an active kite flier and spends most of his time in winter at a Florida retreat flying kites with friends.

Ben Kocivar, New York City, one of the ablest and most imaginative kite photographers and writers.

Rev. Joseph C. W. Lee, P.O. Box 148, Clarkston, Washington 99403. Methodist pastor of Korean ancestry who incorporates kite activity in his church program, staging kite-flies and conducting Oriental kite-building classes. Makes beautiful hand winders.

A. Alan Leveen, 241 Main Street, Hackensack, N.J., is a delightful spokesman for kite flying in his area. He presides at a luncheon club which features kite flying and telling lies about kite flights.

Hal Levine, head of Alan Whitney Kite Company, 165 Dwight Street, New Haven, Connecticut. Introduced variation of French Military Kite in America.

Captain Bob Lewis, North Miami, Fla., veteran inventor of kite for use in boat as outrigger.

Ken Lewis, 66 Simie Crescent, Port Credit, Ontario, Canada, is an Englishman who knows the breezes of Lake Ontario and gave up motorcycle racing for kite making and windhooking.

Michael A. Markowski. Author/illustrator/designer. He is a graduate aeronautical engineer. He has worked for Douglas Aircraft Company on the DC-10 wind tunnel model program as a design engineer; Sikorsky Aircraft Company as a research engineer of advanced vertical lift concepts; and as a design engineer for a Massachusetts engineering firm.

Ann McCandlish, 3411 Consear Rd., Lambertville, Mich. 48144. Widow of E. A. "Mac" McCandlish who was one of the greatest kite fliers of all time. Ann preserves Mac's workshop and has carefully distributed many of his kites to worthy individuals, keeping some favorite ones to show visitors. Is a continuing disciple of kite flying as a therapy and excellent "busy work" for the retired.

Jim Moran, New York City, bearded, wildly enterprising press agent who introduced kites as an advertising medium and flew midgets to demonstrate kites as such.

Frank Mots, 3141 West Juneau Ave., Milwaukee, Wis. 53208, who flies his own kites. He dresses in swallowtail suit and top hat, like Fred Astaire.

David Omick, 723 Dayhill St., Bayard, N.M. 88023. This young man, who recently graduated from high school, is a genius in working out problems with kites and has developed successful parachute systems using the Rogallo Para-Wing as model. Made his first parachute drop in Dallas, Texas, as a graduation gift for himself. Flies with Bob Ingraham, AKA head, at the Silver City, N.M., headquarters.

Howard Norville, 240 Ward Street, San Francisco, Calif. 94134. One of the greatest of all kite enthusiasts. Has entire family enrolled in kiting and makes yearly trek to various parts of the country with a Dodge van. Carries huge supply of rollup kites and is setting a record of flying at least once in every county of every state he visits. Has completed California, Nevada and New Mexico thus far and authenticated such. Is an electronics expert on the 747 jumbo jets, working for a large airline at its San Francisco base of operations.

Samuel Perkins, 229 Harvard Street, Quincy, Mass. 02170, who carries on with kites in the tradition of his late father who used kites for advertising.

Les Phillips, P.O. Box 10800, Houston, Texas 77018. Pioneer kite manufacturer who heads the Gayla Company in Texas.

G. H. Pilch, 54 Broomhill Road, Hucknall, Nottinghamshire, England, is stimulating new interest in kite flying there. His kite is featured in this book.

Albert F. Riederer, 3437 Amber Street, Philadelphia, Pa. 19134, 48-year-old enthusiast who works with Sam Fox in the production of the annual demonstration on Ben Franklin Day. Keeps kite flying active in Philadelphia and is good publicity man for kiting in general.

Richard S. Robertson, 5401 Shoalwood Ave., Austin, Texas 78756. Dick works unceasingly in his community to make kiting a continuing activity. Every child is a winner at the annual Exchange Club contest in Austin.

Frank Rodriguez, 150 West 82nd Street, New York, N.Y. 10024, pioneer in use of plastic material in esoteric as well as traditional kites. One of the best Occidental fliers of Indian fighter kites.

Francis M. Rogallo, Route 1, Box 1520, Kitty Hawk, N.C. 27949. Nonrigid kite inventor, cited throughout this book.

Nicholas St. John Rosse, 16 Woodville Road, London, N.W. 11, England, is probably the foremost kite painter, or painter of kite scenes. His "Kites on the Heath" is a lovely kite scape.

Harry C. Sauls, 1245 159th St., N. Miami Beach, Fla. Pioneer and inventor of the barrage kite and other startling flying vehicles.

Frank Scott, Columbus, Ohio, collaborated with his late father in developing the famous Scott sled, a kite that has runner on each side like a real sled.

Eugene Seder, 1945 Whitney Avenue, Whitneyville, Conn. 06517. Kite-flying scholar and authority on Benjamin Franklin and his kite flight.

Harvey Sellers, 510 East Wabash Avenue, Decatur, Illinois 62525. President of the world famous Hi-Flier Kite Company.

Keith Shields, 1340 Adams Drive, Ambridge, Pa. 15003. Retired draftsman. Builds falcon-type kites and flies in all weather, even in snow. Does drawings for kite designs for *Kite Tales*.

Mendel Silbert, 1210 Frederick Avenue, Salisbury, Md. 21801. NASA employee at Wallops Island, flies big parafoils carrying banners admonishing polluters. Fights airplane pilots who would abolish all kites.

John LeRoy Smart, 3503 Pinehaven Drive, Charleston, S.C. 29405. Deputy sheriff. Builds and gives hundreds of kites away to children in addition to promoting kite flying for kids. Was honored by Harold Alexander with a kite in the exact shape of a deputy sheriff complete with uniform and decorations. It is called the "John Smart Kite."

Francis B. Smith, 2727 Broadway East, Seattle, Washington 98102. United Airlines navigator who spends all spare time flying kites. He represents kite fliers in the air transport industry.

Jane Yolen Stemple, my darling daughter, who lives at Phoenix Farm, 31 School Street, in Hatfield, Mass. Author herself of one of the great kite-flying books, *World on a String*, as well as fiction, *The Emperor and the Kite* and *The Seventh Mandarin*. She has continued her interest in kites and kite fliers through her three children, Heidi, Adam and Jason, and her lectures on the subject in schools and libraries.

Michael Stoltz, 3439 Amber St., Philadelphia, Pa. 19134. Friend and neighbor of Al Riederer in Philadelphia and third man of the team there promoting kite flying in general and Ben Franklin event.

Jim Talcott is the editor at Omega Press, which published the great *The Giant Kites* on its own presses in Tustin, Calif. 92680, P.O. Box 613.

Bill Thomas, kite writer.

Paul E. Thomas, 1106 S. Pine, York, Pa. 17403. Retired senior citizen craftsman who makes beautiful bird kites. Rated cover photo on *Kite Tales* for the superiority of his work.

Antonio Toledo is the winner of first kite-flying trophy in the First Hawaiian Championship in 1972. He is in Seattle, Washington, area where he works for Barb Enterprises when he isn't making special kites for the kids in the neighborhood.

Marjorie Waters, Festival Committee for the Better Use of Air, 23 Arrow Street, Cambridge, Mass. 02138. Along with Gil Fishman, Mike

Sands and Lionel Spiro coordinated the Greater Boston Kite Festival, one of the most imaginative and lighthearted kite affairs in America.

W. E. Waters, Manhawkin, New Jersey, has been flying since 1910, and is an exponent of gang kiting, flying four to ten kites at a time.

Frank Wattlington is the Dean of Bermuda kite fliers and is author of the fascinating *Bermuda Kites*.

David S. Williams, 111 West Court St., Lawrenceburg, Ky. 40342. Developed the circle kite which is a modified full-size parachute. Sticks to this one thing and won't fly any other kind of kite. He is a sort of adventurer, cave explorer, airplane pilot, an engineer in a manufacturing plant tending power equipment.

Fumio Yoshimura, Japanese designer of imaginative concepts of sculptured kites. Husband of author Kate Millett, Westport, Conn.

E. R. Young, a kite fancier whose father was responsible, with Colonel Bill Cody, for designing a kite in 1914 that towed the lesser-known buffalo hunter across the English Channel in a canoe.

Ted Zell, 2010 Southwest Vista Vue, Portland, Oregon 97201, is a jeweler in that town who loves to travel with kites. He demonstrated AKA parafoil and banner kites in the great Honolulu meet.

Tony "The Kiteman" Ziegler, of Monroe, Mich., is the Pied Piper of kiters in that area. Most beloved Tony has converted his backyard into a flying field where he exhibits his huge kites and instructs the neighborhood in kiting and good sportsmanship.

v KITE MANUFACTURERS, LARGE AND SMALL

Kite fliers in the old days made their own kites; the practice is now confined to the hobbyist. Today, most people, young and old, prefer to buy ready-made kites and over the past twenty years the total number of commercial kites sold has quadrupled. Kites can be found in most candy stores, toy stores, novelty stores and the like. Sports goods stores now sell huge kites for fishing, sailing or riding.

For those people who want to buy rather than make their own kites, following is a list of manufacturers who make commercial kites. Because of the volatile nature of the business, some of the companies may have moved or disappeared by now. So don't send money until you write for a catalogue of their wares first.

In many cases you will be referred to local distributors. On the other hand, some of the smaller manufacturers like to deal directly with kite fliers. The huge manufacturers such as Gayla and Hi-Flier work through jobbers and dealers. Al Hartig in Nantucket, Massachusetts, or Go Fly A Kite Store in New York City like to deal direct with people, by mail or telephone order.

For those interested in foreign kites, write for the Pax-Drachen catalogue at an address that will stagger you: Gebrüder Schmol, Spielwarenfabrik, D-7320 Göppingen, Wurtt, West Germany.

One of the colorful kite makers is L. J. Denmire who features a pair of cloth box kites and a small tissue-paper kite when he isn't involved in what he calls "scoop and pitch custom farming" and "hammer and tongs blacksmithing." Furthermore, he also advertises "push and pull conservation" contracting. His kites are name "Kro-Flies."

Another unusual character and manufacturer is Frank Mots, whose colorful kites, which he and his wife make, are a feature of many kite-flying exhibitions in the United States.

There are many individual regional kite makers, whose output is very small. They are enthusiasts who keep the spirit of kite flying alive even though they earn only a skimpy livelihood from it.

California

Synestructics Ind., 9559 Irondale Ave., Chatsworth, Cal. 91311.

Aircraft Spruce & Specialty Co., P.O. Box 424, Fullerton, Cal. 92632.

Gaines G. Co., 226 Kellogg Avenue, Fullerton, Cal. 92633 (714) 879-2885.

Stulken, 501 11th St. Imperial Beach, Cal. 92032. New type kite with twirlers that lift and stabilize.

Gregg, Newtown K., Kentfield, Cal. 94904.

Eipper-Formance Flight Systems, P.O. Box 246, Lomita, Cal. 90717.

Squadron Kites, 12821 Martha Ann Dr., Los Alamitos, Cal. 90720. Craig A. Stratton, pres., makes the old squadron kites such as Sopwith Camel, Red Baron and F3 F2.

International Kites, 1891 Caspian Avenue, Long Beach, Cal. 90810. Tom Joe, prop. Carries all kinds of kites but specializes in great fighter kites. Will custom design upon request.

Plastruck Inc., 1621 Indiana St., Los Angeles, Cal. 90063.

Airtoy Co., 1855 Industrial Street, Los Angeles, Cal. 90021.

Puffer Kites, P.O. Box 253, Pacific Palisades, Cal. 90272. This is an inflatable kite. Try it, you may like it. It goes up like a balloon and then becomes a kite.

The Emperor and the Kite Store, run by Judy Le Veque, Star Route 942, Orange, California, 92667. This is named for Jane Yolen's book *The Emperor and the Kite,* a fairytale about a little Chinese girl who rescues her father, the emperor, from a prison tower by means of a kite.

W.B. Products Co., Astrozoomer, 560 S. Helberta Avenue, Redondo Beach, Cal. 90277.

The International Museum of Kites, 122 Geary Street, San Francisco, Cal. 94108. A fascinating enterprise well worth a visit by kite buffs. Call Steven Polinski, proprietor, for details on hours and kites for sale.

Let's-Go-Fly-a-Kite Store, 1510-G Walnut Street, Berkeley, Cal. 94704.

Sunset Line & Twine Co., Jefferson & Irving, Petaluma, Cal. 94952.

Come Fly A Kite Store, 900 N. Point, Ghirardelli Sq., San Francisco, Cal. 94109.

Stern, E. L., ABAA, 2949 Balboa, San Francisco, Cal. 94121.

Colorado

Estes Altiscope, Box 227, Penrose, Colo. 82140, is specially instrumented to determine the height of a kite from the ground. Ask for catalogue item 70L A.1.

Spencer "Speedy" Allen, East Pikes Peak, Colorado Springs, Colo., with the help of Jim Bowers makes special kites on order.

Estes, Box 227, Penrose, Colo. 81240.

Connecticut

Alan-Whitney Co. Inc., Box 447, 780 State Street, New Haven, Conn. 06502. (203) 787-1001. Makes the best French military type kite in various sizes. Will make special designs in bulk orders.

English and Co., Inc., 123 Hulls Highway, Southport, Conn. 06490. Bill English is designer and inventor of *mad* kite, a stickless kite.

Scharr Industries, 48 Newberry Rd., Bloomfield, Conn. 06002.

Delaware

Brandywine Fibre Products Co., 1465 Poplar St., Wilmington, Del. 19801.

Florida

Jalbert Aerological Laboratory Inc., 170 N.W. 20th St., Boca Raton, Fla. 33432. Home of the great parafoil by the master of parachute kites. One of the strongest and best-devised kites, which can be used as riders. Jalbert is a delight himself and is still developing new ideas for kites and kite fliers.

KHK Corp. P.O. Box 398. Delray Beach, Fla. 33444. Kitty Hawk Kite "no stick" plastics, easily assembled.

CLT Airfoils Associates, 50 E. 10th Street, Hialeah, Fla. 33010.

Lewis Products Co., P.O. Box 982, Kendall, Fla. Captain Bob Lewis makes best fishing kite in America. But you must follow instructions very carefully on this expensive ($17.00) kite, rod and reel.

Aero-Foil Systems Inc., P.O. Box 834, Merritt Island, Fla. 32952.

Max Coombs, 17921 85th Avenue, Miami, Fla. 33015. Coombs makes individual riding kites in his home tool shop. His is one of the best-constructed and safest kites. Furthermore, he is an expert of this new exciting sport and has contributed many innovations. He will not sell kites to beginners unless they undergo a series of lessons with him. He builds every one of his kites by himself and checks it out by flying it himself.

Odell Miller, 601 N. Miami Ave., Miami, Fla. He's an interesting innovator specializing in a round kite and riding kites on which he works with Max Coombs.

Harry Sauls, 1345 N.E. 159th Street, N. Miami, Fla. 33162. His special kites are huge affairs which need a winch to handle.

UFO Flying Saucer, JV Mfg. Co., Miami, Fla.

Georgia

Wellington Puritan Mills Inc., 1205 Lagrange Rd., Madison, Ga. 30650.

Hawaii

Viking Tailless Kite, 1123 Young Street, Honolulu, Hawaii.

Illinois

American Cotton Yarns Inc., 5827 S. Western Ave., Chicago, Ill. 60636.

Burcott Mills, 304 N. Loomis St., Chicago, Ill. 60607.

Creative Marketing, 300 N. Washington Blvd., Chicago, Ill. 60606.

Hi-Flier Mfg. Co., 510 Wabash Ave., Decatur, Ill. 62525. One of the most enterprising and cooperative big kite companies. In addition to full line of inexpensive kites, also makes promotional kites with *imprints* of your own design but in bulk orders.

Kite Specialties Co., 433 Avery St., Elmhurst, Ill. 60126.

Molor Products Co., P.O. Box 709, Glen Ellyn, Ill. 60137. (312) 469-5646.

Censable Products Inc., 3930 N. 25th St., Schiller Park, Ill. 60176. (312) 678-1337.

Indiana

Trading Post, P.O. Box 1988 B, Indianapolis, Ind. 46202. Tetra Kites.

Dwyer Instruments, Inc., P.O. Box 373-T, Michigan City, Ind. 46360.

Iowa

Kro-Flies Kites, L. J. Denmire, prop. (handmade) Keokuk, Iowa. Denmire is a character who does custom farming, horseshoeing and other nutty things. But is still making interesting kites.

SIG Manufacturing Co., Inc., 1200 Glen Ave., Montezuma, Iowa 50171.

Kentucky

Jumbo Kites, David Williams, 111 West Court Street, Lawrenceburg, Ky. 40342.

L. G. Striegel Mfg. 1223 Arcade Ave., Louisville, Ky. 40215.

Louisiana

Eagle Kites, 824 Chartres St., New Orleans, La. 70116.

Explorers, 824 Chartres St., New Orleans, La. 70116.

Massachusetts

Home & Bainbridge Inc., 220 Commercial St., Boston, Mass. 02109.

Al Hartig, Nantucket, Mass. 02554. "Kiteman 'n Lady" Store (handmade). The greatest individually crafted kites in the world, with an assist from wife Sheila.

Scott Education, 5 Lower Westfield Road, Holyoke, Mass. 01085. *Kite Flying Stories and Games* is now available through Scott's Score Reading Improvement Series which is for middle-grade students. If kite kits don't blow your mind, they also have a course on trampoline jumping.

The Kiteworks on Beach Rd. Vineyard Haven, Martha's Vineyard Island, Mass. 02568 specializes in American Box and Oriental Fighting Kites—Write to Hani Dzubas.

Michigan

Wheaton Blue Print & Supply Co., 446 Portage St., Kalamazoo, Mich. 49006.

A. D. Goddard, P.O. Box 133, Otsego, Mich. 49078. A storehouse of information about kites and kite manufacturing and where to buy special equipment.

Missouri

Alox Mfg. Co., 6160-80 Maple Avenue, St. Louis, Mo. 63130.

Crundin Martin Mfg. Co., P.O. Box 508, St. Louis, Mo.

Hobby Saucer Kite, Box 4563, Kansas City, Mo. 64127.

New Jersey

Butler, A. H., Aircraft Specialties, R.D.2, Box 174, Blairstown, N.J. 07825.

Boy Scouts of America, North Brunswick, N.J. 07902.

Remco Industries Inc., Cape May St., Harrison, N.J. 07029. (201) 484-1700. Importers.

New Mexico

Yahtay Industries, Box 235, Jemez Pueblo, New Mexico 87024.

Airplane Kite Co., 1702 W. 3rd Street, Roswell, N.M. (505) 622-7529. Very inventive and best flying hawks ever made. Small company but very strong on research and enterprising as well as innovative.

New York

Educational Design, Inc., 47 W. 13 Street, New York, N.Y. 10011. (212) 255-7900 MINILABS Division's *Flying Machines Kit* contains 18-inch model of Rogallo hang glider. Available in many store hobby or toy departments.

Sky-Way Products, 739 E. New York Ave., Brooklyn, N.Y. 11203. (212) 772-0442.

Blum, Paul Co., 317 Larkin, Buffalo, N.Y. 14210.

Rolex Co. Inc., 65-37 Austin Street, Forest Hills, N.Y. 11374. Importers of kites.

Ruco Division, Hooker Chemical Corp., 8 N. South Rd., Hicksville, N.Y. 11802.

Aqua Flite Sailcloth, Inc., 57 Leonard, New York, N.Y. 10013.

Emporium East, 19 Mott Street, New York, N.Y. 10013 (212) 962-2029. Handmade Oriental kites, dragons, etc., owls that fly and other shapes.

F.A.O. Schwarz, 5th Ave. at 58th St., N.Y., N.Y. Always has important but expensive imported kites.

Go Fly A Kite Store, 1434 Third Avenue, New York, N.Y. 10028. Andrea Bahadur, widow of the great Indian kite flier, has one of the largest collections of commercial kites in the world.

Polk's Model Craft Hobbies, 314 5th Avenue, New York, N.Y. 10001. Small distributor of foreign kites.

Ed Grauel, 774 Elmwood Terrace, Rochester, N.Y. 14620. Makes paper, nonrigid kites and a bullet kite which is a joy.

Ohio

Netcroft Co., 3101 Sylvania Ave., Toledo, Ohio 43613.

Charles R. Stiple, 3006 E. Mound Street, Columbus, Ohio 43209. Makes a simple hand-over-hand reel specially for kites.

Troyer Kite Supply, 4174 Kent Road, Stow, Ohio, 44224. Specializes in kite reels.

Oregon

North Pacific Products Inc., Bend, Oregon, 97701. (503) 382-3231. House of "Glite" kite.

Pennsylvania

Model Distributors, 64 E. Cayuga St., Philadelphia, Pa. 19120.

Rhode Island

Corbin Kites (handmade), Rt. 44, Greenville, R.I., or Harmony, R.I.

Texas

Maciag, E., 3720 Porter Ave., El Paso, Texas 79930.

Gayla Industries, P.O. Box 10800, Houston, Texas 77018. (713) 681-2411. One of best of large kite companies.

Washington

Fairhaven Kite Co., 1487 Telegraph Road, Bellingham, Washington 98225.

Lee's Custom Kites and Reels, P.O. Box 148, Clarkston, Wash. 99403.

The Kite Factory, P.O. Box 9081, Seattle, Wash. 98109. (206) 284-5350. Enterprising company which packages great kites and sets up kite tours to the Orient and other glamorous places.

Wisconsin

Mots Acrobatic Kites, 1418 N. 68th Street, Milwaukee, Wisc. 53213. Mots makes a wonderful colorful kite in a mom and pop shop.

Rayco Reels, 7320 W. Lloyd Street, Wauwatosa, Wisc. 53213.

FOREIGN

Canada

Sturgeon Air Ltd., 36 Airport Rd., Industrial Airport, Edmonton, Alberta, Canada.

Condor Industries Ltd., 3914 St. Peters Rd., Victoria, B.C., Canada.

Flow Form, 53 Frazier Ave., Toronto, Ontario, Canada. Nonrigid kites and accessories.

England

Sewell & Seager Ltd. & Brookite Ltd., Frances Ter., Junction Rd., London N 19, England.

Yachtmail Co., 7 Cornwall Crescent, London W. 11 1PH, England.

VI HANG GLIDING INFORMATION

For a young industry, hang gliding has done right well for itself in the way of publications. Here are some of the more vital ones, according to Bob Goodness, of Man-Flight, one of the big Eastern manufacturers:

Hang Glider Weekly. Edited by veteran Joe Faust, this is considered the bible of this breed of fliers. From the beginning, Joe has been everywhere and seen everything in hang gliders and has reported it weekly—or almost weekly—for many years. A real national trade publication. Address: Box 1671, Santa Monica, California 90406.

Ground Skimmer. P.O. Box 66306, Los Angeles, California 90066. Founded by Lloyd Licher, probably has the largest circulation—about 10,000 monthly. It is the official organ of the U.S. Hang Gliding Association.

Soaring Magazine. P.O. Box 66071, Los Angeles, California 90066. It is the voice of the Soaring Society.

Kite Tales. P.O. Box 1511, Silver City, New Mexico 88061. The beloved quarterly of the American Kitefliers Association, edited by the equally beloved Bob Ingraham, is now devoting more space to the activities of the hang kiters, although it is primarily the bible of the conventional kiters.

Hang Glider. 3333 Pacific Avenue, San Pedro, California 90731. A colorful quarterly published by Cowboy Star Publications, it is the class publication of the industry, although it has come out only twice so far. The editor is Bob Smith.

HANG KITING CLUBS

This is a growing sport, and clubs seem to form overnight. For more information, it is suggested that you get in touch with the dealers in your area.

John J. Montgomery Hang Gliding Association
c/o Jim Spurgeon
5590 Morro Way
La Mesa, California 92401

Self-Soar Association
59 Dudley Avenue
Venice, California 90291

Wings of Rogallo Soaring Club
1137 Jamestown Drive
Sunnyvale, California 94987

The Soaring Society of America, Inc.
P.O. Box 6601
Los Angeles, California 90069

Boston Sky Club/Skysurfer Publications
P.O. Box 375
Marlboro, Massachusetts 01752

Polish Hang Glider Pilots' Association
c/o Skysurfer
Box 872
Worcester, Mass. 01613

HANG KITE DEALERS

California

Free Flight Systems: 12424 Gladstone Avenue, Sylman, California 91324
Eipper-Formance, Inc.: P.O. Box 246, Lomita, California 90717
Bill Bennett Delta Wing Kites: P.O. Box 483, Van Nuys, California 91408
Flight Realities: 1945 Adams Avenue, San Diego, California 92116
Manta Wings: 1647 E. 14th Street, Oakland, California 92116
Sail Wing Sky School North: 2631 A. Rancho Road, Redding, California 96001
Ultralite Products, Inc.: El Segundo, California
Sunbird Ultralight Gliders: Canoga Park, California
Dyna-Soar, Inc.: Hollywood, California
Seagull Aircraft: Santa Monica, California
True Flight: San Jose, California
Hawk Industries: San Diego, California
J.L. Enterprises: San Mateo, California
Sport Kites, Inc.: Santa Ana, California

Omega Aircraft and Kite Systems: Santa Monica, California
Victor F. Musser: Fresno, California
Gary D. Daniel: Downey, California
W.B. Products: Redondo Beach, California
Pacific Gull: San Clemente, California
Walt Wilson: Pacifica, California
Chandelle West, Inc.: Irvine, California
Howe and Bainbridge: Newport Beach, California
Bird Feathers: Santa Monica, California
Colver Soaring Instruments: Costa Mesa, California

Colorado

Get High, Inc.: Box 4551, Aspen, Colorado
Roack Mountain Marine: 5411 Leetsdale Dr., Denver, Colorado 80222
Sun Sail Corp.: Denver, Colorado
Chandelle Corp.: Golden, Colorado

Connecticut

Zephyr Aircraft, Inc.: Glastonbury, Connecticut

Kansas

Pliable Moose Delta Wings: Wichita, Kansas

Massachusetts

Sky Sports: P.O. Box 441, Whitman, Mass. 02382
Man-Flight Systems, Inc.: P.O. Box 375, Marlboro, Mass. 01752
Dan Poynter: North Quincy, Mass.

Michigan

Foot-Launched Flyers: Brighton, Michigan
A & A Flight Systems: New Buffalo, Michigan

Montana

Upward Bound: P.O. Box 2009, Missoula, Montana 59801

North Carolina

Emory Gliders: Raleigh, North Carolina

Ohio

Chuck's Glider Supplies: Columbia Station, Ohio

Pennsylvania

Sutton Brothers: Marysville, Pennsylvania

Virginia

Kitty Hawk Kites, Inc.: 309 Gilpin Avenue, Norfolk, Virginia

Washington

Sun Valley Kites, Inc.: Seattle, Washington
Chandelle Northwest, Inc.: Seattle, Washington
Delta Wing Kites, Inc.: Monroe, Washington

Wisconsin

Bonn Industries, Inc.: Oak Creek, Wisconsin

Extracontinental

Stan Truitt: P.O. Box 7, Kula, Hawaii 96790
Muller Kites, Ltd.: Calgary, Alberta, Canada
Kartway Park, Ltd.: Edmonton, Alberta, Canada
Tod Mountain Flying School: Kamloops, B.C., Canada
L. Gabriels: Hollywood, Oldham, Lancashire, England

BIBLIOGRAPHY

Abbe, C., "Another Use for the Kite." *Monthly Weather Review*, vol. 28, no. 6., June 1900.

————, "Captain Dansey's Kite for Stranded Vessels." *Monthly Weather Review*, vol. 25, no. 5, May 1897.

————, "Espy and the Franklin Kite Club." *Monthly Weather Review*, vol. 24, no. 9, September 1896.

————, "The Franklin Kite Club." *Monthly Weather Review*, vol. 24, no. 10, Nov. 1896.

————, "Kerkan's Kites with Rocket Signals." *Monthly Weather Review*, vol. 25, no. 5, May 1897.

————, "New Use for Kites—the Telephone Kite." *Monthly Weather Review*, vol. 26, no. 6, June 1898.

————, "The Use of the Kite in Meteorology." *Monthly Weather Review*, vol. 24, no. 11, November 1898.

Arlington, L. C., "Note on the Origin of Chinese Kites." *The New China Review*, vol. 3, no. 1, February 1921.

Bacon, G., *Balloons, Airships and Flying Machines*. London: 1905.

Cody, Sam, *The Flying Cathedral*. London: Arthur Gould Lee, Methuen and Co., Ltd.

Cole, F. C., *The Peoples of Malaysia*. New York: Van Nostrand Reinhold, 1945.

Downer, Marion, *Kites—How to Make and Fly Them*. New York: Lothrop, 1959.

Drummond, J., "The Kite, Man's First Aeroplane." *Air B. P.*, no. 27, n.d.

Eddy, W. L. A., "A Record of Some Kite Experiments." *Monthly Weather Review*, vol. 26, no. 10, October 1889.

Fowler, H. Waller, Jr., *Kites*. New York: Barnes Sports Library, Ronald Press, 1965.

Garber, P. E., *The National Aeronautical Collections*, 10th Edition. Washington, 1965.

Gunther, Max, "The Manly Art of Windhooking." *True*, April 1962.

Hart, Clive, *Kites: A Historical Survey*. New York: Praeger, 1967.

Hunt, Leslie L., *88 Successful Play Activities*. New York: National Recreation Association, Inc.

————, *Flying High*. New York: National Recreation Association, Inc.

————, *25 Kites That Fly*. New York: Dover Publishing Co., 1971.

Inglis, A., "Trials of an Inventor in Australia: The Case of Lawrence Hargrave." *Records of the Australian Academy of Science*, vol. 1, no. 1, December 1966.

Jue, D. F., *Chinese Kites: How to Make and Fly Them*. Vermont and Tokyo, Japan: C. E. Tuttle, 1967.

Martin, Ben, "Go Fly a Kite." *Today's Living*, July 12, 1959.

Marvin, C. F., "A Weather Bureau Kite." *Monthly Weather Review*, vol. 23, no. 11, November 1895.

Priestly, J., *The Papers of Benjamin Franklin*. New Haven: 1961.

Pyral, J., "Letter on Kite-flying With Wire." *Bradford Observer Budget*, March 13, 1897.

Rend "Applications of the Kite to Various Useful Purposes." *Mechanics Magazine*, vol. 15, no. 406, May 12, 1831.

Rogallo, Francis M., "First Flexible Kite." *Ford Times*, March 1951.

Rotch, A. L., "The Use of Kites to Obtain Meteorological Records in the Upper Air at Blue Hill Observatory, U.S.A." *Quarterly Journal of the Royal Meteorological Society*, vol. 23, 1897.

Seder, Eugene, "Franklin Experiments." *Kite Tales Magazine.*

Smith, Red, "Gone to Fly His Kite." *The Sign*, April 1961.

——, "Kite King." *New York Herald Tribune*, February 1961.

Watlington, Frank, *Bermuda Kites*. Bermuda: *Island Press.*

Wagonvoord, James, *Flying Kites in Sun, Art and War*, New York: Macmillan.

Yolen, Jane, "I Fly a Kite With the Champ." *Popular Mechanics*, June 1961.

——, "I Fly a Kite With the Champion." *Ford Times*, March 1962.

——, *World on a String*, New York: Collins-World, 1969.

Varney, G. J., *Kites, How to Make and Fly Them*. Boston: 1897.

INDEX